D1330204

CONSTRUCTIVIST

[LEARNING]

DESIGN

WITHDRAWN FROM
THE LIBRARY

UNIVERSITY OF
WINCHESTER

!09

10

10

KA 0336420 8

CONSTRUCTIVIST

Key Questions for

LEARNING

Teaching to Standards

DESIGN

GEORGE W. GAGNON, Jr.
MICHELLE COLLAY

Foreword by Richard A. Schmuck

CORWIN PRESS
A SAGE Publications Company
Thousand Oaks, California

Copyright © 2006 by Corwin Press

All rights reserved. When forms and sample documents are included, their use is authorized only by educators, local school sites, and/or noncommercial or nonprofit entities who have purchased the book. Except for that usage, no part of this book may be reproduced or utilized in any form or by any means, electronic or mechanical, including photocopying, recording, or by any information storage and retrieval system, without permission in writing from the publisher.

For information:

Corwin Press
A Sage Publications Company
2455 Teller Road
Thousand Oaks, California 91320
www.corwinpress.com

Sage Publications Ltd.
1 Oliver's Yard
55 City Road
London EC1Y 1SP
United Kingdom

Sage Publications India Pvt. Ltd.
B-42, Panchsheel Enclave
Post Box 4109
New Delhi 110 017 India

UNIVERSITY OF WINCHESTER

370.152
GAG

03364208

Printed in the United States of America

Library of Congress Cataloging-in-Publication Data

Gagnon, George W.
Constructivist learning design: Key questions for teaching to standards/George W. Gagnon, Michelle Collay.
    p. cm.
Includes bibliographical references and index.
ISBN 1-4129-0955-4 (cloth) — ISBN 1-4129-0956-2 (pbk.)
  1. Constructivism (Education) 2. Instructional systems-Design.
I. Collay, Michelle. II. Title.
LB1590.3.G33 2006   2005018389

This book is printed on acid-free paper.

06   07   08   09   10   9   8   7   6   5   4   3   2   1

Acquisitions Editor:	Faye Zucker
Editorial Assistant:	Gem Rabanera
Production Editor:	Beth A. Bernstein
Copy Editor:	Freelance Editorial Services
Typesetter:	C&M Digitals (P) Ltd.
Proofreader:	Katherine Pollock
Indexer:	Rick Hurd
Cover Designer:	Michael Dubowe
Graphic Designer	Lisa Miller

Contents

Foreword

Will you, won't you, will you, won't you, will you join the dance?

—Lewis Carroll,
Alice's Adventures in Wonderland

This small, precious book is big and seminal. Small and precious because it modestly, pointedly, and succinctly enhances a slowly escalating revolution in how educators think about teaching and learning. Big and seminal because it contributes hundreds of original strategies to a quarter-century-old educational paradigm shift, a shift from behaviorism-inspired, omniscient teaching to engaged, intrinsically motivated student learning.

George Gagnon, a math teacher, and Michelle Collay, a music teacher, are teachers of teachers as well as seasoned school consultants, but they are much more than that. At home, they are a loving, married couple and the caring, conscientious parents of two young children; they are understandably concerned that their children, Von and Nina, reap the benefits of healthy and effective learning environments at school. As professionals with the creative flair of a mathematician and a musician, they are close and interdependent partners; one might say that they are metaphorical choreographers and dancers in the creative design and implementation of teaching for learning.

The content of this well-written ballet-of-a-book is not about the staged allocation of M&M candies or the lock-stepped use of stopwatches to render timely reinforcement as we might see in the theater of direct instruction, teacher control, and extrinsic student motivation. No, in their musical score, we do not hear the claps, clicks, murmurs, and barely audible yeses of B.F. Skinner's disciples. Nor do Gagnon and Collay ask us to imagine students as what Paulo Freire (1970) cynically called bank deposit vaults storing teacher-delivered knowledge. No, this book tells how to encourage all students to dance together to support one another's deep learning.

This book should be read by neophyte and seasoned teachers, by teacher educators in colleges of education, and by trainees in preservice programs. It should also be read by school administrators for insights into how to improve teacher supervision and staff development, by open-minded behaviorists looking for alternatives to direct instruction, by liberal arts professors who what to learn how to teach so that their students want to keep on learning, and by parents with children in school or with children they are schooling at home. For that matter, everyone concerned with formal education should read this book unless, of course, they already have signed the Faustian pact to search only after the qualities and techniques of authoritarian, direct instruction.

This book's theme is constructivist learning design (CLD), which embodies Gagnon and Collay's foundational concepts. Constructivist refers specifically to the assumption that humans develop by engaging in the personal and social construction of knowledge. We humans make personal meanings for ourselves and we create shared meaning with others. Thus, humans construct knowledge; we do not receive and internalize predigested concepts without simultaneously reacting to them and engaging them within our own mental maps and previous experiences. Learning signifies that the primary goal of schooling is student development and improvement. Teaching should be but one means to that end and as such is secondary in importance to it. Gagnon and Collay point out that it is better to be a guide on the side than a sage on the stage. Design denotes the overall structure and outline, sequence of parts, and general forms through which educational activities flow. It is like the composer's or arranger's score for the dance of students and teachers learning together. In other words, Gagnon and Collay's CLD aims to present teachers with a constructivist perspective on how to arrange classroom events for student learning.

CLD is composed of six basic parts flowing back and forth into one another in the actual operation of classroom learning: situation, grouping, bridge, task, exhibit, and reflections.

1. The Situation frames the agenda for student engagement by delineating the goals, tasks and forms of what Gagnon and Collay call the learning episode.

2. Groups are the social structures that create opportunities for interaction and bring students together in their involvement with tasks and forms of the learning episode.

3. Bridge refers to the surfacing of students' prior knowledge before introducing them to the new subject matter. The bridge is at the heart of the constructivist methodology; students are better able to refocus

their energies on new content when they can place it within their own cognitive maps, values, attitudes, expectations, and motoric, skills.

4. Tasks are the "heart of the matter" and, flanked by a clear purpose and authentic assessments, are the centerpiece of CLD. Although powerful questions are used throughout CLD, they are absolutely critical in crafting challenging and interesting tasks to facilitate student learning.

5. An Exhibit asks students to present publicly what they have learned; this social setting provides a time and place for students to respond to queries raised by the teacher, by peers, or by visitors about what Gagnon and Collay call the "artifacts of learning."

6. Reflections offer students and teachers opportunities to think and speak critically about their personal and collective learning. They encourage all participants to synthesize their learning, to apply learning artifacts to other parts of the curriculum, and to look ahead to future learning episodes.

Although the six features of CLD are vital to its effective implementation, Gagnon and Collay wisely caution us about the absolute necessity of establishing a positive, affective climate as an integral feature of it. A sense of trust, safety, and community in the class and school must be wrapped around and woven though CLD for deep student learning to take place. In classrooms, students and teachers must build a culture of social support and mutual helpfulness complemented by an appreciation of diversity as accompaniments of CLD. Trust between teachers and students and among the students is critical to CLD's success. A collegial sense of support, mutual helpfulness, and an appreciation of diversity also should develop among staff members of a school if classes are to benefit from CLD. Gagnon and Collay help us understand that their creative work on learning circles supports the realization of these conditions.

I invite you now to do as I have done. Read this fine book three times. Read it first for a general understanding of its concepts. Read it again and reflect on your own practice. Read it a third time to engage its ideas as you would engage dance partners. Then keep the book at your side for reference to its many action ideas. Will you, won't you join Michelle and George in the creative dance, so that you can use CLD in dancing with Nina and Von and other young students as they construct their own learning?

Richard A. Schmuck,
Professor Emeritus,
University of Oregon

Preface

Classroom-based teaching is a profoundly demanding enterprise that challenges beginners and experienced teachers alike. Reform efforts add complexity to the landscape on which teachers walk, but the challenge of teaching for student learning existed long before current mandates appeared. Reforms include outcome-based education, charter schools, national and state standards, performance assessments, mandated national tests in reading and writing, national board certification of teachers, revised graduation requirements in several states, state testing of reading and mathematics, and small-school initiatives. Bold experiments to disrupt the most inequitable schooling are under way in several urban areas and may be sustained. But few educational reform efforts have succeeded in changing how schools are organized or how students are taught. Whatever level of reform surrounds teachers and schools, a learning-centered approach to classroom teaching is a necessity.

Constructivist Learning Design (CLD) is based on the assumptions and processes of constructivist learning theory, a naturally occurring and real-world way of thinking about learning and teaching. The teacher acts as choreographer: He or she teaches basic steps, shares cultural traditions, and organizes the production, but even the youngest dancers must bring themselves to the dance and give the art form life. Experienced dancers arrange their own choreography. Many teachers are aware of the pioneering work of Jean Piaget and Lev Vygotsky, psychologists who offered theories of constructivist learning. They maintained that students actively construct their own knowledge; teachers don't just transfer knowledge to students. Individual students connect what schools expect them to learn with their own experiences and consciously engage in the cultural construction of knowledge. They make personal meaning for themselves, discuss social meaning in peer groups, decide on shared meaning with other students in class, and then reflect on the standard meaning as they consider their thinking and learning with a teacher. This is a synopsis of what we mean by "designing for constructivist learning" and "teaching to support learners."

Piaget (1976) focused on the personal construction of knowledge in such works as *To Understand Is to Invent*, while Vygotsky (1934) emphasized the social construction of meaning in his work on *Thought and Language*. They both accepted the intimate relationship of individual and interpersonal learning and recognized the power of "reflective abstraction" and "shared reflection." Reflection is a deliberate, self-conscious analysis of life experience. Reflection can be either individual or collective. In either case, reflection is key to constructing knowledge.

Some teachers deliberately design learning activities so their students can make personal and shared meaning, and they welcome the constructivist learning perspective. These teachers invite students to explain phenomena for themselves before examining textbook views or experts' theories. Students work together to develop their own ideas rather than merely accept textbook summaries. When students encounter experts' theories and explanations in original source material, they are better prepared to critically analyze those ideas.

One of the difficulties with constructivist learning theory is adapting it to classroom teaching. Teachers are making the transition from "expecting listening" to "supporting learners" by examining their practice and reframing their approach to teaching. Vito Perrone (1991a) wrote, "teachers will teach the way they are taught." He explained why it is difficult for teachers to change perspectives from "planning for teaching" to "organizing for learning." For most teachers, their images of teaching have been shaped by years of being students. They learned about teaching by being participant observers for six years in elementary school, six years in secondary school, and four or more years in college. The images they have of constructivist teaching are memories of teachers who explored what students knew, engaged students in learning, expected students to think for themselves, and supported students as they made meaning of their learning. These experiences are few and far between in school. Such teaching often occurs in performing arts, athletics, or shop class, and those experiences stand out powerfully in memory. Constructivist Learning Design offers teachers an image of how to organize for student learning and thinking that is consistent with this remembered experience.

WHY WE WROTE THIS BOOK

Thoughtful, reform-minded educators expect students to solve problems, think critically, communicate effectively, and collaborate well with others. These processes require an approach to learning that is much more complex than memorizing facts. Our system of education has often confused memorizing with learning. Being able to recall something does not mean that you understand it or know how to use it. Giving students information and testing their memory of facts does not offer opportunities for them to collaborate productively and undertake complex tasks. Receiving and remembering information does not engage students in learning. Often, we see students succeed in high school with grades and test scores high enough to get them into prestigious colleges, but they avoid mathematics and science courses when they get there. These students report that their conceptual understanding of math and science is much weaker than their ability to memorize formulas or remember algorithms as procedures they can complete but do not really comprehend.

Landmark research by John Goodlad reported in *A Place Called School* (1984, 2004) confirmed that classrooms are often boring places for students. His teams conducted in-depth interviews with students, parents, teachers, and administrators in 13 triads or clusters of a high school, a feeder middle school, and a feeder elementary school. He found that about 90% of the time, teachers told students about information found in textbooks and then tested them on memorized material. Students cited fine arts, physical education, and industrial technology courses as their favorites because they got to do something. Larry Cuban (1984), in *How Teachers Taught*, described few changes in classroom practice throughout the 20th century. He found some interesting experiments in elementary schools, but most involved no more than one teacher in five and lasted no more than a few years.

For most of the 20th century, educational practices were driven by behaviorist psychology. The essence of behaviorism is that only observable and measurable behavior can be considered evidence of learning. Behaviorists assume that the focus of teaching is a broad cultural transmission of knowledge rather than an individual and personal construction of knowledge. School learning is presented as a process of operant conditioning based on a stimulus-and-response model with reinforcement of desired behaviors.

As cognitive psychology emerged during the second half of the 20th century, research and writing about rarely observable or measurable mental processes occurred more frequently. Studies of learning now consider mental phenomena such as dreams, daydreams, images, emotions, values, beliefs, learning styles, and processes of thinking or reasoning. Acknowledgement of these mental processes is important if we are to make classrooms interesting places where students actively engage in learning and construct their own knowledge. Constructivists believe that knowledge is dynamic rather than static, a process rather than a thing, a pattern of action rather than an object. Seymour Papert (1993) encouraged this movement toward "constructionism" and away from the "instructionism" of behaviorist psychology.

"Knowing" is a more appropriate term than "knowledge" to describe what a learner does. What we think of as a static body of knowledge has evolved during the centuries of recorded history. First, the oral tradition was very fluid, and stories changed with each retelling as they were passed on from one teller to another. Second, written language has changed enormously over time, and only a few scholars can translate early writing and thinking. Third, the paradigms of recent scientific thought are shifting radically. One example in the past century is the movement in physics from Isaac Newton's laws to Albert Einstein's theory of relativity, to Niels Bohr's quantum mechanics, to Murray Gell-Mann's quarks. The evolution of genetic biology during the same period demonstrates another paradigm shift as we move from Mendel's identification of genes to microbiology, to genetic engineering, to cloning, and now to mapping the human genome. In the same hundred years, our communications technology has moved from telegraph wires to telephone lines, to transistors, to microwaves, to fiber optics, to wireless cells, to low-orbit satellites. Even our laws, taxes, and codes change regularly, with great political debate about the anticipated impact on society. Clearly, what is considered knowledge changes with each generation.

If knowing is a process of constructing meaning rather than memorizing a body of knowledge, then our whole approach to teaching must be rethought. For education to emphasize learning rather than teaching, our role as teachers must change. No longer are we a "sage on the stage," but a "guide on the side." Instead of planning to teach a lesson by telling or showing students what we know, we should organize for learning by actively engaging students in making meaning to construct their own knowledge. Teachers must have a clear image of knowing and learning from a constructivist perspective to appreciate our process of learning design.

By challenging some cherished beliefs about knowledge and learning inherent in our current system of schooling, teachers can move toward a new paradigm for education. Teachers must challenge outmoded beliefs of the greater society in which they teach. The most important things people still expect students to learn in school are processes of one sort or another. The three Rs—reading, 'riting, and 'rithmetic—are certainly important, but they offer only a basic foundation for real life. Perhaps the real-life Rs of the new millennium should be reasoning, relating, and re-creating, while recognizing that reading, writing, and mathematics are necessary to learn these three. There is just too much information to expect students to be filled with a body of cultural knowledge, as some have advocated

(Hirsch, 1987). Instead of teachers "covering" curricula and requiring students to memorize a huge collection of specific information, they need to design curricula that require students to "uncover" new learning and apply new understanding (Wiggins & McTighe, 2005).

Constructivist Learning Design is grounded in a formal system of philosophy: Knowledge is composed of patterns of action; learning is the process of creating these patterns; and teaching is supporting students to construct their own knowledge. Teachers as learners can embrace the belief that education means to draw out rather than to put in. A teacher's role must then focus on organizing for student learning rather than planning for teacher telling. Because we believe that teaching is a process of supporting learners, we offer our CLD as a way for teachers to think about how they can design for constructivist learning to actively engage students.

In *Who Will Save Our Schools?* (1997), Linda Lambert and colleagues agreed that real reform in education will take place only because of grassroots efforts by classroom teachers to change classroom practice. If they are right, the lasting reform of the past decade will be educators who focus on what students are learning, not what teachers are teaching. As classroom teachers, we found that designing for learning rather than planning for teaching demanded challenging the status quo at all levels of the profession. As teacher-educators, we have accepted the challenge and developed a way for teachers to use CLD to be intentional about designing for learning. This book explains the six elements of our learning-design process and the connections between these elements.

THE HISTORY OF CONSTRUCTIVIST LEARNING DESIGN

Constructivist Learning Design is the product of extensive dialogue between the two of us and among dozens of teaching colleagues about ways teachers organize for learning in their classrooms. As teacher-educators working with prospective teachers, novice teachers, and veteran teachers seeking to improve their practice, we share a commitment to engaging students in learning. Thus, CLD is a guide to organizing for learning using six elements: Situation, Groups, Bridge, Task, Exhibit, and Reflection. Each of these six elements represents an important process in moving constructivist learning theory into classroom practice. We described the fourth element, Task, as "Questions" in previous versions. However, feedback from teachers and students encouraged us to describe it as a Task so the chronological nature of CLD is clear. The CLD outlines an agenda for engaging students in active learning throughout a classroom learning event. We hope you enjoy the same process of learning by working through this book.

We use this approach to organizing for learning with prospective teachers to engage them in all dimensions of planning. Students in math and science and technology methods courses have used versions of our CLD format to describe the units they prepared for elementary and middle school students. Novice teachers have carried CLD into apprenticeships with cooperating teachers and then used CLD in their own classrooms. Experienced teachers have recognized their own values in how we organize adult learning experiences with CLD and have seen applications with students. Many were motivated to teach because they wanted to overcome their own limited experiences in school by engaging students in learning rather than telling them what they needed to know. In that respect, CLD provides a consistent framework for accomplishing that goal.

One focus group of teachers described how they modified the CLD to meet their own needs. Some teachers extended the timeline of one lesson as far as two weeks. Many teachers used CLD for new sessions once every week or two. Other teachers changed the order of the Elements to fit the way they preferred to teach or to meet a series of standards (Gagnon & Collay, 1996). These teachers were excited to have an alternative to the typical lesson-planning format most districts use for evaluation. Because their principals saw a positive effect on student learning, they were willing to accept the CLD in lieu of a more traditional lesson plan.

LINKING AUTHENTICALLY TO STUDENT INTEREST WHILE MEETING STANDARDS

Many veteran teachers have taken risks with new approaches to learning and teaching, only to be criticized by parents or administrators or to see their innovations trampled by the next wave of reform. We believe CLD can be aligned easily with current thinking about standardized outcomes and goal-centered curriculum. The topic for each learning event is selected because our students want to learn it, because as teachers we feel it is appropriate to their development, or because we are required to teach it. As college teachers, we confront the same dilemma as our colleagues in elementary and secondary classrooms. How do we teach something that is developmentally appropriate or identified in a standard so that students are interested, are engaged in active learning, and can demonstrate what they have learned? How do we address school goals, district outcomes, state frameworks, graduation requirements, exit examinations, and national standards? How do we teach mandatory content so students find it interesting rather than boring? How can students become engaged in learning about standards-based concepts, processes, or attitudes rather than just being told what to remember for the test? How do students "show what they know" rather than being tested and graded on what they don't know? Constructivist Learning Design offers a way for teachers to describe the purpose for learning something; determine what specific topic should be learned; think about what students can do to learn this concept, process, or attitude; and decide how student learning will be assessed.

Some theorists argue that constructivist learning is appropriate only if students initiate and direct their own learning and decide what and how they want to learn. In our experience, few teachers are in classrooms where students can completely initiate or direct their own learning. Our work in urban schools over the last dozen years has been with classroom teachers who are most concerned about how students will be able to accomplish a district outcome, state framework, or national standard during a particular class. With the passage of the No Child Left Behind Act, we have seen teachers visited routinely by district "curriculum cops" who make sure they are on the exact page dictated by curriculum "pacing guides." Many teachers question the value of keeping on pace when students are functioning at least two years below grade level. Teachers are not concerned with how students will initiate or direct their own learning, but with students who do not have the skills to meet each standard. As teachers consider their role in classroom learning, they need to focus on what the students are supposed to learn and what students can actually do to learn a particular topic.

We believe that our CLD can assist teachers who work in classrooms that are now based on teaching to standards. We reframe each standard as a concept, process, or attitude that becomes the topic for a Situation, so students think about and explain the topic before they encounter the "official" explanation from the teacher or textbook. We find that most students are interested in figuring things out for themselves, working together to think about an explanation, sharing their thinking with others, and reflecting on their thinking and learning. As students listen to different explanations by peers, they revisit their own thinking and confirm or reformulate their ideas about a topic. Constructivist Learning Design provides a way to address the teaching dilemmas of balancing the required learning of educational mandates with authentic learning.

An additional dilemma is presented by the use of educational jargon: Readers should question the accepted usage of certain terms in educational writing, research, and standards. We deliberately use the phrase "concepts, processes, and attitudes" to convey different dimensions of knowledge. The accepted educational language used in current National Council for Accreditation of Teacher Education (NCATE) standards is "knowledge, skills, and dispositions." This may imply that skills and dispositions are somehow separate from knowledge or something different than knowledge. Is knowledge merely a collection of facts or information unrelated to what you do with it or how you feel about it?

Perhaps some of the confusion derives from Bloom's (1956) taxonomy of objectives in the cognitive domain that begins with knowledge and proceeds through a hierarchy of comprehension, application, analysis, synthesis, and evaluation. Again, this language is accepted as a standard by many educators. Bloom later classified objectives in the affective domain and the psychomotor domain as well. This left us with a legacy of knowledge as separate from how we feel about it or what we can do with it. Updated versions of this work retain a similar interpretation of knowledge (Marzano, 2000).

This separation of knowledge into distinct domains continued in the 2000 draft of the NCATE standards, which asks, "What should elementary teacher candidates know and be able to do to have positive effects on student learning?" A common phrase in these standards is "Candidates know, understand, and use . . . ." This phrase implies that understanding and using knowledge is different than knowing something. We would argue that what NCATE and Bloom refer to as knowledge is really information and that the other levels are different ways that learners construct knowledge for themselves and may not be discreet and hierarchical as Bloom suggests. However, these classifications can serve as important guidelines for moving the goal of education beyond the recitation of information.

We contend that an understanding of education should begin with epistemology rather than relegate it to the province of philosophy as an academic pursuit. Constructivist learning implies an initial concern with what knowledge is and how learners actively construct knowledge. Advocates of constructivism agree that acquiring knowledge is an active process of constructing meaning rather than the passive receipt of information. For these reasons, we use the phrase "concepts, processes, and attitudes" throughout this book to represent different dimensions of knowledge or knowing.

THE PURPOSE OF CONSTRUCTIVIST LEARNING DESIGN

The purpose of CLD is to offer teachers and students of teaching a way to think about organizing for learning in standards-based classrooms. If learning is a process of constructing knowledge, then teaching must involve supporting learners in ways that assist them in making meaning to construct knowledge. The teacher's role is to guide, facilitate, or coordinate learning rather than dispense information. Our CLD offers a basic framework to help teachers think about organizing for learning and a way to enact the basic processes of constructivist learning in the course of a lesson. It also incorporates assessment into each design element rather than seeing assessment as an end product or closing activity. The most important consideration is what teachers believe about learning. If you see yourself primarily telling students about the wisdom of the ages, then you probably don't agree with us that students construct their own knowledge. Perhaps an example from teacher learning in real life will challenge your assumptions.

Think about your first year of teaching. Most first-year teachers report that they learned more about teaching during that year than they had learned during their entire preservice experience. They also cite student teaching as the most valuable part of their teacher education. Much of what they learned was through on-the-job training. They had to sink or swim in their own classroom using their own knowledge, interpersonal processes, humor, and mental agility. They constantly kept their wits about them to survive. There is so much to learn. How do you manage 20 to 40 different personalities, sometimes five or six periods a day? How do you "cover" the prescribed curriculum in a way that interests students and keeps them actively engaged in learning? How do you assess individual learning and interpersonal processes? How do you communicate with parents? How do you keep up with changes in the profession and your subject matter? How do you learn to remove yourself from the external world of adult interaction and community activity eight or nine hours a day? How do you learn to function in professional isolation without the benefit of working with colleagues or team feedback? The answers to all of these questions lie in doing your own learning, constructing your own knowledge, and making your own meaning about teaching.

WHO IS OUR AUDIENCE?

This book is for students of teaching, teachers, administrators, and parents who want to know how to apply constructivist learning theory in classrooms. You can apply CLD to your work whether you are a veteran teacher or a novice teacher who is interested in organizing for learning by youth and adults. You might be thinking about another way of approaching teaching, applying the principles of constructivist learning theory in your classroom, or using a different format for lesson planning and evaluation. Some teachers already do many of these things but have inconsistent results from lesson to lesson. Constructivist Learning Design offers a consistent framework for thinking strategically about engaging learners in their own meaning making. We see our CLD being used in any classroom at any grade level. Teachers from all disciplines use this process to organize for learning by their students: primary teachers in self-contained classrooms, intermediate social studies teachers in teams, middle school language arts teachers, high school physical education teachers, and specialists in art and music.

Staff development coordinators and school administrators have used this approach to organizing for learning. Constructivist Learning Design offers a framework for educators to engage adult students in learning and compels us to establish assessment procedures to document that learning. Teacher-educators can incorporate our CLD into a basic methods course in any elementary area or secondary subject. They also can use it with experienced teachers who are studying for advanced degrees and considering different ways of designing for learning. Parents who home school their children or who are active participants in their children's education will also be interested in CLD as a resource for thinking about the processes of learning.

THE SCOPE OF THIS BOOK

Educators are moving beyond teaching to "objectives" with easily measured outcomes and toward accepting the multiple dimensions of "knowing" that occur in classrooms and in life. Constructivist learning theory emphasizes the processes of learning rather than the content or objectives of teaching. Theoretical assumptions about the processes of informal learning during life experiences guide how we organize for formal learning in educational settings. In the Introduction, we describe several theoretical assumptions about constructivist learning and map these assumptions directly to the six elements of our CLD: Situation, Groups, Bridge, Task, Exhibit, and Reflection. We describe each element separately in Chapters 1 through 6. The Introduction and Chapters 1–6 are organized using the six elements of our CLD as main headings. Under each heading are extended descriptions of how to organize for learning. We close the book with a discussion about the importance of questions in learning and a description of how a CLD unfolded for three of our colleagues. We hope you find your journey through designing for learning by your students, your colleagues, and yourself quite worthwhile.

—George W. Gagnon, Jr. and Michelle Collay

ACKNOWLEDGMENTS

We wish to acknowledge the teachers and students who shaped our thinking and teaching. As learners, we have admired good teaching since we joined the profession as young adults. We strive to model and teach students in ways that will make our mentors proud. These great teachers include Pat and Dick Schmuck, Linda and Morgan Lambert, Diane Dunlap, Rob Proudfoot, Liz Wing, and Vito Perrone.

Colleagues who encouraged us in this endeavor and whose teaching we admire include Kyle Shanton, Jan Lewis, Cathy Yetter, Sandra Gehrig, Valerie Lesniak, Sherry O'Donnell, Virgil Benoit, Christopher Dill, Helen LaMar, Joanne Cooper, Gail Gallagher, Heidi Boley, Steve Chin, Dan Fleming, Jake Dissten, Mark Salinas, Joel Baum, and Tania Gutierrez.

We also appreciate the ongoing support and careful editing of our friends and neighbors, Barbara Joan Tiger Bass and Marty Perlmutter.

As teacher-educators, we have worked with hundreds of teachers in school classrooms, professional development learning communities, and graduate programs. We have learned most of what we know about good teaching from them. Thousands of students have also taught us about constructivist learning, creating learning designs, and teaching learning episodes. Our current work for educational equity in urban settings has strengthened our commitment to supporting diverse learners who think in different ways and need opportunities to fully explain their individual meaning making.

We also wish to thank Caroline Barrit for the CLD template design and Will Hall for the graphics.

Corwin Press gratefully acknowledges the contributions of the following reviewers:

Clive Beck
Professor, Curriculum
Teaching and Learning
OISE/University of Toronto,
    Canada

Linda Kroll
Professor
Department of Education
Mills College
Oakland, CA

Geraldine Lefoe
Senior Lecturer
Centre for Educational
    Development and Interactive
    Resources
University of Wollongong
NSW Australia

Bruce Marlowe
Associate Professor
Educational Psychology and
    Special Education
Roger Williams University
Bristol, RI

About the Authors

George W. Gagnon, Jr., is a math models designer and math educator who directs Pre-Engineering Partnerships for the College of Engineering at the University of California, Berkeley. He has been an educator for 35 years as a classroom teacher, school administrator, university professor, learning community consultant, classroom coach, and academic equity advocate. His research interests include math learning, teacher professional development, constructivist epistemology, appropriate assessment, and communities of learners.

Michelle Collay is Associate Professor in the Department of Educational Leadership at California State University, East Bay in Hayward, California. A former music teacher, she is a teacher-scholar who seeks to align teaching and scholarship in higher education and K–12 schools. Her research focus is teacher professional socialization with attention to how gender, class, and race shape teachers' lives. She coaches principals and teacher leaders engaged in professional learning communities, constructivist teaching and leading, and other school reform efforts.

Introduction: Learning Design

Education is a natural process spontaneously carried out by the human individual, and is acquired not by listening but by experiences upon the environment.

—Maria Montessori,
Education for a New World (1963)

Teachers who embrace constructivist learning constantly seek ways to create the environment Montessori describes. Many educators have deepened our understanding of constructivist learning (Brooks & Brooks, 1993; Fosnot, 1996; Lambert, 1998). They described their theoretical assumptions about constructivist learning and offered principles for applying this theory in teaching and administrative practice. Our work with PreK–12 teachers has shown us that many already design classroom learning experiences for students using a constructivist philosophy. However, few teachers can articulate how they design for student learning, produce consistent results, or link learning to standards. After 15 years of studying planning strategies with our teacher colleagues, we have refined a replicable process that engages students in an active learning episode that we call Constructivist Learning Design (CLD). We deliberately use the words "learning episode" rather than "lesson" because we focus on active engagement by the student learners rather than instruction by the teacher.

The CLD framework is based on three key questions:

1. What are your students expected to learn?

2. Where are your students now in their learning?

3. How will students make meaning about what they are expected to learn?

These key questions are the core of CLD. As you respond to them, your answers will guide your thinking and shape the elements of CLD.

This chapter introduces the process of CLD. The next six chapters describe each element in detail using an interactive process of Constructivist Learning Design to engage you in making meaning. We have designed space for you to write, review, and revise each element of your own CLD. Chapters include an opportunity for drafting, note taking, thinking, editing, crafting a final version, and reflecting on each element. To explicitly model CLD, we invite you to identify a successful lesson you have taught before and use it throughout this process as a foundation for new learning.

The *Situation* section of each chapter describes the purpose, topic, and assessment for each element. You will write a draft of that element in Learning Record A, Element Draft.

The *Groups* section of each chapter provides practical considerations for you to think about with your reflective partner. You can record notes or ideas from this conversation in Learning Record B, Element Notes. We encourage you to meet with a group of reflective partners in a teacher inquiry group, a colleague study group, or a "Learning Circle," as we have described previously (Collay, Dunlap, Enloe, & Gagnon, 1998).

The *Bridge* section of each chapter poses questions about your prior knowledge in Learning Record C, Element Questions.

The *Task* section of each chapter lists characteristics of each element to guide a revision of your element draft in Learning Record D, Element Revision.

The *Exhibit* section of each chapter offers specific examples of elements from different grade levels and subjects. You will write a final version of your element in Learning Record E, Element Final.

In the *Reflection* section of each chapter, we explain the historical precedents for each element from prominent educators and related theory to encourage you to reflect on your thinking and learning as you moved through the chapter and write your reflections in Learning Record F, Element Reflection. Finally, we make some Concluding Remarks to close each chapter.

Chapter 7 is an extended metaphor about CLD as a dance rehearsal so you can visualize the relationship of teaching and learning in a different setting. As you watch one CLD unfold in three different ways, three teachers in separate classrooms portray the art and science of designing for learning.

SITUATION SECTION: CONSTRUCTIVIST LEARNING DESIGN

The notion of constructivist learning is not new. Jean Piaget introduced the idea that children construct their own knowledge in his book *The Construction of Reality in the Child,* first published in English in 1954. Learners construct their own meaning in acquiring knowledge rather than just memorizing information offered by a teacher. Most of us are familiar with learners who memorize well and can restate facts, but they still struggle to articulate the meaning because they do not understand the concept. This is particularly evident in young children who cannot yet speak. We expect them to communicate what they need so we can understand them. As children engage in dialogue, they gradually build up a repertoire of words and phrases until they are speaking in sentences. Just as we don't teach them how to walk, we don't teach them how to speak. We support their learning and celebrate their progress, but they learn to speak by themselves. Children construct their own meaning through interactions with others. Much of the learning of young children occurs by imitating the modeling of adults and rehearsing the patterns they see and hear.

The concept of CLD is based on our belief that learning is both an individual and social process of constructing meaning. Think of this work as organizing for learning rather than planning for teaching because the focus is on what students will do to learn and what the teacher will do to inspire and support that learning. Much classroom practice is driven by teacher talk and does not engage students. High dropout rates and academic failure have been linked to the boredom of classroom-based instruction: sitting in class and listening to a teacher talk rather than thinking and talking with others (Goodlad, 1984, 2004). The 45 or 50 minutes of class six or seven times a day remains the standard unit of instruction in many high schools and middle schools. Teachers tell themselves and their students that they have "covered the material," and they assume they have taught it properly until they test students. Often, they are disappointed by how little learning students can demonstrate and may then blame students for their lack of motivation. Constructivist Learning Design assumes that learning takes place as students reflect on what was taught and construct

their own meaning as they study with peers or apply new learning outside of school. When students attempt to make meaning without the benefit of interaction or feedback on their thinking, there may be little evidence
of understanding. Some undergraduates at the University of California,
Berkeley, report that they got good grades and test scores in high school
math classes to gain admission, but they never took a college course in
mathematics because they did not truly understand the concepts.

The purpose of this chapter is to introduce the six elements of Constructivist Learning Design. The Situation element is designed to answer
three key questions so that you can determine your purpose, topic, and
assessment. The topic is understanding the six elements of CLD and the
relationship between them. The assessment of learning is your definition
of each of the six elements. Each chapter element contains three key questions to answer as a concise guide to thinking about that element of a
CLD. The next section of this chapter is an overview of how to design for
constructivist learning episodes by using the six elements of CLD.

Elements of the Design

Table I.1, Constructivist Learning Design Template, on the next page,
is the framework we use to arrange the six elements in a sequence that
organizes your thinking about designing for learning.

The following description summarizes the six elements of CLD:

1. Designs a Situation that describes the purpose, determines a topic,
   and decides an assessment for student learning;

2. Organizes Groups of students, materials, and furniture to facilitate
   meaning making;

3. Builds a Bridge between what students already know and what
   they are expected to learn by describing students' developmental
   level, socioeconomic circumstances, and cultural background,
   surfaces their preconceptions, and makes connections to their lives;

4. Crafts a Task for students to accomplish that anticipates questions from students as they engage in tasks, considers responses
   to these questions so that students will sustain thinking, and
   describes how students are learning by making social meaning
   during tasks;

5. Arranges an Exhibit for students to demonstrate the results of
   their collaborative thinking by producing artifacts as a result of
   their learning, making presentations of these artifacts, and offering
   explanations about how they made social meaning; and

Table I.1   Constructivist Learning Design Template

Level:
Subject
Title:
Designers:

Situation	
Groups	
Bridge	
Task	
Exhibit	
Reflection	

Figure I.1   CLD Schematic

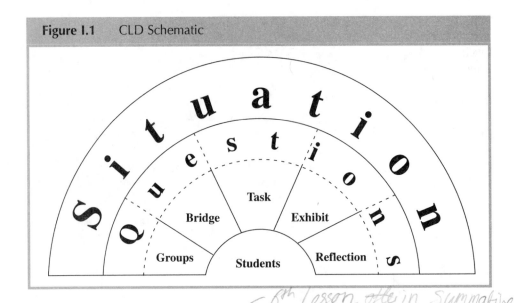

[handwritten note: 6th lesson often in Summative assessment]

6. Invites Reflection by students on their process of thinking during the learning episode through feelings in their emotional and physical responses, images in their sensory representations, and languages in their consideration of shared and common meanings.

Figure I.1 depicts the relationships among the six elements and the chronological sequence we recommend for designing and supporting constructivist learning episodes.

The CLD begins with a Situation or a comprehensive overview of your learning episode, a clear statement of your purpose for the topic you expect students to learn, and the assessment for student learning that has taken place. As you can see from the schematic, details of the learning episode unfold chronologically through the five other elements.

The CLD continues with your Groups of students, materials, and furniture, then moves to your Bridge between prior knowledge and current learning. Next, you elaborate on the Task that students will accomplish by thinking together. As learners accomplish this Task to your satisfaction and theirs, they create an Exhibit of their thinking. Then you arrange individual and collective student Reflection on their thinking. Your focus in designing a learning episode is structuring the work so students can think together about accomplishing the Task. The Task itself will allow students to demonstrate mastery of standards.

Please use Learning Record I.A, Element Definitions Draft, on the next page, to create a brief definition, in your own words, for each element. You will revise and write a final version of these definitions as you proceed through this chapter.

Learning Record I.A	Element Definitions Draft

How do you define the Situation element in your own words?

How do you define the Groups element in your own words?

How do you define the Bridge element in your own words?

How do you define the Task element in your own words?

How do you define the Exhibit element in your own words?

How do you define the Reflection element in your own words?

Copyright © 2006 by Corwin Press. All rights reserved. Reprinted from *Constructivist Learning Design: Key Questions for Teaching to Standards*, by George W. Gagnon and Michelle Collay. Thousand Oaks, CA: Corwin Press, www.corwinpress .com. Reproduction authorized only for the local school site or nonprofit organization that has purchased this book.

The following section offers ideas about learning for you to consider with your reflective partner or Learning Circle. The Groups section of each chapter encourages colleagues to co-construct their understanding of learning design.

GROUPS SECTION: LEARNING CONSIDERATIONS

The chapters in this book are designed as working guides to write elements of a CLD and include several Learning Records to document your thinking. We assume you have at least one reflective partner in a Learning Circle with whom to review these learning considerations and clarify your thinking about constructivist learning. You can use constructivist processes to frame learning episodes around people, places, products, and phenomena of interest to students. Content standards determine how students' work will be assessed. A learning episode is a distinct learning event that is part of a larger learning event or one of a series of learning events. You can design learning episodes to engage learners in constructing their own understanding of real learning events. The topic of study should be accessible in a variety of ways, opening many possibilities for the learning episode to become a real-life learning experience. Constructivist learning theory compels teachers to engage learners in formal learning at school, just as they engage informally in learning during life experiences outside of school. Teachers can use a consistent framework to build bridges from student interests and engage students in the kinds of formal, standards-based learning expected at school. Constructivist learning leads to deep, internalized knowledge, which requires the teacher to engage learners in truly making meaning. The following is one example.

Think about how you learned to ride a bicycle. Our experiences were very similar, with a few interesting differences. One of us had an old Schwinn with training wheels. The other learned on a pass-around bike that had no training wheels and was virtually indestructible. It was short with hard rubber tires and rotated through the neighborhood among children who were learning to ride. Both of us had used three-wheeler tricycles, so we already knew how to pedal and steer. One was the oldest child, so the parents had to buy the first bicycle in the family. The other was a youngest child, so all the older kids had bikes of their own. Both of us remember a lot of ceremony around learning to ride. We both pestered our families to get us a bicycle of our own. Training wheels were a great comfort and allowed for a feeling of confidence in being on a bicycle. They also gave one of us a sense of what it felt like to balance on two wheels with the security of outriggers in case we faltered.

Parents were there to help put the training wheels on and take them off when the rider was ready to solo. We both received a lot of support from our parents in learning to ride, including giving verbal directions and encouragement, holding the bike while running along behind, showing concern when we lost our balance, and expressing great satisfaction when we could actually balance by ourselves. The important point is that the experience of learning to ride a bicycle is deep knowledge, something that we can still do without riding every day. Our parents or brothers were our teachers, but they couldn't do it for us. We had to learn to ride a bicycle ourselves.

Thoughtful school learning leaves us with the same kind of deep, internalized lifelong knowledge. Watching another child ride a bike tells you something about it, but you have to experience riding for yourself to learn. You constructed patterns of action for balancing the bicycle and turning the pedals at the same time. You had to feel what it was like for yourself. Even a great description could not give you the knowledge you needed to learn about riding a bicycle. Your knowing came from doing the Task yourself and constructing your own pattern of action.

Recently we encouraged our six-year-old son and his two friends as they learned to ride their bikes without training wheels. Different sizes of bikes, different levels of tolerance for risk, and different attitudes toward failure all influenced their speed and success in learning to balance and pedal on only two wheels. Moving their learning environment from a narrow urban sidewalk to a wide school parking lot with a gently inclined driveway gave them more confidence. Some wanted us to hold them up as we ran alongside, while others didn't want us to do more than give them a safe start. They first learned to turn circles and fall without hurting themselves. Then they learned to coast down the driveway to get a feeling of balance on two wheels. After they were comfortable coasting, they started pedaling the bike before the momentum was gone to maintain speed and balance. In the end, all three learned to ride their bikes, some more quickly and confidently than others, but each in his own way.

In this bicycle example of a learning event, the role of the learner is to create knowledge, not to consume information. Learners want to do what is necessary to succeed and will risk making mistakes and even take some falls to be successful. Others can tell or show learners how to ride a bicycle, but those learning must choose what advice to take. School learning requires the same level of engagement. When children learn to read, write, and do arithmetic, their experience is very much the same as learning to ride a bicycle. Young children are very excited to learn these basic skills if they are offered in a compelling way. Once engaged, the struggle is worth their effort, and they are much more likely to accept coaching about reading, writing, and figuring. If they aren't engaged, then teaching can be a difficult proposition.

Take some time now to think about these considerations and talk with your Learning Circle colleagues or reflective partner about how real-life learning experiences compare to school learning. Think about whether you agree or how you would change these considerations based on your understanding. Fill in Learning Record I.B, Notes on Learning.

Learning Record I.B	Notes on Learning

Write your notes and ideas about how school learning compares to life learning.

Copyright © 2006 by Corwin Press. All rights reserved. Reprinted from *Constructivist Learning Design: Key Questions for Teaching to Standards*, by George W. Gagnon and Michelle Collay. Thousand Oaks, CA: Corwin Press, www.corwinpress .com. Reproduction authorized only for the local school site or nonprofit organization that has purchased this book.

The next section of this chapter raises questions about your understanding of learning.

BRIDGE SECTION: WHAT IS LEARNING?

We described constructivist learning theory in the Preface and at the beginning of this chapter. In this section, we ask you to answer several questions about how you understand learning and to compare your understanding with this description of constructivist learning. These questions should guide your thinking as you compare your own ideas with ours. This should surface your prior knowledge of learning and support you in connecting with the concepts of learning we encourage you to analyze. Take time to write your answers to the questions in Learning Record I.C, Learning Beliefs.

Learning Record I.C	Learning Beliefs

How do you define learning?

What do you believe about learning?

(Continued)

Learning Record I.C   (Continued)

How is learning related to teaching?

How does constructivist learning differ from your definition of learning?

How does our description of teaching compare to your experience?

Copyright © 2006 by Corwin Press. All rights reserved. Reprinted from *Constructivist Learning Design: Key Questions for Teaching to Standards*, by George W. Gagnon and Michelle Collay. Thousand Oaks, CA: Corwin Press, www.corwinpress .com. Reproduction authorized only for the local school site or nonprofit organization that has purchased this book.

When you finish writing, continue on to the next section of this chapter.

TASK SECTION: LEARNING CHARACTERISTICS

The principles of constructivist learning led to the following characteristics about learners engaged in real-life learning events:

- Learners think individually to make personal or self-meaning about learning events.
- Learners think collaboratively with others to make "social" meaning of learning events.
- Learners connect their prior knowledge and previous experience to learning events.
- Learners pose and answer questions as they think together about accomplishing group tasks during learning events.
- Learners present their thinking about learning events to others and make shared meaning with a class.
- Learners reflect on their individual and collective thinking during learning events and consider standard meaning with a teacher.

These six characteristics about learning through real-life experience must be the foundation for school learning episodes. Each element of CLD addresses one characteristic of learning during real-life events. School learning is most powerful when it clearly parallels real-life learning. We recently reminisced with some former students at one of the first alternative public schools in the country, the Evergreen Open Living School in Jefferson County, Colorado. Many of these now 40-year-olds had not attended college and were successful entrepreneurs who ran their own businesses. Several thoughtful conversations addressed the condition of the environment, the economy, and the education system. Their perceptions and life paths were very consistent with the school's value for lifelong learning and caring between students and teachers and community members. Their schooling experiences included undertaking tasks such as building greenhouses, and this learning was preparation for life. These former students talked about how their school-based experiences were reflected in their worldview and their parenting. They led their children through life learning with love and respect for both learner and learning. They recognized the value of real-life learning experiences provided at our school, and they now "carry the torch with their own children."

To educate is to draw out what is within by articulating and clarifying thinking. Education should be all about learning! Our friend Fred Jacob talks about working with campesinos in the rural mountains of Nicaragua who are not educated but are trained to maintain the water purification systems. They cannot solve problems or complications they have not encountered in training. So when unusual circumstances disable the system, the campesinos wait for the "Norte Americanos" to arrive and figure out what is wrong and then tell them how to fix it. Their training was based on memorizing a routine, not on theoretical understanding.

Constructivist learning is based on learners constructing their own meaning as they think together to accomplish a Task. The nature of the Task should be demanding or challenging enough to engage their attention and focus their concentration. Working with urban youths in schools that are embedded in tough inner-city neighborhoods has challenged some of our mainstream cultural assumptions, but it has not shaken the profound conviction that in any setting, every learner constructs his or her own meaning. The preconceptions and sometimes misconceptions that students carry into classrooms are as much a part of the learning process as what they carry out of the classroom. Another way of framing this goal is to ask, what real learning do you want the kids to take out the door? Seldom is the answer information from a textbook or a short homework assignment; rather, teachers plan for deep, conceptual understanding that is developed over time and can be applied in the real world.

Students must make meaning in classroom settings and apply that learning to their lives. Such academic learning must be realistic, compelling, and credible to students. Many urban learners have little adult support, time, or space at home for schoolwork. Parents often defend their children against accusations made by the school administrators or teachers. Undereducated parents want their children to do well, but they have few models of productive schooling themselves. Math may be a worst-case scenario because few parents of any class feel they learned much math in school, particularly algebra, and fewer think their children will use it very often in either their personal or work lives. Schoolwork is most useful and compelling when it applies to real life. Formal learning must be structured around thinking and making meaning just as informal learning is outside the classroom. Dan Fleming has taught Oakland public school students for 10 years in a self-contained eighth-grade classroom. He successfully moved their collective level of academic success two to three grade levels in one year by relating their school learning to their life experiences.

We now market algebra to students in middle school as a "way of thinking about what you don't know." This approach offers more than solving for x. Instead, learners are required to understand how what they know is related to what they don't know and to determine whether they have enough information to find the answer. Math may be one of the last bastions of a classical education and a powerful gatekeeper that prevents undereducated students from attending college. Like Latin or Greek, it is a school language spoken and used by formally educated people but rarely part of daily life. Education used to be the great equalizer, but now cash may be. Prisons are filled with young and not-so-young men who did not learn algebra or even basic math in school. Another friend, Marty Perlmutter, taught math to inmates in San Quentin and reports that few have a grasp of fundamental arithmetic concepts, such as fractions, integers, and proportions, that are prerequisites for algebra.

In 1997, former Secretary of Education Richard Riley reported research in a white paper (policy report) that recognized the completion of advanced math courses beyond algebra as the most reliable predictor of success in college admission, regardless of ethnic or economic background. Why do our efforts in educational equity miss this mark? Even fully committed and well-trained math teachers find it difficult to interest kids in math. How is it relevant to their lives? Who uses it in their family or community? What outcomes does it offer that street smarts can't buy? How do we convince kids that they need math to survive and succeed? We can't continue to teach algebra and math the way it was taught 150 years ago in the common schools of Massachusetts.

Teachers don't need to be experts in explaining or telling what they know. Instead, teachers should be experts in learning and know how different individuals learn. We continue to present the illusion that every child learns the same way by structuring classroom learning one way. The learner experiences school as a department store that has general merchandise that may or may not fit. Only the privileged can choose to shop at specialty stores. Imagine shopping at a large department store for men's shoes. You can only get a medium width in sizes 8 to 12. If your feet are smaller or larger or narrow or wide, you are out of luck. You can go to a special shop for shoes, but we have few specialty public schools. How do we measure the fit of the learning model to the student? What kind of learning is being measured? Who sets the standard?

Students with good memories can regurgitate factual information about what teachers or textbooks have told them. Such short-term memorization required of them is fairly easy to measure. However, retelling facts does not lead to deeper learning, and more authentic assessments are essential to learning design. A few tests now measure problem-solving ability and require students to describe their thinking or explain their answers. These tests cannot be scored by a computer scanner. Students need individual, expert analysis by competent peers and teachers. Comprehensive and timely assessment that captures how students learn what they know is central to our design.

Based on these learning characteristics, rewrite your definition of each CLD element and explain its order in a CLD in Learning Record I.D, Revised Element Definitions, which begins below.

Learning Record I.D   Revised Element Definitions
Situation definition and explanation of why it is first:
Groups definition and explanation of why it is second:
Bridge definition and explanation of why it is third:

(Continued)

Learning Record I.D (Continued)

Task definition and explanation of why it is fourth:

Exhibit definition and explanation of why it is fifth:

Reflection definition and explanation of why it is sixth:

Copyright © 2006 by Corwin Press. All rights reserved. Reprinted from *Constructivist Learning Design: Key Questions for Teaching to Standards*, by George W. Gagnon and Michelle Collay. Thousand Oaks, CA: Corwin Press, www.corwinpress .com. Reproduction authorized only for the local school site or nonprofit organization that has purchased this book.

Now proceed to the next section to prepare a final version of your CLD element definitions and explanations.

EXHIBIT SECTION: FAIRY TALES LEARNING EPISODES

Here is a sketch of an exemplary CLD. A team of three middle school language arts teachers designed it for several ninth-grade classes studying different genres of literature. In this section, we describe how individual learning episodes based on the same CLD unfolded for one teaching team. We will revisit this same team in the last chapter.

Ellen, Gail, and Sue had met to design a constructivist learning episode that would introduce the elements of fairy tales to their ninth-grade classes. For homework, they asked their classes to write essays about personal experiences with fairy tales. The next day, each teacher opened class by describing her own experiences with fairy tales. Ellen related the story of her Irish grandfather, who had told her about the "little people" and made them seem so real that she would look for them in likely hiding places. Her class also offered their personal experiences with fairy tales. Next she asked her class to arrange themselves in groups of four and had each group list the common elements in fairy tales and develop a definition of what made a fairy tale. Then each group wrote their list and definitions on a transparency, presented it to their classmates, and debriefed their thinking with Ellen.

In another classroom, Gail had her groups of four share their personal experiences with fairy tales and collect large chart paper, markers, and tape. Then she asked them to develop their own definitions of a fairy tale and to identify the common elements in fairy tales. Her class met for about 15 minutes of discussion while Gail moved among the groups and answered their questions or asked clarifying questions. She directed them to tape their charts to the wall and to present their definitions and common elements to their peers. Gail invited her class to discuss their choices and their rationale for each choice.

In a third classroom, Sue first told a story about how she had enjoyed listening to fairy tales when she was a small child. She asked her class what they remembered about fairy tales as listeners, readers, or storytellers. She had them meet in writer's workshop groups and asked them to compare their personal experiences with fairy tales, to make lists of common elements, and to agree on a definition of a fairy tale. After each group selected one person to report on its work, Sue led a discussion comparing the different elements and definitions.

Then each teacher handed out articles from their files by experts who defined fairy tales and listed their common elements. They asked their classes to read the articles and then compare and contrast their own definitions and lists with the experts' thinking. After 10 minutes, they led a discussion about group observations and reflected on how the group definitions and elements were similar to those of the experts.

In each classroom, teachers asked their classes to answer two questions for the next day:

1. What would you add to your group's definition and list based on ideas from your peers and experts?

2. Which definition is more meaningful to you in preparing to write your own fairy tale?

At the end of the day, the teachers talked together about the how the learning episode had gone in each of their classrooms. They spoke about the level of student engagement and how collaborative thinking seemed so much more meaningful than when they had lectured about the elements of fairy tales. They identified students who seldom participated in the day-to-day activities of class yet were excited to offer ideas to their small group based on their own experiences with fairy tales. They talked about the importance of capturing the students' new knowledge in ways that documented their individual grasp of this area of literature. Ellen, Gail, and Sue had high hopes that their students were now prepared to write interesting fairy tales. Table I.2, Fairy Tales CLD, on the next page is the framework of elements the teachers used to design their constructivist learning episode.

Use this example of a complete CLD to analyze your definitions and explanations for each element. Then write your final revision in Learning Record I.E, Final Element Versions, which begins on page 21. You may see evidence of how your thinking evolved as you progressed through this chapter. Most teachers rearrange the order within the design as they consider different points or after test-driving the design with one group of students. Continue on to the final section of this chapter.

REFLECTION SECTION: PRECEDENTS FOR CONSTRUCTIVIST LEARNING DESIGN

Renowned educators such as John Dewey, Maria Montessori, Paulo Freire, Eleanor Duckworth, Theodore Sizer, and Maxine Greene have advocated for similar elements within educational design. Teachers worldwide are heeding their advice to think differently about designing for learning rather than planning for teaching. None of these ideas is new—rather,

Table I.2   Fairy Tales CLD

Level:	Middle School
Subject	Language Arts
Title:	Fairy Tales
Designers:	Ellen, Gail, Sue

Situation *50 minutes*	The purpose of this Situation is to engage students in analyzing fairy tales so they develop an understanding of core elements and common themes that define this area of literature. Students will consider their previous experience with fairy tales, develop their definition of a fairy tale, and identify a list of common elements that are found in fairy tales. Students will assess their learning by comparing their definitions and characteristics against experts.
Groups *5 minutes*	Students will put themselves into groups of three or four. The students will be given large sheets of chart paper and markers to write their group definition of fairy tales and lists of common elements found in fairy tales and tape to put them up on the white board for the exhibit. Copies of articles by experts defining fairy tales and listing common characteristics will be distributed to individual students following the exhibit. Desks will be turned toward each other in groups of four.
Bridge *10 minutes*	The teacher will describe personal experiences with fairy tales and ask students to read what they wrote for homework the previous day about their personal memories of fairy tales.
Task *15 minutes*	Students will organize into groups and get paper, markers, and tape. They will develop their definition of a fairy tale and will list common characteristics of fairy tales. Teacher questions: What were your previous experiences with fairy tales? How would you define a fairy tale? What are common characteristics in fairy tales? How do your definitions compare to experts'? Were your definitions or lists as precise? After seeing and reading others what would you add to your own definition or list? Which definition was more meaningful to you and would be more helpful in writing your own fairy tale? Why are we studying fairy tales? Where did fairy tales come from? What are fairy tales from other cultures?
Exhibit *10 minutes*	Student groups will tape the chart paper with definitions and lists of common elements on the white board and present their thinking to the rest of the class.
Reflection *10 minutes*	Students will read the articles and discuss the comparisons and contrasts with their own definitions and lists. Then they will write about what they would add to their definitions or lists from other groups or from the article. Students will describe why their own definition or the expert's definition was more meaningful to them as they think about writing their own fairy tale.

Learning Record I.E   Final Element Versions

Situation definition and order explanation:

Groups definition and order explanation:

Bridge definition and order explanation:

(Continued)

Learning Record I.E (Continued)

Task definition and order explanation:

Exhibit definition and order explanation:

Reflection definition and order explanation:

Copyright © 2006 by Corwin Press. All rights reserved. Reprinted from *Constructivist Learning Design: Key Questions for Teaching to Standards*, by George W. Gagnon and Michelle Collay. Thousand Oaks, CA: Corwin Press, www.corwinpress .com. Reproduction authorized only for the local school site or nonprofit organization that has purchased this book.

CLD organizes the thinking of many scholars of teaching into a framework that is sequenced and accessible.

In addition to the writing of these scholars, researchers working directly with schools have identified very similar patterns of learning design. Several excellent examples of how constructivist processes have been used to frame learning episodes are available from the Annenberg Foundation videos on teaching math in North America (Harvard-Smithsonian Center, 1987) or the TIMSS videos of Japanese and German classrooms (NCES, 1998). These vides documentation of international teaching address the importance of designing for learning that leads to an agreed-upon standard of performance. Some argue that learning episodes designed to meet national standards or curriculum outcomes can't really be constructivist. However, the concepts, processes, or attitudes selected as the topics of learning episodes are more powerful if teachers and students know what is expected. Teachers have always been challenged to design educational experiences that support learning at a high level. Standardized tests do not always measure this kind of deep, conceptual learning, but competent students should be able to demonstrate learning on both standardized and comprehensive assessments. Progressive educators often argue about the limitations of standardized testing, but their own children are coached to succeed in any kind of assessment. Educators must take responsibility for ensuring that all students, not only those from privileged backgrounds, can meet contemporary international standards required of a global education in this new millennium.

A brief history of modern lesson planning often begins with the work of Ralph Tyler's (1949) "rationale" or the underlying reason for shaping curriculum. His thinking was complex, illuminating the need for a grounding philosophy and matching processes required to educate. He is best remembered for his ideas about measurable objectives. Tyler believed that teachers cannot teach effectively unless the curriculum is well-defined and learning objectives are measurable.

Robert Gagné (1985) also described the difference between education needed to learn simple tasks and education required to learn complex tasks. He suggested that teaching should be structured to involve problem solving and to ensure higher-level understanding. Gagné specifies nine relevant "instructional events" that vary according to the specific content and the expected outcome:

1. Gaining attention

2. Telling learners the learning outcome

3. Stimulating recall of prior learning

4. Presenting the stimulus

5. Providing learning guidance

6. Eliciting performance

7. Providing feedback

8. Assessing performance

9. Enhancing retention and transfer to other contexts.

James Block (1971) offered the field of education "mastery learning." He believed that knowledge is acquired on a continuum from simple to complex and that instruction should be structured to reflect these levels of knowledge. He collaborated with Bloom and others and used his hierarchy of educational objectives with "knowledge" at the bottom of the ladder, representing facts and tables, and "synthesis" at the top, representing the most complex action by the learner. Such "instructional programming" frameworks emerged from an era that Case (1996) called the "cognitive revolution." This philosophy suggests that teaching behaviors and student learning can be structured and measured, from the most simple to the most complex.

In contrast to these precedents, constructivist learning theory focuses on the development of individual self-meaning, group social meaning, class shared meaning, and the public standard meaning in the cultural construction of knowledge. In this philosophical framework, teaching becomes a process of surfacing prior knowledge, actively engaging students in new learning, and connecting the two for as many students as possible.

Now reflect on your thinking and learning as you wrote your definitions for the six CLD elements (Situation, Groups, Bridge, Task, Exhibit, and Reflection) and your explanations for the order of CLD elements. Revisit your answers to the three CLD key questions introduced at the beginning of this chapter:

1. What are your students expected to learn?

2. Where are your students now in their learning?

3. How will students make meaning about what they are expected to learn?

Reviewing your answers should remind you of the feelings thoughts in your spirit, the images thoughts in your imagination, and the languages thoughts in your internal dialogue. Please describe these thoughts in Learning Record I.F, Thoughts on CLD, on the next page.

Learning Record I.F Thoughts on CLD

As you were answering the three key questions about CLD,

Describe the feelings thoughts in your spirit.

Describe the images thoughts in your imagination.

Describe the languages thoughts in your internal dialogue.

Copyright © 2006 by Corwin Press. All rights reserved. Reprinted from *Constructivist Learning Design: Key Questions for Teaching to Standards*, by George W. Gagnon and Michelle Collay. Thousand Oaks, CA: Corwin Press, www.corwinpress .com. Reproduction authorized only for the local school site or nonprofit organization that has purchased this book.

CONCLUDING REMARKS: WHERE DO WE STAND?

We position ourselves on three related continuums:

1. Instructional design

2. Constructivist learning

3. Educational assessment

The continuum of instructional design includes the macro-level planning of a curriculum or course, the mid-level planning of units or themes, and the micro-level planning of one class or lesson. The last category focuses on thinking about how to learn a single topic or idea in one class period or lesson, referred to as a *learning episode*. Older educational theory, derived from military experience, arranged lessons in 50-minute-long configurations with a 10-minute break between each lesson. The notion reflects a belief that learners and teachers do better if they have a short break in the class. Current high school classes still run 45–90 minutes, depending on single- or block-period scheduling. Some modern fitness theory says that workouts should last only 30 minutes rather than 90 minutes because both interest and endurance begin to wane shortly after half an hour. Many of the example CLDs reflect short periods of about 10 or 20 minutes to engage students as they think together to accomplish a Task and then share their thinking and reflect on what they have learned. The balance of the episode can take another 20 minutes or a few hours. Pacing engagement is an important part of creating the learning environment, so the design keeps things active and interesting for students.

The constructivist learning continuum extends from radical constructivists on one end to social constructivists on the other end. This perspective balances individually constructed personal meaning, collaboratively constructed social meaning developed in a group, and collectively constructed shared meaning. There are also culturally constructed standard meanings held by the larger community or society. Teachers need to relate these broader societal values to the shared meanings that are constructed collectively by a class. Personal meanings and social meanings are powerful for individuals and groups, but to be useful to others, these meanings must be communicated and understood. An important goal of education in a democracy is that students know that others have thought about these concepts before and have developed a cultural or standard meaning that has been derived and accepted over time. Broader societal practices that continue to marginalize certain races or cultures can be challenged and disrupted only if their history is fully examined.

The third continuum of educational assessment is polarized and political. One end is quantitative, with standardized test scores and grade point averages, while the other end is qualitative, with artifacts of student work or performance on open-ended problems available for teacher and parent analysis. We rely extensively on teacher observation and judgment about students, but we realize that these professional assessments must be documented and translated into easily understood frameworks to demonstrate accountability for those who are not as skilled at evaluating education. Most standardized, norm-referenced tests are designed to be easily administered and scored. Classroom criterion-referenced tests are usually easy to give and grade. Both of these approaches to testing are too simplistic to measure conceptual understanding. A more comprehensive approach that includes multiple measures and individual information about the learner is required to tailor teaching that supports real learning.

This chapter has walked you through a process of CLD for answering three key questions: What are your students expected to learn? Where are your students now in their learning? How will students make meaning about what they are expected to learn? Math and science teachers usually see this approach as relevant for their subjects. Language arts, social studies, and fine arts teachers have also used this process to design engaging learning episodes for their classes. Teachers from almost every grade level and subject area, including physical and special education, have used this CLD framework. We encourage you to use our six-step CLD process and see how your students respond.

The next six chapters discuss each element in the process of designing a CLD. The Situation, or the overarching theme that is central to learning design, is presented in Chapter 1. The other five elements follow in subsequent chapters. Readers walk through a process of writing each element as they draft, consider, answer questions, review characteristics and revise, finalize, and then reflect on their thinking and learning about each element. This interactive process is designed to familiarize you with the CLD process and let you practice enough to feel confident organizing for student learning using our CLD framework.

1 Designing Situations

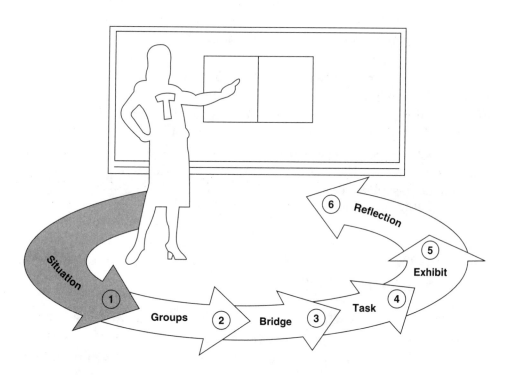

The only true education comes through the stimulation of the child's powers by the demands of the social situations in which he finds himself.

—John Dewey, "My Pedagogic Creed" (1897)

Constructivist Learning Design (CLD) seeks to satisfy Dewey's pedagogic creed. The first CLD element or Situation connects formal school learning with his "only true education" of real-life learning in social situations. This Situation element of CLD focuses on organizing learning episodes that produce "stimulation of the child's powers by the demands of the social situations." This chapter describes the first and overarching element of CLD, the Situation that frames and connects the other five elements. We considered other terms such as problem, experience, and event before settling on Situation. Later in this chapter we review many precedents for this term.

Constructivist Learning Design begins with this element because choosing a powerful Situation is the most important decision teachers make as they design a learning episode for students to construct meaning about a relevant topic. A Situation answers three key questions:

1. Purpose: Why are you engaging students in this learning episode?

2. Topic: What is your specific focus for student learning?

3. Assessment: How will you assess student learning?

In this chapter, you will move through a cycle of Constructivist Learning Design in order to connect your knowledge with the experiences of your colleagues and the authors. You are encouraged to draft, revise, and finalize a Situation element for your own CLD, and we offer considerations, questions, characteristics, and examples for you to review as you refine your writing. Then, some educational precedents for the Situation element are described to use in reflecting on your thinking and learning as you wrote this element of your CLD.

SITUATION SECTION: DEFINING GUIDING QUESTIONS

The initial element of CLD is called a Situation, and this overarching description frames and binds together the other five elements. The primary concern in drafting a Situation element is to describe the purpose of your learning episode for students. The second concern is to determine a topic so that students can think together to make meaning and fulfill your purpose. The topic you select will become the core of a Task for students to accomplish. This Task can be framed as a problem to solve, a question to answer, a decision to make, a metaphor to create, a conclusion to draw, a goal to reach, a characteristic to identify, a definition to prepare, an essay to write, a physical challenge to complete, a puzzle to figure out, or any other active engagement in learning. The third concern is to decide how student learning will be assessed. Generally, students prepare an artifact of their thinking for presentation to class. This Exhibit could be a chart, a poster, an overhead, a PowerPoint presentation, a drawing, some photographs, a diagram, a cartoon, a graphic, a calculation, an audio tape, a videotape, a film, or some other depiction of their thinking. The depiction must be accompanied by an explanation. Student work can then be assessed against a rubric determined by one or a combination of the following: an individual performance of the concept, process, or attitude to be learned; the class; a review panel of peers, teacher analysis, the industry standard, or an examination. Students must know the criteria they will use for assessment of a completed Situation.

Purpose of a Situation element

The Situation sets up the other five elements in the CLD. The purpose of a Situation can be quite varied. Sometimes the purpose is for students to understand a concept, other times for students to perform a process, and still other times for students to examine an attitude. Sometimes the purpose is for students to explore a topic and other times for students to understand a topic in depth. The purpose may encourage students to be wildly creative, expect students to craft a specific product, or ask students to explore their attitudes toward cultural values. Rarely is the purpose just to offer students an experience, but rather to engage students in examining big ideas or analyzing relevant events.

Teachers design a Situation to ensure that students learn the concepts outlined in content-based standards, to strengthen a specific set of processes defined by district- or state-mandated outcomes, or to examine a personal or social attitude embedded in curriculum objectives. Standards must be broken down into meaningful parts. Teachers may weave together a series of learning episodes into a theme or project so learning is more meaningful. Research suggests that students are more likely to retain new knowledge when the learning is applied, meaningful, and builds on their prior experience. Connecting sometimes disparate standards requires care and creativity. As you and your colleagues align specific learning episodes into one Situation, you walk the fine line of structuring purposeful learning for students while holding yourself and them to a high level of achievement against measured content standards.

Topic for a Situation element

Determining a worthwhile topic for students to learn is fundamental to Constructivist Learning Design. A topic is the concept, process, or attitude that you select for students to learn by thinking together to make meaning. The topic must be appropriate to students' developmental level but challenging enough to engage their interest in accomplishing the learning. A topic should involve students in making meaning about the concept, process, or attitude that is the focus of your learning episode. Students should participate in learning, not passively listen to explanations by experts. The more students can construct knowledge by making their own meaning, the more they will learn and understand about the topic.

Teachers often begin to plan a lesson by thinking about an activity, exercise, or project that they will have students do. If this activity is just following a recipe, memorizing a passage, practicing an algorithm, duplicating a craft, copying definitions, or doing other activities that don't include meaning making, then the opportunity for learning is diminished. An activity becomes a topic for making meaning when students have to think for themselves and display their thinking for others. In the previous examples, students would make more meaning if they created a recipe, wrote a passage, explained an algorithm, created a craft, or wrote definitions in their own words. Selecting worthwhile topics to engage students in learning is like choosing the most fitting music before rehearsing the dance. Careful thought up front leads to a well-crafted outcome.

Assessment in a Situation element

As teachers design and guide learners through a Situation, they must decide how student learning will be assessed on several levels:

- Teachers assess what their students need to learn. For their grade level or subject area, teachers must consider the expectations of the community, the outcomes specified in their district curriculum, any markers or checkpoints toward state graduation requirements, and the curriculum standards from professional organizations such as the National Council of Teachers of Mathematics, International Reading Association, National Council of Teachers of English, National Science Teachers Association, National Council of Social Studies, and International Society for Technology in Education. Teachers may use district or national standards as they design curriculum and evaluation for their classrooms.

- Teachers assess the developmental level of their students both individually and collectively. Teachers are constantly evaluating the developmental status of their students and what they are capable of understanding. There are no quick inventories that teachers can use; rather, they must observe and make judgments about how learners are thinking and measure that learning against a continuum of appropriate development. Elementary teachers assess whether their learners are thinking perceptually or conceptually by analyzing explanations. Are students' explanations based on perceptions of sensory appearance or on mental concepts constructed through experience? A common standard for assessment is Piaget's classic conservation of number, length, mass, and volume; these skills emerge sequentially about ages 7, 8, 9, and 10. Do students see objects as equivalent depending on their appearance, or do they realize that appearances can be deceptive and conserve the quantity even if it appears to be transformed? For example, do students think there is more rice if it is poured from a wide, short container into a narrow, tall container? Secondary teachers assess whether their students think through concrete or formal operations. Are their decisions based on acquired experiences or logical structures? For example, do students think a can of tennis balls is taller or further around?

- Teachers assess what captures the interest of their students or piques their curiosity. Teachers know the culture of the children or teenagers in their community: where they like to go, what they like to do, what's hot and what's not, who is in and who is out, and what the trends are in their world. Many teachers also know about the lives of their students on a personal level. What is their home life like, how are they supported by adults in their lives, what chores or jobs do they have, what are their sports or activities, and what are their hobbies or interests? Such background is gathered through informal conversations or interactions and influences how teachers arrange a Situation. Some teachers use surveys to gather such information.

- Teacher judgment is the most important factor in selecting an appropriate Situation. Teachers may use formal assessments and informal observations to select a pertinent and compelling Situation for their students. They might consult with colleagues to review and refine their choices. Research on the practice of nurses and teachers has identified tacit knowledge as a critical factor in professional judgment. Just as nurses may know implicitly when a patient is deteriorating although doctors are not aware of the condition, teachers are able to judge the appropriateness of a lesson based on subtle student responses such as facial expressions, body language, or the general tone of a class. These informal teacher judgments often are more reliable than other assessments in evaluating the appropriateness of a design or the extent of learning.

After reviewing key dimensions of a Situation, draft your own element with a purpose, topic, and assessment of student learning in Learning Record 1.A, Situation Element Draft, on the next page. Don't be concerned about the final content right now, just get started.

Learning Record 1.A Situation Element Draft

Write a rough draft of a Situation element, including your purpose, topic, and assessment of student learning.

Copyright © 2006 by Corwin Press. All rights reserved. Reprinted from *Constructivist Learning Design: Key Questions for Teaching to Standards*, by George W. Gagnon and Michelle Collay. Thousand Oaks, CA: Corwin Press, www.corwinpress .com. Reproduction authorized only for the local school site or nonprofit organization that has purchased this book.

In the next section, reflect with at least one other colleague before you revise the Situation element for your CLD.

GROUPS SECTION: CO-CONSTRUCTING THE CLD

There are several ways to apply new learning to your teaching. You are encouraged to identify reflective partners or a group of colleagues with whom to do reflective work. This reflective group can be considered your "Learning Circle." The specific membership of this group directly affects the quality of your product. Not only will different colleagues have different approaches to teaching "big ideas," they can consider ways, means, and assessments that will strengthen everyone's work and, subsequently, your students' learning. Talking with a trusted colleague over time as you refine how you teach challenging, important concepts is energizing and powerful.

Your partner or teammates may be teaching the same content or grade level, or they may be working with the same student population. Share dilemmas that are sure to arise as you craft your CLD.

Considerations for designing a Situation element

To design your Situation, you and your reflective partner or team should choose a learning episode from your current curriculum and use it throughout the design process. Choose a lesson or unit that you have experience teaching, that is based on a big idea in your curriculum, and that requires learners to document their learning. The length may be 30 minutes, one hour, 30 minutes each day for five days, an all-day workshop, or a several-day unit. If you choose a lesson that has worked well for you in the past, you may feel more confident in your design. You may want to take advantage of the design process to start new work.

Preparing a Situation element

The planning cycle requires imagination. Many teachers start curriculum design with a student activity in mind. Teachers are now required to be familiar with grade-level and content standards and to show connections among the curriculum, instructional strategies, and learning outcomes. Choosing a thoughtful Situation with a focused topic is always a challenge, but the level of accountability many teachers now face makes the choice even more daunting.

When you and your class unfold your learning design, different students will reach the goal in different ways. Draw from your experience with productive lessons to choose a powerful Situation. Our advice about setting up a thoughtful Situation that is standards-based comes from observing good teachers; from learning theory; from creating project-based learning, cooperative learning, or active learning; or from freely trading teaching approaches back and forth among disciplines. No Situation is foolproof, but little powerful learning can happen without a clear purpose, topic, and assessment.

Framing a purpose for the learning episode

New teachers sometimes identify an engaging activity but don't explicitly link it to the purpose. Colleagues asked a group of preservice secondary teachers to generate a list of activities to use during the first few days of school to engage high school students. The list was quite long and inventive, and many said the exercise had been one of the most meaningful and useful that semester. They saw firsthand the benefits of borrowing from other disciplines, something that is not typical of veteran secondary teachers. Their next step was to make the purpose of the activity or "hook" more explicit. Some of their Situations included the following:

• High school English students ask family, friends, and neighbors about their favorite poem, favorite author, or favorite type of literature. To modify an activity into a Situation, they added an explicit purpose: *The purpose is for students to realize that adult role models read these different genres and understand what they are, for teachers to show connections to students' culture, race, or gender that may not be evident, and for the teacher to build individual knowledge of each student.*

• Middle school social studies students interview five members of different households and ask them how many people live in their house and how many televisions they have. *The purpose of this Situation is for students to behave as social scientists by framing research and collecting data and to use the tools of survey research they will need later in the semester.* This activity becomes a Situation when students study the correlation between school success and hours of television watched and make an informed decision about their own habits.

• Elementary students examine three different kinds of clay pots—coiled, thrown, and pinched—and analyze the tools used to shape clay. Each student chooses one they'd like to re-create, speculates on the tools that they will need to make that pot, and then experiments with clay to reconstruct it. *The purpose is for students to learn language for describing others' artwork and to derive and differentiate among techniques for fabrication.* The activity becomes a Situation when students begin a social studies unit about different Native American cultures and varied methods of cooking.

Deriving rules from examples

Another approach to designing a Situation is giving students several examples and asking them to derive rules for classifying or determining patterns or characteristics. Rules derived are rules understood.

- Primary students develop rules to sort a collection of buttons into different categories and to build number sense and vocabulary.
- Intermediate science students examine several different rocks and develop rules to classify these rocks into distinct categories.
- Middle school math students measure the circumference and diameter of several circular or cylindrical objects, such as plates, bowls, clocks, cans, bottles, jars, or lampshades. When they divide the circumference by the diameter, they produce a rough approximation of pi (3.14) as the relationship between those two dimensions.

- High school foreign language students look at several different examples of regular verbs in the present, past, and future tenses and determine rules for forming those tenses with other verbs or for identifying irregular verbs.

The purpose for each Situation is to have students construct knowledge rather than receive information. Now that you've read these considerations, talk with your reflective partner or Learning Circle about designing a Situation. Write your notes or ideas in Learning Record 1.B, Situation Element Notes, on the page below.

Learning Record 1.B	Situation Element Notes

Write your notes and ideas about designing a Situation element.

Copyright © 2006 by Corwin Press. All rights reserved. Reprinted from *Constructivist Learning Design: Key Questions for Teaching to Standards*, by George W. Gagnon and Michelle Collay. Thousand Oaks, CA: Corwin Press, www.corwinpress .com. Reproduction authorized only for the local school site or nonprofit organization that has purchased this book.

In the next section of this chapter, answer questions based on your choice of Situation.

BRIDGE SECTION: QUESTIONS FOR ANALYZING SITUATIONS

As you revise your Situation element, use the following questions to analyze the purpose, topic, and assessment you have chosen. Review and answer in Learning Record 1.C, Situation Element Questions below. Your answers will evolve throughout the design process, so capture your first thoughts and clarify your thinking later.

Learning Record 1.C	Situation Element Questions
What do you want your students to take out the door?	
How will you know that students have fulfilled your purpose?	
How will you pre- and post-assess student learning?	

Copyright © 2006 by Corwin Press. All rights reserved. Reprinted from *Constructivist Learning Design: Key Questions for Teaching to Standards*, by George W. Gagnon and Michelle Collay. Thousand Oaks, CA: Corwin Press, www.corwinpress .com. Reproduction authorized only for the local school site or nonprofit organization that has purchased this book.

After you draft your answers, talk with colleagues about your ideas. Then review the characteristics of a Situation element in preparation for revising your rough draft of this element. Assessment of how to design for learning occurs in the Bridge section. Someone facilitating your Learning Circle might ask you to describe your current beliefs about the "whys and wherefores" of a Situation. Others might ask you to describe your most productive teaching, your greatest student success, or how you learn best as a professional. Those assessments will guide your next steps. Use these or similar prompts with your partner or team.

TASK SECTION: REVISING A SITUATION ELEMENT

A Situation is a purposeful topic chosen for students to learn by thinking together to make meaning. A Situation should provide connections to daily life and actively involve them in making their own meaning. A Situation should be developmentally appropriate for students so that it corresponds with expectations for their level of understanding. In response to Dewey's pedagogic creed, a Situation should be related to a real-world context as much as conditions of the learning episode permit. A Situation also includes a framework for assessing what students have learned.

Characteristics of a Situation element

Each of the characteristics is important for you to consider when arranging a productive Situation. We elaborate on each characteristic so the significance is clear as you think about revising your draft of a Situation element.

A Situation fulfills a specific purpose

When experienced teachers design a learning episode, they first think about what they want their students to do. They often refer to such an event as an activity, exercise, or project. We recommend that teachers start to design for learning with the following questions:

- What is your purpose for the learning episode?
- Why should students fulfill your purpose?
- How will you know that students have fulfilled your purpose?
- How will students "show what they know?"
- What will students "take out the door?"

Once these questions are answered, it is much easier to think about the topic that you want your students to learn. Usually your purpose addresses a specific expectation. Often that purpose reflects your own learning experience and a synthesis of several expectations described in textbook objectives, school themes or projects, district outcomes, state requirements, or national standards. You should state the purpose as what the student will accomplish using terms such as "demonstrate," "explain," or "express." Your experience with a class of students and your familiarity with content standards will determine what will connect students with your purpose. How does the Situation relate to their youth culture or apply to events in their lives? You can start with a hook or theme that is relevant. Then you should determine what your students will take out the door that would fulfill your purpose. Next, decide what data you need from students to show what they know and convince you that they have fulfilled your purpose. What can students produce that will demonstrate their learning? In the language of constructivist learning, your answers are "constructs" because you construct you own meaning about the purpose of the learning episode and how students will fulfill your purpose.

Teachers who ask more sophisticated questions such as these create purposeful learning episodes. A clear purpose challenges students to learn the same way they do in real-life events. Clarifying the purpose of the Situation before the design is complete promotes opportunities for deeper reflection and analysis and gives you confidence in your decision making.

A Situation focuses on a topic for student learning

A productive Situation is not a group of questions with right answers. A Situation usually involves a single topic for students to learn about. What particular topic is your focus for student learning? A topic is the key concept, process, or attitude that you expect students to learn by thinking together to make meaning for themselves. Just as teaching is both an art and a science, there is artistry in designing for learning so that the topic may be learned in many ways. More learning takes place when students think through a challenging topic than when they memorize one "right" way to do something. How will you frame the topic as a problem to solve, a question to answer, a decision to make, a goal to set, or a metaphor to create so that students will take out the door what you want them to learn? This question becomes the key to framing the Task element later in the process of designing your learning episode.

A Situation compels interest by challenging students

A Situation should also represent big ideas that are worthy of consideration and require collaboration to accomplish. Students must engage in learning as members of a community rather than as individuals competing for the highest scores. Many students are turned off by competition among individuals to give "right answers" with speed and accuracy. Teachers can organize students, big ideas, and classroom space to develop a Situation that requires noncompetitive collaboration. When students think together to make meaning about an open-ended topic, they think and learn in deeper ways. Making meaning with other students is more compelling than working in isolation. When teachers can present the content as a challenging topic for learning, students are more interested. Content may include other concepts, processes, and attitudes that become part of the thinking needed to make meaning about a topic. Choosing a compelling topic makes it possible for students to accomplish worthwhile learning.

A Situation is developmentally appropriate for most students

Choose the next lesson from your curriculum or textbook and ask your students to develop their own ideas about it. For example, what does democracy mean to students? What is the right to vote? Why is it important? How do students see people in their lives exercising their voting rights or being denied their voting rights? How can students find out if people vote or don't vote in their own community? What inventory or survey could students develop to understand why? A primary teaching concern, of course, is that learning episodes must correspond with outcomes or objectives of the curriculum at particular grade levels.

Open-ended questions offer learners of varying abilities a point of entry into the topic to be learned. More sophisticated students can opt for more complex responses, while less sophisticated students or those who are more challenged can work productively at different levels. Students with limited reading abilities, for instance, can draw a graphic representation of the "answer" or describe their ideas in a story. As they make meaning about such topics, students improve their social skills and gain self-confidence as learners. English Language Learners can work in their home language to understand more complex issues, then work with a peer to translate their work into English.

A Situation connects student learning to real-world experience

If you want students to explain what friendship means to them, there are many ways to connect it with their life experiences. Students could script and perform a short play, write an essay and read it on videotape, audiotape comments and opinions of peers, create a visual metaphor for friendship, or make a list of what they expect from a friend during tough times. Students can determine what might be a good test of friendship, create criteria for a friend, list words that are attributes of a friend, or decide how far they would go to save a friend's life. Students could debate whether they would donate a kidney to a friend or read some classic works on friendship and decide whether those characters meet the criteria that they used. These are all ways of connecting learning to real-life experience.

A Situation describes a format for assessment of student learning: How will you determine what your students have actually learned? Even though teachers specify a particular topic for their learning episode, students may actually learn many other concepts, processes, or attitudes as they think together to make meaning about that topic. Much of the assessment framework may depend on teacher observations and informal questions about student thinking. However, what you expect each group of students to present during the Exhibit is a key to assessing their thinking and moving from a shared meaning to a common meaning for the topic. This format for assessment will guide you in deciding what artifact students will create during the Task element and present as an Exhibit.

In summary, a Situation with a clear purpose, a definite topic, and a realistic assessment can define the entire learning episode. The other elements of the CLD help you to think about the important questions for designing an effective learning episode and how it might unfold chronologically. Experienced teachers grasp this notion of a Situation more easily than less experienced teachers. It takes practice to predict the many ways that a comprehensive learning episode could begin with a single question or topic that may be answered or addressed in several different ways. Structuring learning to allow for diverse responses remains a challenge for all teachers. Design topics for open-ended learning in content areas where you have the greatest confidence. In all cases, the teacher is not required to have all of the answers before proceeding! Again, the following are characteristics of a Situation element:

- A Situation fulfills a specific purpose.
- A Situation focuses on a topic for student learning.
- A Situation compels interest by challenging students.
- A Situation is developmentally appropriate for most students.
- A Situation connects student learning to real-world experience.

Now that you've reviewed the characteristics, go back to the first notes you made about the purpose of your Situation. Does it have these characteristics? Use Learning Record 1.D, Situation Element Revision on the next page, to revise your draft of a Situation element. Use the questions you answered before and the summary of characteristics listed above to guide your writing. After you are finished, return to the next section on Situation examples and compare your element to examples in the next section.

| **Learning Record 1.D** | Situation Element Revision |

Write a revision of your Situation element draft.

Copyright © 2006 by Corwin Press. All rights reserved. Reprinted from *Constructivist Learning Design: Key Questions for Teaching to Standards*, by George W. Gagnon and Michelle Collay. Thousand Oaks, CA: Corwin Press, www.corwinpress .com. Reproduction authorized only for the local school site or nonprofit organization that has purchased this book.

EXHIBIT SECTION: EXAMPLE SITUATION ELEMENTS

This section includes 12 Situation elements from the complete CLDs provided in the Resources. These designs address four levels of learners. The primary (K–3) elements are from Reading/Retelling the Story, Fine Arts/ Drawing Animals, and Physical Education/Imitating Animals (Examples P-1, P-2, P-3). The intermediate (3–6) examples are from Science/Moon View, Media Technology/Logo, and Special Education/Vending Machines (Examples I-1, I-2, I-3). The middle school (6–9) samples are from Language Arts/Fairy Tales, Math/Base Blocks, and Industrial Technology/Scooter Motor (Examples M-1, M-2, M-3). The high school (9–12) illustrations are from Social Studies/Trading Partners, Foreign Language/Spanish Songs, and Business Education/Creating Spreadsheets (Examples H-1, H-2, H-3). Examples from 12 different teaching areas were deliberately chosen to emphasize the utility of the CLD. Choose one or two CLDs that fit with yours. Other elements are presented in subsequent chapters so that you can watch CLDs unfold. Refer to the 12 examples on the following pages.

	Situation Element Examples
Situation *50 minutes* P-1	The purpose of this sequence of three Situations is for young students to make further meaning of the rhythmic, patterned story *Brown Bear, Brown Bear, What Do You See?* "Brown bear, brown bear, what do you see? I see a yellow duck looking at me." They engage in rich literature activities by listening to the story or song, drawing new animals, writing a parallel phrase, acting out new behaviors, describing these new behaviors in words, and retelling the story through new pictures and words. The topic is for students to choose a new animal and a color for that animal and then create a page for a book about new animals. In the assessment, the teacher or assistant collects the sheets into a book and students write on their page or dictate a story pattern for their new animal and color.
Situation *50 minutes* P-2	The purpose of this sequence of Situations is for young students to make further meaning of the rhythmic, patterned story *Brown Bear, Brown Bear, What Do You See?* "Brown bear, brown bear, what do you see? I see a yellow duck looking at me." They engage in rich literature activities by listening to the story or song, drawing new animals, writing a parallel phrase, acting out new behaviors, describing these new behaviors in words, and retelling the story through new pictures and words. After drawing new animals in the previous learning episode, the topic is for students to think about how their animal moved, where it went, and what it ate after it saw the next animal. For example, the red goat might bounce to the garden and eat flowers after seeing "a pink salmon looking at me," and the grey goose might waddle off to a pond and eat slugs after seeing "an aqua elephant looking at me." In the assessment, individuals act out what their animal did after it saw another animal looking at it, and then the whole class imitates each action in the order of the new book.
Situation *50 minutes* P-3	The purpose of this sequence of three Situations is for young students to make further meaning of the rhythmic, patterned story *Brown Bear, Brown Bear, What Do You See?* "Brown bear, brown bear, what do you see? I see a yellow duck looking at me." They engage in rich literature activities by listening to the story or song, drawing new animals, writing a parallel phrase, acting out new behaviors, describing these new behaviors in words, and retelling the story through new pictures and words. The topic is for students to use a new sheet of paper to draw a picture of their new animal and then to write down how their animal moved, where it went, and what it ate after seeing another animal. The words should describe the story they made up when imitating their animal's actions in the previous learning episode.

(Continued)

(Continued)

	Situation Element Examples
Situation *90 minutes* I-1	The purpose of this Situation is to provide investigation of a basic science concept rarely understood by adults and often explained with misconceptions relating to shadows of the earth on the moon. The topic is for students to work in groups to determine the relationship between the sun, the earth, and the phases of the moon. In the assessment, groups are asked to explain their thinking through a diagram.
Situation *90 minutes* I-2	The purpose of this Situation is to let students feel competent as creators of computer programs, not just consumers of software others have made. The topic is to introduce students to programming in the Logo language and to challenge them to accomplish some basic tasks such as measuring the screen vertically, horizontally, and diagonally. Next, they preview the repeat command and try to write a program for the largest equilateral triangle that they can make on the display screen. Then they preview a recursive program and write one for the largest circle they can make on the display screen. In the assessment, students will present their programs and show the results on screen.
Situation *90 minutes* *(plus travel)* I-3	The purpose of this Situation is for each student to learn independent life skills and to do some basic problem solving when confronted with a new challenge. The topic is for developmentally delayed students to choose what to eat from vending machines and then manage money to use vending machines. In the assessment, students are given a $5 bill and use three different vending machines to get a sandwich, a drink, and dessert or chips.
Situation *50 minutes* M-1	The purpose of this Situation is to engage students in analyzing fairy tales so they develop an understanding of core elements and common themes that define this area of literature. The topic is for students to consider their previous experience with fairy tales, develop their definition of a fairy tale, and identify a list of common elements that are found in fairy tales. In the assessment, groups present a poster of their definition and common elements.
Situation *1 week* M-2	The purpose of this Situation is to engage students in a deeper exploration of number sense and place value in a different context than base 10. The topic is that students work with models of a different number base, from base 2 to base 7 and then use these models to show how they would solve basic problems requiring addition, subtraction, multiplication, and division. Each group is asked to model the problem, a solution, and the relationship between the two and explain it to their peers.

(Continued)

(Continued)

	Situation Element Examples
Situation *1 quarter* M-3	The purpose of this Situation is for students to understand how a small gas engine works. This Situation is structured over one quarter as the theory of small engines is reviewed and applied. The topic is for students to take apart and reassemble a small gas engine. First, teams test and replace specific parts of the engine, next bench test it, and then test it on a machine such as a scooter that they make themselves. In the assessment, teams demonstrate their engine and machine for peers and parents.
Situation *6 weeks* H-1	The purpose of this Situation is to investigate how global trade will influence students' future employment. The topic is for students to explore international trade between continents and determine how it might affect their future jobs. Teachers specify regions, goods or services, and jobs. The students list jobs of family and friends, review the want ads to see the kinds of positions that employers are seeking to fill, and then choose an occupation and company for the duration of the unit. In the assessment, students list ways that their occupation and company are linked to international trade.
Situation *2 weeks* H-2	The purpose of this Situation is to explore the influence of Hispanic language and culture on American music. The topic is for students to transcribe a contemporary Spanish song by Selena in the *tejano* style popular with Mexican Americans and some mainstream audiences. Students first create an English translation of the lyrics to fit the melody and rhythm of the original Spanish version. Then students conduct research on the Internet to consider how Hispanic musical styles have influenced mainstream American music. In the assessment, students videotape their song and research summary for presentation to peers and parents.
Situation *1 week* H-3	The purpose of this Situation is to familiarize students with creating spreadsheets using categories, formulas, and charts to make and account for a personal budget. The topic is for students to create a spreadsheet with categories for all their income and spending for a week. Each day they record in a notebook the money they get and spend and then transfer this information to their spreadsheet during class. In the assessment, students create a DVD for presentation to their families.

Review these Situation examples and note that each includes a purpose, a topic, and an assessment. Then consider how the examples align with the characteristics. Are they open-ended, do they compel interest, are they developmentally appropriate, do they expect use of prior knowledge, and are they connected to real-world experiences? They may be appropriate for some student populations and less so for others. These examples are offered for you to revise your draft of a Situation element. Study these 12 Situation examples and compare them to your draft of the Situation element. Then use Learning Record 1.E, Situation Element Final, to refine your previous revision based on what you noticed as you compared these examples with your writing.

Learning Record 1.E   Situation Element Final

Write the final version of your Situation element.

Copyright © 2006 by Corwin Press. All rights reserved. Reprinted from *Constructivist Learning Design: Key Questions for Teaching to Standards*, by George W. Gagnon and Michelle Collay. Thousand Oaks, CA: Corwin Press, www.corwinpress .com. Reproduction authorized only for the local school site or nonprofit organization that has purchased this book.

Now that you have crafted and revised a Situation, review the educational precedents behind this element.

REFLECTION SECTION: PRECEDENTS FOR A SITUATION ELEMENT

In most texts, "theory" is presented first, sending the message that, "Here is the theory, now go and apply it." Classroom teachers often start their planning with thinking about an activity for students, so the CLD framework was crafted in response to that practice. Although deep knowledge about the practice of teaching is often tacit, it is not "atheoretical." You have constructed a Situation that is based on prior knowledge of the topic and how students learn. As you sit with your version of the Situation, revisit some of the work that influenced this work.

Dedication to structuring an effective learning Situation has a rich history. Looking only at the last 100 years, John Dewey used the term "Situation" in his essay "My Pedagogic Creed." He focused on situating new learning in the natural world of the child. He described building on children's experiences in the home by continuing to re-create similar activities at school and never portrayed education as acquiring a set of skills. In 1897, Dewey wrote,

> I believe that education must be conceived as a continuing reconstruction of experience; [and] that the process and the goal of education are one and the same thing. (p. 434)

Donald Schön (1983) is best known for his theories about reflection-in-action by professionals. He also conceptualized the Situation in a very constructivist way. He studied professionals, such as architects, who are challenged to solve problems in real-world Situations rather than merely apply theoretical rules to abstract problems. Experienced practitioners face a variety of learning events in their work and bring a repertoire of problem-solving strategies and ways of thinking to each new Situation.

Eleanor Duckworth (1987) used situations to engage learners in "the having of wonderful ideas" about science. She observed that, when children were left to their own imaginations, they would construct and reconstruct their own meaning of the world around them. Children's efforts to explain situations resulted in creative, innovative, and theoretically sound understandings of the natural world. Steffe and D'Ambrosio (1995), researchers of constructivist learning, built Situations for learners to explain new understandings of math concepts.

Catherine Fosnot (1996) invited several contemporary philosophers to write about their understanding of constructivism. In addition to chapters on the disciplines of science, mathematics, and language, she broadened the conversation to include the fine arts. Maxine Greene (1995) provided examples of real-world learning from the fine arts. She thought deeply about how children create, interact, and learn to make meaning within the fine arts, reminding readers that children learn from experience, and experience should include interactions with the aesthetic side of life: "Where education is concerned, large-scale solutions hold little relevance for situation-specific undertakings. Local knowledge and local coming together ought to counter the tendency toward abstraction, as should a conscious concern for the particular, the everyday, the concrete" (pp. 68–69). As we described at the beginning of this chapter, the tradition of creating or recognizing a Situation to engage students in learning can be seen in all fields of study. Professionals in all fields use case studies to guide class learning.

Constructivist Learning Design entails teaching for purpose rather than teaching to objectives. Constructivist teachers engage students in a Situation and understand what students will do with their new learning. Such a teaching strategy involves more than stating an objective to be learned or an outcome to be demonstrated. The Situation embodies your purpose in creating a learning event for students. Most CLDs are built around a big idea and often have multiple purposes. Teachers can't predict or limit what students will learn while they are engaged in open-ended activities, so it can be difficult to specify measurable outcomes. For that reason, CLD purposes are broader than objectives and involve introducing, exploring, or understanding concepts or ideas rather than demonstrating one particular behavior.

Creating Constructivist Learning Designs may not be supported in some schools. Behaviorist beliefs and high-stakes standardized testing have limited what might be learned by mandating strict use of instructional minutes. Experienced teachers realize that what students are expected to learn is not necessarily what they will learn, especially with more than 30 students in a classroom. However, the likelihood that students will learn increases if they are engaged and interested in a Situation they have co-constructed. The pursuit of broad purposes such as defining, experiencing, and investigating creates more authentic and transferable learning than does the pursuit of specific objectives that have been predetermined by a district curriculum or a mandated textbook series.

Some vestiges of behaviorist thinking include notions that concepts are static, that they can be described objectively, and that they can be learned in the same manner by all students. For example, if the fourth-grade curriculum introduces fractions in mathematics, textbook authors assume that all fourth graders will meet the objective of adding and subtracting fractions. They also assume that, by following the textbook instructions, most teachers will find success at teaching students to add and subtract fractions. The objective is for students to demonstrate through a test that they can manipulate the algorithms and obtain a correct answer. Such a measurable objective can be reached by some students. What isn't known from such behaviorist practice is whether students have a conceptual understanding of how fractions work, even when they obtain a correct answer. Nor do you know what the students with the incorrect answers understand and can do with the concept. Unfortunately, teaching to an easily measured objective perpetuates the myth that clear objectives reflect good teaching practice. The large number of high school students who still cannot add and subtract fractions makes clear that there are flaws in this thinking.

In practice, teachers know that all children learn differently, make meaning of concepts in different ways, and learn at different rates. Yet the same teacher who knows this truth about learning will find solace in the idea that an objective defined is an objective that can be reached. Working with comprehensive standards is more challenging and it makes it more likely that students will reach benchmarks and widely held standards of achievement.

What kinds of thinking will provide teachers with the courage to move toward CLD? The first step is putting aside the notion that concepts are tangible objects that can be transferred from one person to another with mere explanation. Paulo Freire (1970) called this the "banking" model of education: Teachers make a deposit into students and expect them to give back the funds on demand. Personal knowledge is the patterns of action constructed individually by students who make their own meaning. Knowledge is not a set of objects that can be transmitted in a neat little package from teachers to students. The role of the teacher is to light a candle rather than to fill a piggy bank. Teachers who embrace the constructivist philosophy have moved beyond dispensing information and have entered a partnership for learning with each student. Recognize your own relationship with learning and make sense out of your own journey to understanding. Creating a Situation is much more than setting up an opportunity to experiment with ideas—the learning episode you design represents your values, beliefs, and dreams about our place in the world. Education is a complex social process of human interactions about meaningful ideas.

Most teachers consider three main areas when they plan a lesson as depicted in Figure 1.2, Teaching Plan Triangle, on the next page.

The sides of the triangle represent the components of a static lesson before it is taught: expectations, materials, and evaluations. Expectations are the base of the triangle and encompass the continuum of national standards, state requirements, district outcomes, and teacher objectives for the lesson.

Figure 1.2   Teaching Plan Triangle

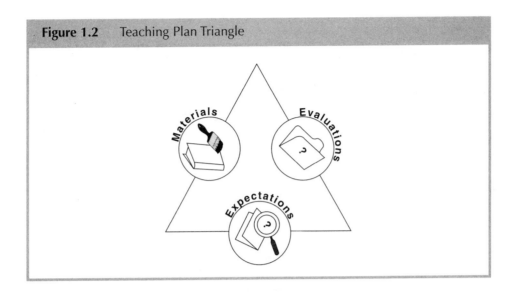

Materials include the resources available for teachers to use with that lesson, such as textbooks, teacher manuals, anthologies, articles, or curriculum guides. Evaluations include the typical tools for determining student learning from the lesson, such as homework, quizzes, exams, and regional, state, or national standardized tests. The visual metaphor often used to describe these components is a three-legged stool. This is an apt representation because many lessons are conducted as the teacher sits on a stool, has students read the material, explains the material to the students, and then evaluates students' understanding of the materials. Modify this representation in your mind as you look at Figure 1.3, Learning Design Pyramid on the next page.

This depiction adds a fourth side representing students and asks you to imagine not just looking at a flat figure on a page, but rather a three-dimensional Learning Design Pyramid. Not only have students been added to the influences on the design, but also the previous terms have evolved to resources, purpose, and assessments. You develop your own purpose for each learning episode as you derive meaning from all of the expectations bearing on your teaching. Resources for the learning episode depend on the topic you determine and may include original source writings, physical models, graphic materials, community members, and technology, among others. You decide which assessments to use throughout the learning episode, such as profiles, portfolios, presentations, proposals, paragraphs, or performances. Students become the fourth side of the base of the pyramid. Their diversity as individuals reflects cultural and ethnic backgrounds, personality types, thinking styles, and developmental levels or maturity. Individual learners have emotional, social, and disciplinary needs that also become factors in the learning design.

Figure 1.3   Learning Design Pyramid

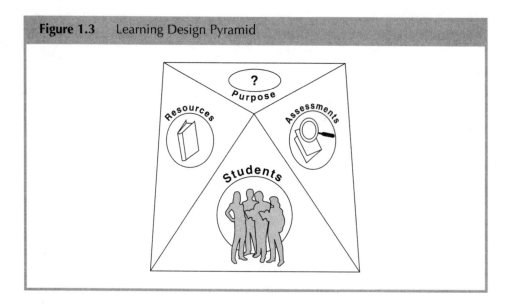

The Learning Design Pyramid also represents movement through time as these four factors interact and your Constructivist Learning Design unfolds in a dynamic process of thinking and learning. When you move students through the steps of a learning design during a real-time learning episode, you act as a choreographer, and your students enact the interpretive dance you have planned. The performance moves your learning design from theory to practice, from generic to specific, from ideal to actual. This visual metaphor showing the relationship of students to other dimensions of a Situation moves them from the audience onto the stage.

After getting a sense of the educational precedents and theory that are the foundation for this Situation element, reflect on what you were thinking and learning as you were writing a Situation element in this chapter. In Learning Record 1.F, Situation Element Reflection (on the next page), write about the feelings, images, and languages in your thoughts about designing a Situation to engage students in learning.

CONCLUDING REMARKS: THOUGHTS ON DESIGNING SITUATIONS

Does your Situation structure learning new knowledge that is applicable in the real world? Does the assessment align with standards? Knowing when and how to bring information to students is essential to supporting learning. Textbooks, for example, are most useful when teachers have a clear purpose for student learning and mediate which content to use and in

Learning Record 1.F   Situation Element Reflection

As you were thinking and writing about your Situation element,

What were feelings thoughts in your spirit?

What were images thoughts in your imagination?

What were the languages thoughts in your internal dialogue?

Copyright © 2006 by Corwin Press. All rights reserved. Reprinted from *Constructivist Learning Design: Key Questions for Teaching to Standards*, by George W. Gagnon and Michelle Collay. Thousand Oaks, CA: Corwin Press, www.corwinpress .com. Reproduction authorized only for the local school site or nonprofit organization that has purchased this book.

what order. Other source materials, such as internet articles, are best used as a reference, not as a centerpiece of instruction. Print materials sometimes give explanations before students have a chance to think about a topic for themselves. One way to "tweak a textbook" is to have students think about a topic before reading the text as a reference or resource.

- Primary students could determine how many different ways to form a hexagonal pattern block as an introduction to basic fractions.

- Intermediate social studies students scheduled to learn about India could begin with a world atlas and topographic map of the country. Before reading the source materials for information about cultures, languages, dress, food, and other aspects of Indian life, students can spend some time generating ideas about the climate. Over several sessions, they can first discern the characteristics of the climate and geography and then determine what cultural characteristics they would anticipate finding in a country that has large, arid regions with few rivers or other sources of water. Information in the textbook would then connect to their thinking.

- Middle school math students could use the examples in a chapter to solve as groups before reviewing the explanations or solutions.

- High school chemistry students could sort index cards showing pertinent information about individual elements into a rough approximation of the periodic table as an introduction to that topic.

Reflection is intended to capture your thinking in feelings, images, or languages as you work through the process of designing a Situation. Our colleague Kyle Shanton adopted the Constructivist Learning Design in his literacy methods course. Students resisted using this constructivist method at first. They saw this approach as more appropriate for math or science teaching because those subjects seem to be based on solving problems or explaining Situations. With some experience, however, they created ways to engage their own students in making meaning of story and language rather than memorizing or word calling.

An example from Kyle's class is useful as he models how to teach a story to young children. In the story, "The House on Mango Street," a young Mexican American girl tells about her neighborhood. Kyle asks the adult students to think about what young children might already know about their neighborhood, and then they discuss it. Next he reads the first chapter. Between each chapter, he takes time for conversation about the young girl's experiences and invites the adult students to expose their assumptions about the girl, the culture in her border town, and how they might approach teaching this story. Kyle's thorough, step-by-step learning episode is designed to move students from liking or not liking a story to a deeper level of decision making. They have been challenged by this Situation to think like practicing teachers who are mature and culturally competent rather than students doing an assignment.

Now that you've designed a Situation, check in with your partner or Learning Circle for some feedback before drafting the five elements that support it. Go back and review the characteristics and see whether your Situation meets some or all of those. Revisit your initial purpose for the Situation you chose and reflect on how the purpose could be clarified or possibly modified. Step into the rest of the design knowing you've created a powerful and real experience in which you and your students can situate new learning. This "walk-through" of the dance will make subsequent rehearsals more productive.

As we indicated in the Introduction (see Figure I.1, CLD Schematic), the Situation is an overarching framework that determines how the other elements of the CLD will unfold. Beginning teachers are initially prepared to specify objectives, "cover" the mandated curriculum, and strive to produce students who can learn important material and pass standardized tests. More states are evaluating academic achievement in comprehensive ways that require teachers to assess students differently. Whether teachers begin with the evaluation overview and work backwards or choose key curriculum concepts from the year's offerings, our CLD is more likely to prepare students for the higher-level assessments they now face.

You should now have answers to the three key questions for designing a Situation element:

1. Purpose: Why are you designing this learning episode?

2. Topic: What is your specific focus for student learning?

3. Assessment: How will you assess student learning?

The Situation can be designed to reflect your strengths and interests and to prepare your students to demonstrate their learning or to show what they know in ways that will be evident to parents, administrators, and community members. To formalize a CLD is not to disregard the realities of schooling. You can ensure that certain topics or ways of knowing are experienced and practiced without relinquishing your personal values about learning. With the pressures of testing and evaluation more and more prevalent in schools, you can be easily discouraged about charting a course of quality education for your students. Constructivist Leaning Design's overarching Situation offers you the freedom to build strong curricula and to be confident that students will learn what teachers will teach.

2 Organizing Groups

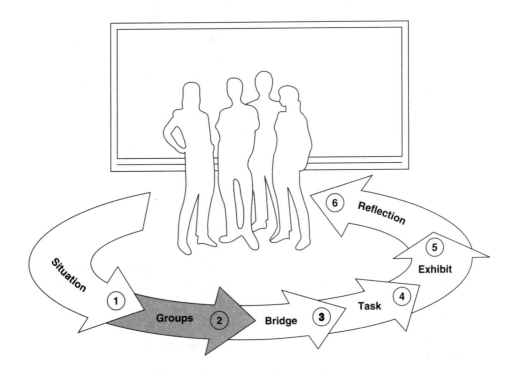

The ultimate purpose of a teacher's guiding a group of learners through the different stages of development is to maximize the learning ability of the individuals by developing group norms and procedures that encourage all learners to do their very best.

—Dick and Pat Schmuck,
Group Processes in the Classroom (2001)

This chapter describes the second element of Constructivist Learning Design (CLD), Groups. As the Schmucks suggest, the way students are grouped and supported to think together in making meaning is central to designing for learning. Use of Groups for structuring learning is not as common as it should be, even in culturally homogeneous communities. In their book *Small Districts, Big Problems: Making School Everybody's House* (1992), Pat and Dick conducted research in rural schools around the country. They expected to find many classrooms using group process and were very disappointed when they visited only a few teachers who did. In urban classrooms, where students are often grouped by primary language for instruction, cultural and racial differences are reinforced unless teachers act deliberately to integrate students by language, race, ethnicity, and gender so they can learn from and with cultural groups different than their own.

Configuring small Groups of students for both social and intellectual purposes is also a key equity strategy—norms that lead to higher achievement by every class member are established for the whole class and must be reinforced in all settings. In addition to developing cross-cultural competence, students learn differently from peer instruction, have regular opportunities to articulate their ideas, and build deeper conceptual knowledge when they are engaged in a structured group. Research on English-Language Learners identifies "student talk" as a critical dimension of language acquisition. We invite you to read this chapter and talk about your thinking as you read with a reflective partner or Learning Circle. Then use the Learning Records in this chapter to guide you through crafting your own CLD Groups element.

The three key questions to answer in writing a Groups element ask designers to think about groupings of students, materials, and furniture:

1. Students: How will you organize students into groups?

2. Materials: What materials will students use to make meaning?

3. Furniture: How will you arrange furniture to facilitate learning?

These questions should guide your thinking in organizing Groups. Your Task in this chapter is to write a final version of a Groups element for your CLD. First, prepare a draft of this element in the Situation section. Then discuss considerations with colleagues and write notes in the Groups section of this chapter. In the Bridge section, you will answer some questions. Next, you will revise your draft in the Task section of this chapter based on specific characteristics. In the Exhibit section of this chapter are several Groups elements from other designs for examples as you prepare a final version of your own Groups element. Finally, you have an opportunity to reflect on your thinking and learning in the Reflection section of this chapter before considering our concluding remarks.

SITUATION SECTION: DECIDING ON GROUPS

Putting students in Groups is common in some classrooms and more prevalent in primary and intermediate grades. Small group work becomes less frequent in middle and high school classes, where instructional times are shorter and less flexible. Whole-class grouping is so common teachers may not think of it as a "group." The teacher-to-students dynamic common in large classes reflects and reinforces certain assumptions about school-based learning. When teachers present primarily to a whole class, call only on raised hands, question individual learners, and explain answers to everyone at the same time, they must assume that each student learns the same way and will make the same meaning of the information. After the teacher's explanation, individual students often are asked to work on their own to complete an in-class assignment or to get started on homework. When students receive information as a whole group and then do worksheets in isolation, they have little opportunity to co-construct meaning. This ubiquitous whole-class learning experience is a powerful symbol of school-based learning for many—and one of the least effective ways to structure teaching and learning. Indeed, we do teach as we were taught. When provided with small-group models, organizing strategies, and assessment frameworks, however, most teachers find that their capacity to structure small-group learning grows quickly.

Purpose of a Groups element

The purpose of a Groups element is to decide how students should be organized to think together to make meaning about the topic. Small-group structures provide a forum for students to develop personal meaning into shared meaning through the social construction of knowledge. A large group seldom offers the security or interaction necessary for students to be open or candid with one another about their thinking. Students can be grouped in several ways depending on both social and intellectual purposes. Ongoing assessment of the quality of interactions and students' knowledge of the topic displayed in their exhibits of learning dictate when and how to create and modify membership.

Use different ways of forming Groups to engage students in thinking together about the topic as they accomplish the Task crafted for your CLD.

Students can be grouped in several ways depending on your purpose. The class might begin in one grouping and evolve into another. For example, the Bridge can be done with the whole class before students separate into small working Groups based on topics, questions, or interests. Other times, the students might be assigned to a group first and then asked to work on a Bridge. Whatever configuration and order of Groups you decide to use, think deliberately about how each group will best serve your purpose for intellectual and social learning. School is preparation for the real world, and children learn powerful lessons about how their race, class, gender, and other differences are valued by peers and teachers.

Public education for everyone is essential in a democracy. For individuals to function well as citizens of a democracy, they must have access to accurate information and then work effectively with others to make choices, decisions, and laws based on that information. The Princeton Review (2003) editors list two central characteristics of international business schools: "a strenuous education analyzing business fundamentals [and] a collaborative atmosphere fostering teamwork and innovation." Cohen (1994) described a class of sixth graders who refused to believe that adults often worked together in small groups with people who weren't their friends. Their parents had to convince them it was so. The emphasis we place on Groups in our CLD demonstrates the importance we place on a Task being accomplished in learning teams or task forces so that personal meanings are valued and multiple perspectives contribute to understandings shared by group and class members.

Topic for a Groups element

The topic of this Groups element is how groups function to support individual and shared meaning. When teachers plan for teaching, many consider what they will say to their students, what students will read, and how they will assess students' recall of the lecture or text. As we ask teachers to organize for learning, they think about what their students will do to think together and make meaning about the topic of the learning episode. This shift in focus—from teachers telling to students thinking—is critical to constructivist learning. Planning how students will engage with each other to articulate what they think, compare their thinking, and come to a shared meaning is the nature of the Groups element.

Creating and sustaining learning communities of students has been a central part of classroom practice for decades (Cohen, 1994; Collay, Dunlap, Enloe, & Gagnon, 1998; Johnson & Johnson, 1998). Learning communities are collectives of individuals and smaller groups that have come together to learn and build a larger classroom community—as such, teachers must work student by student and group by group to structure learning. Having functional and productive small Groups is essential to supporting individual learners as they move from direct instruction (from teacher or peer) to guided practice to independent work. Creating a classroom culture with students who respect each other as learners and take responsibility for each others' learning is a complex but worthwhile enterprise.

Why are Groups essential for learning? Most major dilemmas we face in society require analyzing complex systems to move toward acceptable solutions. These problems include challenging economic disparity between the few rich and the many poor, providing equitable and accessible education, offering medical treatment and housing for the most underserved populations, managing the lethal residue of conventional weapons such as land mines and the potential destructive force of nuclear weapons, resolving environmental contamination from toxic chemicals, preventing religious conflicts from erupting into wars and killings, and addressing the worldwide population explosion. None of these problems will be solved until a group of people with different perspectives and values communicate and think together to resolve world problems rather than just taking sides and defending their positions.

All of us have addressed problems in our own lives, such as conflict in a relationship, authority struggles between children and parents, money income and outgo, emergency medical treatment for ourselves or our family, the long-term illness of parents or children, structural home repair or improvement, or recovery from natural disasters. Daily problems include finding and scheduling work around child care, getting training necessary to keep work, keeping a household running, and finding affordable transportation. Whether our problems are major or minor, we often turn to individuals or to a small group of friends or neighbors to listen and give us advice as we try to resolve these problems and figure out what to do. Sometimes just talking through a problem with others helps us sort things out. Other times, we need specific advice or suggestions when we are not sure how to proceed. Your Task is to decide on useful groupings and make your best guess about the power of those Groups of students to think together productively.

Assessment in a Groups element

We address three significant criteria for assessment in a Groups element. You may have others. The first criterion for teacher assessment of group process is: How productively are students thinking and learning together? Rather than grading only the quality of individual or group products or exhibits, assessment of how students create and adhere to group norms is essential. Teachers and students can state what is expected of individual students, what students expect of themselves and each other, how they should interact in a group, and how they should support one another in learning. Teachers assess the interpersonal skills of their students as they watch them interact, communicate, and work with other students in the class. Often, the way students enter a classroom, take a seat, talk with friends, or stow their gear tells observant teachers quite a bit about their mood and attitude. Many teachers stand at the door of the classroom every day and check in with each student personally. This ritual allows teachers to assess the confidence, attention, personality, and ability of students to relate with others by how they carry themselves, engage in conversation with friends, exchange jokes or jibes, listen to others, dominate the conversation, or defer to peers. These observations provide useful information for teachers as they group students who can think together effectively. Sometimes Groups are formed by random assignment early in a term until teachers get to know their students and their interaction styles. Students should be grouped deliberately based on the purpose of the learning within the Situation.

In addition to the factors for grouping already considered, such as primary language and culture, race, gender, or class differences, individual styles of interaction also affect group process. Teachers can put "high talkers" and "low talkers" together so that some students don't always dominate group thinking while others withdraw. Likewise, "quick studies" and "deliberate studies" can be grouped together so that all students have ample time to think things through for themselves. Several different factors must be considered when choosing Groups or structuring opportunities for students to choose their own group. Cultural and interaction differences do not determine students' capacity for intellectual work, but classroom settings may privilege certain types of student behavior. Each grouping decision influences the development of the learning community, the quality of thinking between students, how students think about themselves in relation to others, and the quality of the product or outcome. As the term progresses, teachers become much more knowledgeable about arranging Groups of students based on their previous observations and decisions.

Assess student thinking styles as well: How are students learning the material I am required to teach? What other wonderful things are they learning that are a bonus? Are students "feelings thinkers" who need to do actions themselves before they can imagine or talk about their learning? Are students "image thinkers" who need to watch others and observe their actions before they want to do it themselves or talk about their learning? Are students "language thinkers" who need to listen to descriptions and talk about their learning before doing it themselves or observing others?

This criterion for assessment suggests a simple reduction of our complex theory about symbolic systems. However, teachers can use this distillation to make decisions about how to engage students and how to understand their thinking in order to support students as learners. Putting students with different thinking styles together often produces more creative and divergent thinking because they are exposed to different points of view, strategies, and perspectives. Sometimes teachers put similar thinkers together and then compare the results from different groupings.

Membership in Groups profoundly influences the quality of collaborative thinking and the quality of the product. Students can both explain to one another the individual meaning they construct to understand a concept, process, or attitude and evaluate the quality of their peer teaching. Peer work in a small group allows students to rehearse their new knowledge in safe settings so they can be more confident when "going public" in larger school settings or in the larger community. Peer assessment, whether formal or informal, shapes how students perceive their own goodness and their right or responsibility to judge others.

The second criterion for teacher assessment of group process is what materials are available to support learners in making meaning and constructing knowledge: How do the materials available or the strategic use of them enhance or limit students' productivity? Some classrooms have a rich array of manipulative materials, art and office supplies, scientific instruments and equipment, maps, charts, and graphs, or computer-based technology and Internet access. Other classrooms have insufficient materials, poor-quality textbooks, and maybe limited paper and pencils. Lack of materials is a serious equity issue in many districts, and teachers may need to barter within the existing system to overcome this problem. Talk with other teachers in your school to see what they have or ask where to get materials. Talk with the principal or the district curriculum coordinators to see what materials are available. Ask a parent or community group to fund sets of math models or science kits that can travel from room to room as needed. Use pencil and paper materials inventively to draw diagrams or cut out models whenever possible. Try to find ways for learners to construct models or representations for concepts they are learning, and be conscious about when your choice to group students is limited by a lack of materials or by your own knowledge of how to structure learners' use of them.

Jigsaws, or structuring group process so that each member's information or materials are necessary for the group to succeed, are a good way to move teachers and students away from the competitive model of school. Working independently and completing the assignment first is a trait that only applies to a minority of people in the adult world. The majority of people will need to perform well as teams to succeed in work and in life.

Young people will not succeed in the larger society with conventional, classroom-based competition as their only model.

The third criterion for teacher assessment of group process is the placement of the furniture in classrooms to accommodate different Groups. Some teachers prefer tables and cubbies to individual desks. Others like the convenience of desks for student storage and then just rearrange the desks to form different groupings. Elementary teachers "meet on the rug" for direct instruction before moving back to group work at tables. Some teachers share classrooms that are labs, lecture bowls, gym bleachers, or rehearsal halls for other classes. These venues present challenges and opportunities. Teachers often have to move what can be moved, have students sit on the floor, or sit backwards on stadium seats to work with others. Three to four students around one table is ideal if you can control the setting, yet teachers often have to accommodate less-than-ideal situations. Conventional classrooms are arranged for monitoring behavior and positioning the students to listen only to the teacher, not for having students communicate and work with each other. Try to form the best Groups you can with whatever furniture you have and lobby those in positions to support you for better facilities.

We invite you to write a draft of your Groups element in Learning Record 2.A, Groups Element Draft, on the next page. Jot down the first ideas that come to mind, imagining how your students would best be grouped in the successful lesson you selected. You can revisit your decision later and modify it if necessary.

Now proceed to the next section to continue developing and refining a Groups element for your CLD.

GROUPS SECTION: THE POWER OF COLLABORATIVE THINKING

The value of working in Groups to resolve real-life problems is undeniable. Most of us appreciate the support of family, friends, and colleagues when we need to talk things out. Many major corporations are organized into task forces or working teams to accomplish particular tasks or goals for the organization. Corporate time and money is spent in leadership training or team-building activities designed to make people more comfortable working with one another and cooperating on a project. Complex problem solving in business, industry, science, engineering, law, or medicine requires small teams of people from diverse intellectual and cultural perspectives to work together. Colleges of engineering are now organizing multidisciplinary teams for research and development around topics such as nanotechnology rather than interdisciplinary groupings (Newton,

Learning Record 2.A	Groups Element Draft

Write a rough draft of a Groups element.

Copyright © 2006 by Corwin Press. All rights reserved. Reprinted from *Constructivist Learning Design: Key Questions for Teaching to Standards*, by George W. Gagnon and Michelle Collay. Thousand Oaks, CA: Corwin Press, www.corwinpress .com. Reproduction authorized only for the local school site or nonprofit organization that has purchased this book.

2005). In education, the norm is still an individual teacher working solo in a classroom. Many teachers plan in grade-level or multi-age teams in elementary schools or in interdisciplinary teams in middle schools, yet they usually teach and solve problems by themselves. When teachers reflect with colleagues, they experience the benefits of learning together. As they realize the value of collaborative thinking for themselves, more teachers are encouraged to group their students so they can think and learn together.

We use the term "Learning Circle" (Collay et al., 1998) to describe a group of learners, whether students or colleagues, who think and learn together over an extended period of time. There are generally two kinds of Learning Circles. One is a base group that represents the larger community

groups

mixed ability

and meets regularly throughout a term. These teams are most powerful when they contain members from different roles, experience, and cultural backgrounds, and are truly heterogeneous. These groupings are the "jigsaw puzzle" and combine different parts and perspectives, share specialized knowledge, and focus more on the broader organization's goals. The other common Learning Circle is an interest group or project group that meets to complete a specific task. In schools, this type of group is typical of grade-level or department teams that meet to coordinate and schedule classes or curriculum. Another example is a proposal or design team that may be ad hoc and only meet for a summer or until a particular due date. Role-alike and project-based groupings typically form the heart of learning communities in classrooms, schools, or districts. Base Groups that are cross-role and representative are necessary to create and sustain a learning community, yet they can be more perfunctory and less engaging for members unless their purpose is compelling.

Groups have a variety of purposes, sizes, and time frames. There may be a short-term group where students meet a few minutes or for part of one class period to complete a short activity. Most often, this is a "thinking group." In addition to offering students time to think together, the temporary group allows teachers to observe different combinations of students. Ideas can be brought to the surface quickly and individuals can begin to "think aloud" and get feedback from other group members. Early in the term, students need this time to get acquainted by learning names and finding out a little bit about each other. Such a temporary group generally does not develop the level of trust or intimacy required for deeper or more risky learning, yet these are a necessary part of community building. A long-term group where students meet regularly over a period of time has a different purpose. Within such a group, students support each other's learning through constructive dialogue, honest encouragement, and realistic assessment of one another's work. A real feeling of community develops among these students as they interact, think together to accomplish a task, and present their thinking to peers. Members of a long-term group establish personal rapport and learn to trust each other. A long-term group can be heterogeneous or role- or task-alike.

Considerations for organizing a Groups element

The groupings described offer a basic framework for creating Groups. Here are some other thoughts about Groups for you to consider. Using group dynamics and cooperative processes well in designing for learning is deceptively subtle and exceedingly challenging. We advise teachers to start simply with pairs and work up to more complex Groups and more challenging learning events or Situations after some basic learning has taken place. Students should rarely be in group larger than five, or some won't talk at all or only share their thinking very guardedly. A few students "lead" the conversation, while others hang back and let the high talkers dominate.

Committing to using group process and cooperative learning

Structuring group process requires basic social skills and sophisticated strategies. Sometimes teachers are reluctant to organize Groups because they are unfamiliar with the developmental stages of a group, because they don't have experience with using cooperative learning strategies to teach, or because they feel pressured to "cover content." Both teachers and students may press for getting right to the content, and some may feel the time it takes to set up or work in Groups is wasted. Teaching social skills, conflict mediation, and group interaction strategies is a skill that can be learned. Students must be taught about teamwork and cooperation throughout their schooling, not just in kindergarten. Don't give up on students' capacity to work together or on your ability to facilitate their work! Remember, the most important characteristic employers seek is the ability to work with others. Better and more powerful problem solving occurs when divergent thinkers collaborate. Students can learn these strategies and teachers can learn to teach them. The quality of learning that emerges from collaborative thinking makes the planning required worthwhile.

Using materials to make thinking visible

This section focuses on the materials you will need for Groups. Sometimes you may have only one set of materials and arrange a demonstration or a series of stations so that each group can accomplish a different task. Other times, you may have enough materials so that each student can work on an individual project. Most of the time, you will probably have five to eight sets of materials. Rather than thinking about the whole class, we think about what four or five students can do with a given set of materials to accomplish a Task. How can each group of students use the materials to demonstrate their understanding of a concept, to show a process, or to display their attitude about an issue? Materials can make student thinking visible to small-group members and to others during the Bridge or Exhibit.

Furniture shouldn't be a barrier to grouping

Unless desks are bolted to the floor, most classrooms can be reconfigured so that students can form working Groups. Desks can be moved, tables and chairs can be reorganized, and students can sit on the floor together in different areas of a classroom or outside. We have seen effective group learning conducted in lecture bowls, science labs, auditoriums, and gymnasiums. Students are usually quite willing to accommodate teachers' requests to work in a peer group and will move themselves and their gear as necessary. Sometimes they grumble, but usually they appreciate an opportunity to do something other than sit and listen.

Dan Fleming, an urban science and math teacher, usually seats students at desks or tables in groups of four or five. Recently, he moved all six tables into one large rectangle, and all the students sit around the same table and work in a big group. For his six-classes-a-day format, this seating seems to ground students more quickly. Dan prefers a self-contained eighth grade, which he taught for 10 years and consistently improved math test scores. He believes that middle school students need a significant adult relationship in their lives other than their parents. Today's students need the stability of a familiar teacher and fellow students in a learning community to communicate honestly and effectively as a group. Dan's self-contained approach seems quite sound from the perspective of a teacher who values developing thinking and positive interactions in Groups.

Now that you've read our considerations, talk with your reflective partner or Learning Circle about ways of forming Groups. Write your notes or ideas in Learning Record 2.B, Groups Element Notes, on the next page.

BRIDGE SECTION: QUESTIONS FOR FORMING GROUPS

Here are some questions for you to answer as you prepare a Groups element. Grouping depends on the Situation you design, your configuration of students, the materials you have available, and the furniture in your classroom. Use Learning Record 2.C, Groups Element Questions, on pages 70 and 71 for your answers. After you complete this Learning Record, proceed to the next section, which describes the characteristics of a Groups element in preparation for writing your revision of this element.

TASK SECTION: REVISING A GROUPS ELEMENT

As you revise this element, your Task is to organize Groups of students to think together about the learning framed in the Situation, to organize the materials they will have to make meaning, and to arrange time and space productively. Groups of students, materials, and furniture are connected because how students are grouped often depends on the topic you have determined, the materials available, the space to be used for work, and the length of time students will be together. Groups should be flexible enough to accommodate configurations of any size, from pairs to the whole class, depending on the purpose of your learning episode. An ideal group should be small enough to allow students with divergent thinking styles to talk together effectively but large enough to represent different abilities and diverse perspectives. Teachers should be deliberate in deciding how students will be grouped, whether the grouping is random, by interest, by academic skill, or balanced by race, culture, language, and gender. The basic principle for Groups is that students think together to construct social and intellectual understanding. The next section describes the characteristics of a Groups element as a guide for you to revise your writing.

Learning Record 2.B	Groups Element Notes

Write your notes and ideas about choosing a Groups element.

Copyright © 2006 by Corwin Press. All rights reserved. Reprinted from *Constructivist Learning Design: Key Questions for Teaching to Standards*, by George W. Gagnon and Michelle Collay. Thousand Oaks, CA: Corwin Press, www.corwinpress .com. Reproduction authorized only for the local school site or nonprofit organization that has purchased this book.

The next section asks you some questions to guide your thinking.

Learning Record 2.C	Groups Element Questions

Why are you going to group students to think about accomplishing the Task?

Will students be grouped as a whole class, as individuals, or in collaborative thinking teams of two, three, four, five, six, or more?

Will you group students randomly or selectively?

Will you group students by counting off, choosing a favorite color or fruit, or having similar clothing, shoes, heights, birthdays, or zodiac signs?

Do you want teacher-selected groups based on personalities, academic strengths, or student's choice of topic?

How can you avoid "ability groups," because school-defined ability can separate students into higher- and lower-status groups?

(Continued)

Do you want students engaged with materials by physically modeling, graphically representing, numerically describing, or individually creating?

How many sets of materials do you have, and how many students can work with each set?

What physical layout and furniture do you have, and how many student groups will you form?

How are you going to distribute the materials to groups of students?

Copyright © 2006 by Corwin Press. All rights reserved. Reprinted from *Constructivist Learning Design: Key Questions for Teaching to Standards*, by George W. Gagnon and Michelle Collay. Thousand Oaks, CA: Corwin Press, www.corwinpress.com. Reproduction authorized only for the local school site or nonprofit organization that has purchased this book.

Now use these answers to guide a revision of this element in the next section.

Characteristics of a Groups element

Six characteristics are significant in organizing a Groups element. A summary of these characteristics is provided at the end of the section for you to use in writing this element of your CLD.

Groups vary in configuration

Teachers adjust the size and membership of Groups according to the purpose of the learning episode, the materials available, and the time and space available. Students should know the purpose of the learning episode, comprehend the topic to be learned, and understand the assessment framework. Most effective communication takes place in small groupings of two to five learners. Teachers can form random groupings or selectively assign students to create productive teams. Smaller groups of pairs or trios work well for younger students and respond well to teacher prompts, such as "list three ways to solve this problem." Larger groupings of four or five are better for older students and long-term base groupings or Learning Circles that stay together for a unit, month, quarter, semester, or year. When Groups work together over the long term or on a large project in a Learning Circle format, the time allotted to the Bridge and other elements may be extended.

Groups accommodate differences

There are some questions to ask when configuring Groups. Are students clear about how a group will support their new learning? Is someone facilitating? Students need to spend some time getting to know each other and talking about how they think and learn most productively. They also might describe what support they need from the group for listening, speaking, thinking, or writing. Students need explicit structures and norms to build trust so they can learn openly and without fear.

Are members of the group well acquainted, or are they working together for the first time? This is important because group members build trust by knowing each other's history, beliefs, and experiences. More time is needed for members to get acquainted when Learning Circles are new. Similarly, experienced Learning Circles can move quickly into complex tasks, although community building always requires informal reconnection at the beginning of each session.

How will teachers assign group roles so students engage in learning and develop social skills? Establishing roles of Convener (or facilitator), Process Observer, Recorder, and Reporter address initiating and monitoring the group process and recording and reporting group thinking. Older students can make sure someone is attending to each role while younger or inexperienced students are assigned specific roles. Patterns of participation and leadership will become evident quickly and teachers must be proactive to make sure all students have an equal chance at all roles. "I don't have good handwriting" is not a good excuse for refusing to take notes.

Groups solicit thinking from all members

How are students most likely to share their own thinking with one another? Conditions of trust and respect are important for everyone to feel comfortable contributing their thoughts, particularly if they are unsure of themselves or their thinking. Students should be encouraged to explain what they are thinking and why. Articulating their thinking might expose flaws and misconceptions, so honest communication is very important for students to understand and address in the process of learning. Structures such as "waves" (everyone has a turn) and the use of a timer ensure that time and space is held for each person. "Holding space" is an equity strategy that must be practiced.

Groups account for individual learning

How will each group document its new learning? Many teachers are reluctant to put students in Groups because they can't adequately assess individual performance. A way to hold students accountable for their own learning is to ask them to explain other members' thinking. This assessment captures both group and individual performance. Every student is asked to record group thinking, and teachers choose reporters randomly so that each student must attend to the process of thinking and learning. Students can always complete individual Learning Records representing their own learning or one aspect of the group's learning.

Groups are organized deliberately by teachers

What processes will be used to create Groups? Teachers need to be clear about the size of groupings, how groupings are configured, and when groupings will be reconfigured. There are several approaches to forming Groups. These include random grouping, limited-choice grouping, "hand" grouping, and student choice. In random grouping, teachers assign the students to a group by randomly distributing tokens. Tokens can be different colored index cards or handouts, colored paper clips, colored dots, or colored fabric. Other choices are playing cards, stickers, chapter headings, cartoons, famous quotes, pieces of a puzzle, sentences of a paragraph, related words, or objects from the topic, such as math models or different kinds of mammals. Shapes and stickers that represent the content are useful, such as squares, triangles, rectangles, and so forth to make up math groupings; notes on a staff to make up music groupings; and characters from a story to make up literature groupings whose members will discuss their character's place in a story. Jigsaw pieces are terrific. Cut political cartoons into five pieces each, have students draw them out of a hat, find the holders of the other pieces, and then analyze the cartoon. Cut up quotes or textbook headings and have these groups review that part of the text and share their findings with the rest of the class. Limited-choice grouping is similar, but students have some choice about the group they join. If all the red dots go together, the students have no choice. If every group is required to have one of each color, students have some choice where they go. Students of all ages will trade tokens. Don't let this bother you, but take time to watch who is trading with whom, take note of students who are uncomfortable working with others, and follow up to learn more about why they chose to trade.

Hand grouping is done in advance by teachers because they want a specific combination of students to work together. Some educational theory advises against ability grouping and urges teachers to mix students by thinking styles, ethnicity, gender, experience with a topic, interests, high and low talkers, or age. When students are allowed to choose their own group, values based on race, class, gender, or who is part of the "in group" may exclude some students. We use this method sparingly and only after trust is well established. Give yourself permission to regroup learners at any time if personality conflicts or other group dynamics impede progress too much. Keep in mind your purposes, especially the importance of learning to value others' perspectives. It's not always a smooth ride. Constructivist Learning Designs can move students through a variety of groupings during a single learning episode or a series of learning episodes.

(handwritten margin note: against attainability?)

Groups are allocated specific sets of materials and furniture

Often, the best learning episodes have students use materials to model their thinking or to track events in an experiment. For example, you might use a prescribed set of commercial materials such as pattern blocks, instruments, topographic maps, or microscopes for students to make meaning. Other times, you might use materials such as poster paper and markers to draw maps, paints and brushes to create a mural, jars of beans and rice to estimate, or balances made from rulers, string, and paper cups. The more students use materials to make their own meaning, the more they will be actively engaged in learning. Teachers must consider how each group of students will use available furniture to work together, whether it is desks, tables and chairs, or seats in an auditorium.

Here is a review of the characteristics of a Groups element:

- Groups vary in configuration.
- Groups accommodate differences.
- Groups solicit thinking from all members.
- Groups account for individual learning.
- Groups are organized deliberately by teachers.
- Groups are allocated specific sets of materials and furniture.

Now use Learning Record 2.D, Groups Element Revision, to revise your draft of a Groups element. Capture your current thinking using the questions you answered before and the summary above to guide your writing.

Learning Record 2.D	Groups Element Revision

Write a revision of your Groups element draft.

Copyright © 2006 by Corwin Press. All rights reserved. Reprinted from *Constructivist Learning Design: Key Questions for Teaching to Standards*, by George W. Gagnon and Michelle Collay. Thousand Oaks, CA: Corwin Press, www.corwinpress .com. Reproduction authorized only for the local school site or nonprofit organization that has purchased this book.

Continue to the next section and compare your element to some examples.

EXHIBIT SECTION: EXAMPLE GROUPS ELEMENTS

This section includes 12 Groups elements from the complete CLDs provided in the Resources. The primary (K–3) CLDs are from Reading/Retelling the Story, Fine Arts/Drawing Animals, and Physical Education/Imitating Animals. The intermediate (3–6) examples are from Science/Moon View, Media Technology/Logo, and Special Education/Vending Machines. The middle school (6–9) samples are from Language Arts/Fairy Tales, Math/Base Blocks, and Industrial Technology/Scooter Motor. The high

	Groups Element Examples
Groups *3 minutes* P-1	To create work groups, students pull from a basket an index card naming one of nine animals in the original story. Materials such as markers, crayons, construction paper, drawing paper, and glue are available for the groups to use to create a depiction of their invented animals. Students can create one picture per child or one per group. Students can sit in groups of four or fewer per table.
Groups *1 minute* P-2	Students work in the same small groups as the Drawing Animals learning design to create actions for their new animals. Materials needed are space and clothes for free movement.
Groups *3 minutes* P-3	Students work in small groups of two or three formed by the teacher so there is one writer in each group. Materials include pencils, markers, crayons, pieces of paper to fit in the book, glue, and scissors. Small groups can meet at tables.
Groups *10 minutes* I-1	Students are put into groups of four based on their zodiac signs. Groups work with drawings, pictures, or any objects they spontaneously use to construct models of the relationship. Small groups can push desks together.
Groups *10 minutes* I-2	Students work in pairs determined by self-report of advanced and basic computer skills. Students work in pairs or in small groups on the computer depending on how many are available. Students meet at the computer.
Groups *10 minutes* I-3	The teacher puts students in pairs. When possible, team a more capable or street-wise student with a less able or experienced one. Each student team is also assigned a paraeducator or adult volunteer to accompany them or to shadow them so they are protected or can have assistance as needed. $5 bill or equivalent change per team is needed. Pairs can meet at tables or push desks together.
Groups *5 minutes* M-1	Students put themselves into groups of three or four. The students are provided large sheets of chart paper, markers, and tape so they can write their group's definition of a fairy tale and list of common elements in fairy tales and post these for the Exhibit. Copies of articles by experts defining fairy tales and common characteristics of fairy tales are given to individual students after the Exhibit. Students can push desks together if there are no tables.
Groups *First day* M-2	Students get into six groups by counting off from one to how many there are in the class. Then they divide their number by six and get into groups by remainders: zero, one, two, three, four, and five. Groups work with the blocks that model a base that is two more than their remainder: remainder zero group works with base 2, remainder one with base 3, and so on. Small tables with chairs are the best arrangement for models.

(Continued)

(Continued)

	Groups Element Examples
Groups *First class* M-3	Teams of two or three students are determined by the number of students in the class, the number of engines available, and the amount of hands-on learning each student needs. For instance, one motor could be taken apart by the teacher and each team given one part. One motor could be taken apart several times, once by each team. Or four to five motors could be divided among 20 students. The groups should be small enough that each student can fully participate.
Groups *First day* H-1	Maps of the six inhabited continents are cut into four to six puzzle-like pieces and distributed randomly to students. They organize into six groups by finding others with pieces of the same continent. Accompanying materials include maps, graphs, business pages, and Web site information related to international trade. Students need large library tables or floor space.
Groups *First day* H-2	Students are grouped based on the number of letters in their Spanish names. No group should be larger than four. Each group needs a CD or cassette player and a computer with internet access.
Groups *First day* H-3	Students work in pairs on computers and with each other to develop categories, formulas, and systems to track their income and spending. Then they work in teams of four to record class information. Materials include one computer per pair, notebooks, index cards, and Monopoly money. Students need additional work space such as desk tops or tables.

school (9–12) illustrations are from Social Studies/Trading Partners, Foreign Language/Spanish Songs, and Business Education/Creating Spreadsheets. Refer to the 12 examples on previous pages.

Study these 12 Groups element examples and compare them to your draft of the Groups element. Note that each attends to students, materials, and furniture. Then consider how each example aligns with our characteristics. Do these Groups element examples vary by size, accommodate differences, support collaborative thinking, encourage accountability for individual learning, and specify arrangements for configuring groups, assigning materials, and allocating furniture? Compare the following examples to these criteria and decide whether your Groups of students, materials, and furniture satisfy these characteristics. Then use Learning Record 2.E, Groups Element Final, on the next page, to write your final element draft based on what you noticed as you compared your previous writing with your revision.

Learning Record 2.E Groups Element Final

Write the final version of your Groups element.

Copyright © 2006 by Corwin Press. All rights reserved. Reprinted from *Constructivist Learning Design: Key Questions for Teaching to Standards,* by George W. Gagnon and Michelle Collay. Thousand Oaks, CA: Corwin Press, www.corwinpress .com. Reproduction authorized only for the local school site or nonprofit organization that has purchased this book.

Now proceed to the next section and reflect on your thinking and learning as you wrote this element.

REFLECTION SECTION: PRECEDENTS FOR A GROUPS ELEMENT

The inclusion of this element was guided by the principles of classic social constructivist theory. Vygotsky (1934) articulated ways that learning is a social experience. Individuals thinking alone first make personal meaning. Then they test their thinking in dialogue with others to construct social meaning. Next, they construct shared meaning by reviewing their thinking with the class or in a larger community. Finally, the teacher leads students in considering the standard meaning among local communities and the broader society. Movement through these four phases of meaning making embodies the process of socially constructing cultural knowledge.

Thomas Kuhn (1996) described a similar process of socially constructing knowledge on a worldwide level in *The Structure of Scientific Revolutions.* He explained how many exciting theories of the past century were first proposed by individuals, then debated by people who studied the theory, and finally accepted by the international scientific community. Examples include the theory of relativity, quantum mechanics, plate tectonics, theories of contagion and vaccination, and the standard model in modern physics and chemistry. Most of the problems facing the world today are complex and do not have simple solutions. Teams of people working together and even internationally are conducting research to find solutions. Current examples are the international research on cancer, drug therapies for HIV/AIDS, the Human Genome Project, and string theory in physics. Large research universities are moving out of discipline-based departments to do more multidisciplinary thinking and research.

Constructivist Learning Design subscribes to the constructivist theory of Jean Piaget and his notion of "active" learning (Piaget & Inhelder, 1969). Students learn more deeply when they think with others, when they record their thinking, and when they explain and present an Exhibit to an audience. As students actively engage with others to think together and make meaning, they become more interested in learning.

Members of a group are more excited about learning when they work with materials or models to explain their thinking. They are engaged physically as well as mentally and make their thinking visible for others. Students who think more through their feelings and images than through language benefit most from such "hands-on, minds-on" learning experiences. The movement from self-made meaning to social meaning making is supported when students construct a physical representation of their thinking. Some students use the models to show their thinking, and others give form to their thinking by handling the materials.

The materials that Groups use are often addressed at the end of lesson plans as an afterthought rather than at the beginning as an early consideration. Teachers sometimes reject lessons or activities because they "don't have those materials in our school." Other teachers feel that math models and science equipment are not developmentally appropriate for older students, even those in intermediate grades or middle school. Yet offer the same materials to adults, and they will engage in fascinating discussions about arranging colored wooden blocks to demonstrate their thinking about a mathematical concept. Middle school students come alive when they use materials to construct a metaphor or to make a clear presentation of their thinking to classmates. The use of concrete objects is considered unnecessary by some who believe that working with abstract ideas represents greater intelligence. Students will try and dissuade teachers from using physical models or concrete representations, declaring, "Those are for little kids!" Do persevere. The clarity and visibility of thinking is enhanced when students move beyond verbal explanations to a physical representation of their thinking. The prospects for useful, real-world assessment increase greatly when real materials are part of teaching and learning.

The materials or models themselves have great power to affect the group members' learning. Give a group of people something to handle and play with, and wonderful sharing and talking about learning can emerge. For instance, when math students collaborate to physically represent an abstract idea, their handling of models creates a tangible connection between them. Another use of materials is for a writer's workshop, when teachers give learners "realia" or real objects to handle, create metaphors with, and write about. One favorite from professional development work is a "Basket of Shells." Each person chooses a shell from the basket, sketches it, and writes about how she or he is like a shell. They talk about the shell's shape, history, having been the home to a creature, having layers of calcium deposits, or being spirals. Writers can then extend their understanding of themselves as growing life forms. The choice of materials that students will use to accomplish a task by physical modeling, graphically representing, numerically describing, or individually writing about their shared meaning has a profound effect on the growth of a group. Models and other physical representations help bridge the gap between English-only speakers and English-Language Learners.

Many teachers are familiar with cooperative grouping in classrooms. You may have been introduced to this practice as a child, in teacher education coursework, or as a practitioner. Although learning with others is not new, teachers who support cooperation rather than competition are often seen as radical. The work presented in Roger Johnson and David Johnson's *Learning Together and Alone: Cooperative, Competitive, and Individualistic Learning* (1998), in Robert Slavin's *Cooperative Learning: Theory, Research and Practice* (1995), and in Spencer Kagan's *Cooperative Learning: Resources for Teachers* (1990) reviews the rationale, strategies, and outcomes of cooperating to learn. This research encourages teachers to move away from individualistic learning models and toward cooperative learning models. Students learn content more comprehensively in a cooperative group. Social skills necessary for cooperative learning are taught proactively along with the cognitive focus. For example, every student gets a section of a book, chapter, or article and is responsible for reviewing the information in that section and teaching it to others in their cooperative group. Each student is then tested on the entire text. This "jigsaw" format, initially described by Eliot Aronson (1978), promotes "resource interdependence" yet acknowledges individual contributions. Students must learn and practice group facilitation, such as taking up the role of "encouraging everyone to participate."

Yael Sharan and Shlomo Sharan's (1992) *Expanding Cooperative Learning Through Group Investigation* shows how student learning and inquiry are improved when they are aligned with cooperative learning traditions. Spencer Kagan (1990) compiled this work on cooperative learning in his comprehensive handbook for teachers. Elizabeth Cohen's *Designing Groupwork: Strategies for the Heterogeneous Classroom* (1994) and Mara Sapon- Shevin's *Because We Can Change the World: A Practical Guide to Building Cooperative, Inclusive Classroom Communities* (1999) focus on the importance of creating equity and establishing democratic classrooms, learning communities, or communities of practice. These texts focus on the need to improve equity, access, and inclusion for all students in the classroom. They pay special attention to issues of diversity and use cooperative learning to disrupt racism, sexism, and language-exclusive curricula.

Well-managed Groups within the framework of CLD are a powerful strategy for changing the norms of unequal education experienced by girls and boys. Studies of coeducation and single-sex groups, classrooms, and schools have been around for a generation. Sadker and Sadker (1994) raised the awareness of many teachers about sexism in schools. Constructivist curriculum offers girls and other marginalized groups of students more equitable access to education. Resolving equity issues in all classrooms every day is a challenge, yet our constructivist framework assists teachers in treating students equitably and holding high expectations of all students.

Researchers of bilingual education value the constructivist approach to learning and teaching. The focus on social interaction and cooperation improves learning for all students. English speakers also benefit from classrooms in which every student is legitimized and no student is stigmatized. Collier (1995) and Krashen (1987) advocate grouping bilingual students with English speakers. They focus on the importance of structured, interactive cooperation between learners of both languages.

Dick and Pat Schmuck (2001) describe using group-process strategies in classrooms and schools. They focus on the tensions and possibilities of heterogeneous groups as members strive to find common ground. Their struggle generates powerful learning about self, others, and classes for both students and teachers. They often consulted about organization development in schools, using group processes for professional development of staff, teachers, and principals. School personnel can be more productive members of site councils and other decision-making groups when they use group process. Teachers can use the same group-process strategies to support student learning.

Learning to use Groups effectively is central to constructivist learning and teaching. Because most teachers were taught in a large class, few have images of how small-group learning looks and feels. Keep in mind your real-life learning experiences—generally there are others around to support your learning. Seldom did you learn something new all by yourself. Teachers using cooperative learning have many resources, including colleagues, in their schools. One excellent resource that supports teachers' learning is Celeste Brody's and Neil Davidson's *Professional Development for Cooperative Learning: Issues and Approaches* (1998).

There are many precedents for using materials to support student learning. Friedrich Fröbel organized the first kindergartens in Germany during the mid-1800s. His "gifts and occupations" are beautifully described in Norman Brosterman's *Inventing Kindergarten* (1997). He described the value of materials and models such as clay, blocks, and tokens. Maria Montessori designed specific materials for young children to investigate size, shape, length, weight, and sound, among other concepts. Many of these materials required children to order objects as they replaced pieces. Several of these materials are described in *Dr. Montessori's Own Handbook* (1965) such as pink cubes, brown prisms, sound cylinders, and musical bells. George Cuisenaire was a music teacher who designed a set of graduated centimeter rods for his students who were having difficulty learning mathematics. In the mid-20th century, Zoltan Paul Dienes (1967) developed attribute blocks, rectangular and triangular versions of multibase blocks, and inscribed place-value blocks that have been copied in many different plastic variations. These thinkers had a profound respect for the physical representation of knowing.

After getting a sense of the educational precedents and theories that are the foundation for this Groups element, please use Learning Record 2.F, Groups Element Reflection on the next page. Write about what you have learned by thinking and writing a Groups element. Describe the feelings, images, and language in your thoughts as you learned about forming Groups of students, materials, and furniture for collaborative thinking.

Learning Record 2.F Groups Element Reflection

As you were thinking and writing about your Groups element,

Describe the feelings in your spirit.

Describe the images in your imagination.

Describe the languages in your internal dialogue.

Copyright © 2006 by Corwin Press. All rights reserved. Reprinted from *Constructivist Learning Design: Key Questions for Teaching to Standards*, by George W. Gagnon and Michelle Collay. Thousand Oaks, CA: Corwin Press, www.corwinpress .com. Reproduction authorized only for the local school site or nonprofit organization that has purchased this book.

Now read some concluding remarks and take a break from the CLD.

CONCLUDING REMARKS: THOUGHTS ON ARRANGING GROUPS

Many teachers are using Groups in classrooms; examples from different subject areas include cooperative teams, study partners, project pairs, or presentation teams. Because "teachers teach as they were taught," using small-group configurations to engage students in more powerful learning may be unfamiliar territory. New teachers may have experienced group learning in high school or college, but seldom during their early socialization in schools. Discuss the advantages and challenges of various groupings of students with colleagues.

Some teachers give up after a few attempts because "These students just can't work in groups." Students may protest when asked to learn in a group since their comfort level is disrupted. Learning together can be taught and practiced. Start with a simple activity of "think, pair, share." As pairs complete a quick Task, compliment the quality of teamwork rather than the quality of their product. Discuss the results with your reflective partners and then move to Groups of three or four students. Go carefully but deliberately, and your students will learn with you.

Committees, task forces, and working teams are common in education, but Groups are seldom used in classrooms. Teachers who support students through personal, social, and cultural meaning making ask students to think together about what they are learning. A random group is very useful when a topic is introduced or early in a course of study. As teachers get to know students, they can "hand group" them by personality, attitude, or work habits, mixing or matching these traits to create easy or difficult working conditions for students. This affective aspect of education acknowledges the human interactions involved in communicating, relating, and learning. Competence and humanity in social interaction are just as important as the content to be learned. The way students approach life depends on how they learn to work together and get along with peers during school. Teachers can no longer ignore the social processes of learning and just focus on content. Be thoughtful about how Groups of students, materials, and furniture can be used to successfully complete the Situation you selected for your students.

The three key questions answered in writing a Groups element are:

1. Students: How will you organize students into groups?

2. Materials: What materials will students use to make meaning?

3. Furniture: How will you arrange furniture to facilitate learning?

3 Building Bridges

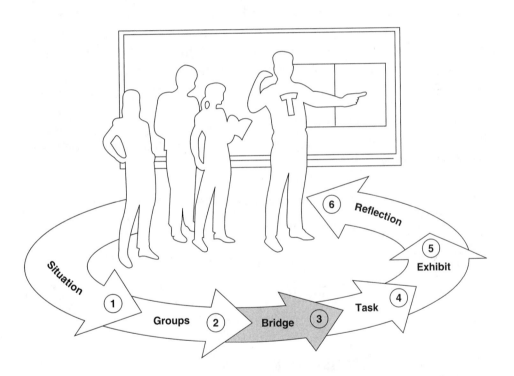

We now understand that learning is a dual process in which, initially, the inside beliefs and understandings must come out, and only then can something outside get in. It is not that prior knowledge must be expelled to make room for its successors. Instead, these two processes—the inside-out and the outside-in movements of knowledge—alternate almost endlessly. To prompt learning, you've got to begin with the process of going from inside out. The first influence on new learning is not what teachers do pedagogically but the learning that's already inside the learner.

—Lee Shulman, "Taking Learning Seriously" (1999)

As Shulman describes, any new learning is based on what students currently conceive, understand, or believe. A good example of this phenomenon is portrayed in a short video made at a Harvard University graduation in 1989 by the Annenberg Foundation. In *A Private Universe*, graduates and professors were randomly selected and asked to explain why there are four seasons. Most of those interviewed gave an intuitive explanation and attributed summer to that the period when the earth is closer to the sun in its orbit and winter to the period when it is farther away. Only 1 person in 20 accurately described the 23-degree tilt of the earth on its axis as the reason for seasons. As the Northern or Southern Hemisphere is tilted inward in the earth's orbit around the sun, that hemisphere experiences summer while the other experiences winter. If teachers hope to organize effective learning episodes, then they must find out what current perceptions, conceptions, or constructions students bring with them. This is essential to surface any misunderstandings and move toward reconstructing clear concepts. Teachers must understand what students actually know or think to engage them in new learning.

The three key questions to answer in building a Bridge element address your audience, their preconceptions, and their connections with personal knowledge:

1. Audience: Who are your students?

2. Preconceptions: How will you surface students' prior knowledge?

3. Connections: How will you connect the topic to students' lives?

These questions should guide your thinking in building a Bridge element.

SITUATION SECTION: SURFACING PRIOR KNOWLEDGE

The third element of Constructivist Learning Design (CLD) is the Bridge. This element is critical to applying constructivist learning theory in a classroom. Before beginning any "new" learning, teachers must invite students to surface their prior knowledge, which serves as "footings" or the foundation for a Bridge between what students already know and the new learning they will build. Students carry an array of information about any topic from previous experiences, including popular media perceptions, folk wisdom, common misconceptions, or partial understandings. Some have bits and pieces of vocabulary, while others have complete definitions that are quite accurate. Sometimes no student in your class really understands the concept or can make connections to their life experience, or one student may be an expert who has specialized knowledge.

Purpose of a Bridge element

The purpose of a Bridge element is to think about effective ways to surface students' prior knowledge or preconceptions and to find out what they already know about what you are organizing for them to learn. The focus of this chapter is to create a Bridge element for your CLD. After reading an initial explanation, you will draft your Bridge element and then discuss some considerations with your reflective partner or a Learning Circle of colleagues. Questions will prompt you to think about how you can get students to describe what they already know about what you want them to learn. After that, you will review some characteristics of this element, write a revision, compare your element to our examples, write a final draft for your CLD, and reflect on your thinking and learning as you wrote your Bridge element.

Topic for a Bridge element

The topic for a Bridge element is to identify prior knowledge that students have about the concept, process, or attitude you have chosen for your CLD. This Bridge element relates directly to the Situation and Groups elements you have already written and will prepare students to move forward with the Task element you design for your learning episode. Some teachers conceive of the Bridge element as an initial warmup or a simple problem to review before they move on to the major Task for the learning episode. Other teachers engage the whole class in a discussion of the topic to be studied during the learning episode. The risks involved in surfacing prior knowledge are personal and real. Many students are not confident enough in their understanding to reveal what they think. This attitude can result from the culture of speed and accuracy that is prevalent in schools, especially in this era of high-stakes testing. As we work with eighth-grade students learning to use an abacus, many do not trust their mental arithmetic and try to conceal their lack of skills by using calculators rather than risk embarrassment by being slow or wrong. If a teacher does not realize what students already know or think about a topic, then it is difficult to address what they need to learn or to assess new learning.

The best Bridge elements we have observed engage students in making connections between their previous experiences and the learning topic by encouraging them to freely describe their thinking and understanding without reservations about being right or wrong. This attitude of trust in the teacher and fellow students arises when teachers purposely include a value for different perspectives and risk taking, so that mistakes or failures are only potholes or detours on the road to success. For example, a group of high school students toured Pixar Studios in Emeryville, California, and during the two-hour visit did not see a single computer. Instead they saw artists thinking: developing characters, locations, and stories; producing rough drafts of their work; and reviewing ideas with colleagues to get feedback and suggestions for improvement. Only after these artists had vetted their ideas with others on their teams did they begin to produce the artistic models that would guide the computer renderings for animated features such as *Finding Nemo* or *The Incredibles*. Their motto was "We succeed at failure," and the results of this attitude seemed to be quite effective and spectacular in the very demanding commercial arena of public opinion. Developing this culture of experimentation with students takes time and trust as students realize the correct answer is not valued as much as a clear explanation of thinking, which other students can review and then respond, react, or relate to in their own thinking.

Assessment in a Bridge element

A math colleague was preparing to teach a learning episode on fractions to seventh graders. As a Bridge to what they already knew, he asked them about selecting half of a sheet cake if it was divided vertically or horizontally, as depicted in Figure 3.1, Vertical and Horizontal Halves, on the next page. His students agreed that both cakes were equal and divided in equal halves, but if they were going to select a piece to eat, they would choose the one on the right, which was divided vertically, "because there was more cake." He talked with them about their concept of a half and equal shares, and they attributed their thinking to how they perceived it rather than to their concept of "half."

This kind of assessment about what students already know or think they know is very important in identifying preconceptions and misconceptions at the start of a learning episode. What students think and why they think that way has a profound effect on what they learn next. Without conducting some basic formal or informal assessment about prior knowledge, teachers search for the right key to new learning in the dark. For example, ask students to sort out a simple problem such as the halves question, have a group discussion, play a game, role play a simulation, or brainstorm a list of connections. Determining what students already know

Figure 3.1   Vertical and Horizontal Halves

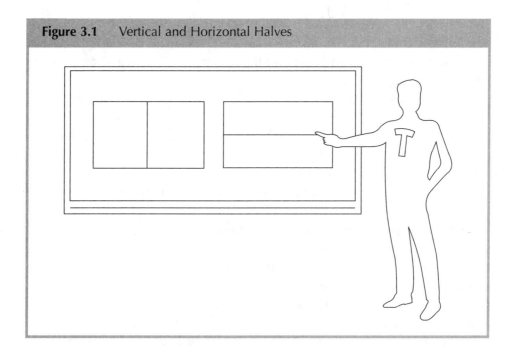

can be done quickly and yields information about prior knowledge that the teacher can use to plan the rest of the learning episode. Students appreciate being acknowledged for what they know and appreciate when someone asks. Teachers and students alike can use this information in making decisions about the rest of the learning episode. Without this initial assessment, it is difficult to determine what is existing knowledge and what previous conceptions or misconceptions are interfering with meaning making about new ideas, how new ideas are being connected to existing knowledge, and what new knowledge is being constructed. These questions are at the heart of constructivist learning.

The following examples are some great ways to create a Bridge between prior knowledge and new learning:

- In social studies, have students draw a map of a country, continent, or the world and fill in everything they can. After they study the material, have them draw the map again from memory and compare the two.
- In science, ask students to decide what will happen if they test a scientific theory. For example, if a ball of clay is dropped into a glass of water, will the water level rise, stay the same, or go down? Then ask the students to change the experiment and predict the results. In the previous example, you could flatten the clay so it sits on the surface of the water and ask students to decide again what will happen to the water level. Then have them experiment themselves to test their theories.

- In art, ask students to draw a human face and describe the relationship of the eyes, ears, nose, and mouth on the face. Then look at faces in the class and consider the commonalities an artist might use in drawing portraits.
- In physical education, have students work in groups to create games with a basketball or soccer ball that require cooperation rather than competition to win. Team skills are essential for winning, and this approach might get players to understand this concept more quickly.
- In math, ask students to count using only the numbers zero to four to surface what they know about place value in base five.

These are just a few examples of building a Bridge to assess what students already know about a topic. If you think about ways that students can show their thinking rather than just tell about it, then you will have a record of their prior knowledge to compare with the knowledge they construct during a learning episode. Students also have a record of their new learning and can effectively reflect on changes in what they know.

Now write a rough draft of a Bridge element in the CLD format. Write your draft in Learning Record 3.A, Bridge Element Draft, on the next page.

After completing your draft, continue on to the Groups section that follows.

GROUPS SECTION: CONNECTING WITH STUDENT THINKING

Perhaps the most important contribution of Constructivist Learning Design to standards-based teaching is the notion that students arrive in the classroom with preconceptions about whatever teachers want them to learn. Many teachers still behave as if students do not know very much about a topic and explain it with little consideration of students' existing knowledge. Constructivist learning theory assumes that students connect everything they are learning with what they already think they know. Often, their thinking is not completely accurate or is partially formed and may contain several misconceptions or shaky preconceptions that teachers must address for students to fully accommodate new learning.

A hallmark of constructivist teaching and learning is creating a productive and trustworthy environment so that students will candidly surface what they do and don't know. Students can express what they already know about a topic individually or collectively. In a typical Bridge, students think together to reveal what they already know about the concept, process, or attitude selected in the Situation. Such collaborative thinking usually stimulates more discussion and raises a broader range

Learning Record 3.A	Bridge Element Draft

Write a rough draft of a Bridge element.

Copyright © 2006 by Corwin Press. All rights reserved. Reprinted from *Constructivist Learning Design: Key Questions for Teaching to Standards*, by George W. Gagnon and Michelle Collay. Thousand Oaks, CA: Corwin Press, www.corwinpress .com. Reproduction authorized only for the local school site or nonprofit organization that has purchased this book.

of ideas than individual thinking. Sometimes students need to reflect privately about their prior knowledge. This strategy is effective for students who are not comfortable speaking out in even the smallest group. Such individual documentation holds each student accountable and offers baseline data for all students. In any case, this strategy can be used periodically for formative assessment. Small-group conversations offer a safe way for students to express their ideas and test their thinking with others, especially if community-building activities have established a strong foundation of trust. In both cases, a prompt or question about the topic will generate some data for the students and for teachers. Each small group is often expected to complete a simple problem, list, or game instead of just being asked to "discuss" the topic. These activities don't take any longer, generate real documentation, and offer a more engaging review and introduction to the Task than a whole-group conversation. Specific instructions and required documentation reduce the "float" possibilities—students chatting about unrelated topics or one student tuning out. Framing the "right" activity—that is, one that results in useful documentation—requires teachers to be very clear about the purpose of the Situation and to be explicit about the quality of the documentation.

A Bridge can take a few minutes if the CLD is one class period, or it could take a day or a few days if the CLD is a unit. Teachers may use a Bridge as the first class session in a two- to three-week unit to firmly ground students in their own thinking before they begin work on a long-term task such as a case study, project report, or fine arts production. How you and your students build a Bridge is not as important as doing it early in the learning episode so that students can connect their prior knowledge to each part of the new learning. Here are some considerations in designing a Bridge element.

Considerations in Building a Bridge Element

This section extends our Bridge metaphor with other ideas about connecting prior knowledge and new learning. At the end of the section, use Learning Record 3.B, Bridge Element Notes, to note your ideas in thinking with a reflective partner about writing your Bridge element.

Engineering Bridges

We are often amazed at what students already know or think they know about the topic of a lesson. They have a variety of learning experiences from inside and outside the classroom. Taking time to find out what some students know and others don't can surface valuable resources for other students. Identify students who might coach others and offer suggestions to "expert" students so they can help other students understand what they know. They also can serve as resources to explain key concepts to others in their group. A backup activity or extension question will engage groups who finish their explanation quickly. Be sure to have students explain their thinking to you and then redirect their explanation or encourage further thinking. Think about how you might engineer a Bridge that spans your classroom membership and connects to the individual Situation.

People Bridges

Doing the Bridge in small groups gives students an opportunity to meet peers who are not in their usual social group and even to form new friendships. Many students feel more comfortable speaking up in smaller groups and participate more fully in the Bridge activity. The small-group format also lets you observe the interactions among group members before the Task is addressed. Your observations can give you valuable information about the strengths and weaknesses of group members, their different languages and cultural perspectives, and how different students relate with each other. In many urban schools, students spend most of their in-school time with language-group peers, even though the school itself may include speakers of several different languages. This is true in elementary schools and major research universities. Teachers must be strategic about when and how to integrate students so they can overcome their assumptions and prejudices about themselves and others and build cultural competence. The Bridge is a time to rethink the configuration of Groups and modify initial plans if needed.

Floating Bridges

On Puget Sound in Washington State, several inland bridges don't span a body of water but float on the surface of the water. The CLD notion of a Bridge also floats in time and depth. If you are already familiar with what your students understand, then surfacing prior knowledge to connect with new learning might be much less substantial. Military engineers also construct such floating bridges that can be dismantled and moved along with the troops as needed. These structures only need to move thinking from one point to another; they do not serve as permanent spans to carry two-way traffic. Sometimes a Bridge takes a few minutes. Other times a Bridge may take a week to set up and carry out and become an integral superstructure for new learning. The kind of Bridge you organize should be consistent with the time and depth of the learning episode you are designing. Don't feel bound by rigid construction specifications or protocols, and feel free to experiment with unique designs.

Now that you've read these considerations, talk with your reflective partner or Learning Circle about designing a Bridge. Write your notes or ideas in Learning Record 3.B, Bridge Element Notes, on the next page.

In the next section, answer questions based on your ideas.

BRIDGE SECTION: QUESTIONS FOR STRUCTURING BRIDGES

Use Learning Record 3.C, Bridge Element Questions, on page 95, to record your answers to these questions. When you have answered these questions, proceed to the next section, which describes the characteristics of a Bridge element and prepares you for revising your first draft of this element.

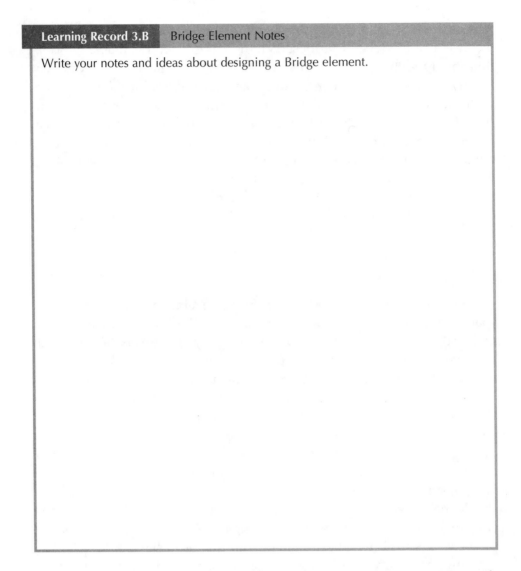

Copyright © 2006 by Corwin Press. All rights reserved. Reprinted from *Constructivist Learning Design: Key Questions for Teaching to Standards*, by George W. Gagnon and Michelle Collay. Thousand Oaks, CA: Corwin Press, www.corwinpress .com. Reproduction authorized only for the local school site or nonprofit organization that has purchased this book.

Your answers should be useful in applying the following characteristics.

TASK SECTION: REVISING A BRIDGE ELEMENT

A Bridge element may be long and low or short and high. A Bridge doesn't need to be elaborate, but the structure should be substantial enough to span the depths of knowledge within each student and to make their knowledge visible to the teacher and classmates. Traditionally, the opening activity or "anticipatory set" of a lesson plan was designed to set up a lesson, not

Learning Record 3.C   Bridge Element Questions

What would you expect students to know already?

Will you determine students' prior knowledge by having students solve a simple problem, define terms, play a game, construct lists, or discuss the topic?

"High talkers" often dominate the conversation in a class discussion. What other ways can students show what they know to examine their prior knowledge?

How will students surface their prior knowledge and analyze what they understand or do not know?

How can students apply their knowledge to the current Situation?

Copyright © 2006 by Corwin Press. All rights reserved. Reprinted from *Constructivist Learning Design: Key Questions for Teaching to Standards*, by George W. Gagnon and Michelle Collay. Thousand Oaks, CA: Corwin Press, www.corwinpress .com. Reproduction authorized only for the local school site or nonprofit organization that has purchased this book.

to find out about prior knowledge. A Bridge must link existing student knowledge to new learning. The design of a Bridge determines the quality of the new learning and should be thoughtfully planned and documented. Each characteristic is an important part of building connections between what the students already know and what you want them to learn.

Characteristics of a Bridge element

Six characteristics of a Bridge element are described in the following sections. Each characteristic is explained in some detail and then repeated in a summary for your reference before you revise your draft of a Bridge element.

A Bridge surfaces students' prior knowledge

All students benefit from the chance to review prior knowledge as they learn new things. Students can connect prior knowledge with new learning to make both more meaningful. Some teachers shy away from too much public description of current knowledge because they fear that articulated misconceptions will become a barrier to correct understanding. They hope to reduce the weight of excess baggage that students bring with them to the learning episode. However, such efforts to bypass existing knowledge allowed some Harvard graduates and faculty members to retain misconceptions throughout their very expensive educations.

Surface any and all preconceptions for several reasons: First, youth and adult students are both honored by the assumption that they already know something. A learning episode that begins with something they know is much more interesting than the usual message of "Here is something else you need to learn about." This is especially true when teachers and students come from different races, cultures, languages, classes, or genders. Second, most student and adult preconceptions contain some elements of truth, and those elements can be the basis for building new learning. Students are more motivated to pursue new learning if they can be convinced their existing knowledge is legitimate. Third, teachers and students together weave a tapestry of understanding when all are encouraged to bring their ideas forward. Ideas can be rewoven in subtle ways that take advantage of existing ideas in the construction of new ones. Facilitated by an artful teacher, reweaving student words diminishes the constant privileging of certain students over others so that those who are so often marginalized can be heard. With opportunity, the second-language speaker, a nonreader, or an emotionally challenged child can make the most colorful contributions to the weaving. Existing and new knowledge includes contributions from all students rather than a mere presentation of privileged knowledge. Fourth, old ideas will not go away without some reconciliation with the new. Whether they are fully formed or half baked, they will continue to lurk in all of us. The good and the bad carry equal weight in our minds and hearts. The final product will be more comprehensive as student thinking is honored and initial understandings are given a place in the development of new learning.

A Bridge refocuses students

Students need to refocus when they come into your classroom or move from one subject to another. This is especially important for secondary teachers, whose students move from room to room or subject to subject every hour or so. Elementary teachers face a similar challenge when creating a transition from recess or lunch to a topic of inquiry or from one area of study to another. The difference between telling students to "open your books to page 143" and having them write or tell a neighbor something they know is evident in their body language, willingness to engage, and attention to one another.

A Bridge organizes students into collaborative groups

A Bridge can be done with a whole class, small groups, or individuals. Many teachers begin with a whole-class discussion of the learning that is the "construct." The advantages of a large-group conversation are time efficiency (for a secondary teacher who has 45 to 55 minutes of class) and the volume of data produced about students' existing knowledge. The disadvantage is that some teachers ask a few high-talking students their opinions and assume they represent the group. The whole-class format may not be a comfortable setting for many students to offer their ideas. Shy students, English-Language Learners, or those who question their understanding are least apt to contribute. A more effective technique is to have each student write down one response in a notebook or on a card. Teachers can call on individual students for sample responses or collect and review the cards.

Having students in a small group can be very useful during a Bridge. Every group could be randomly composed and small enough so that each student can speak in the time allotted. For example, if a teacher only wants to allow three minutes, the dyad is the obvious choice. If a Bridge is setting up a longer unit and the groupings are predetermined by interest or topic assigned, then Groups of three to six are appropriate. Most students discuss their thoughts more easily with a small group of peers than with the whole class. Often just a few students engage in whole-class discussion, but when the class is asked to turn to a neighbor or to talk with people at their table, there is a buzz of activity and ideas. That is one reason the Bridge element comes after the Groups element in CLD.

A Bridge builds community among students

Building a Bridge together also provides an opportunity for students to form a new working group, become familiar with peers, and get comfortable with any new procedures. Using small groups of students to do a Bridge usually takes more time than having a whole-class discussion, but that time is well spent. As teachers move around from group to group and sample the conversations, they have a better understanding of how individual students think and what roles they might play in the group. Use this window of opportunity for community building, and it will pay back big dividends in improved relationships, more respectful interactions, and a greater appreciation for different kinds of students, especially those poorly served by the "fastest and loudest is best" culture.

A Bridge creates a shared understanding and vocabulary

Teachers can make use of the language their students bring into the classroom by creating opportunities for each student to say what they mean when they use a word or idea. Teachers also can encourage two or more students to agree on a definition, but they must allot more time for students to develop a thorough understanding of important concepts. By building a Bridge, teachers reject the old adage of ineffective teaching, "I covered the subject, but the students didn't learn it!" As teachers and students become familiar with what they already know, both are better able to make connections with new learning. When students are in small groups, they can work together on a minor problem or question. This activity serves as an introduction to the topic and gets students thinking about what they already know. Your Bridge could be a puzzle, a game, a definition, a brief explanation, or a list of characteristics.

A Bridge gathers information about what each student knows

This characteristic of a Bridge will influence the rest of the learning design in several ways. First, individual student assumptions and knowledge about the topic are exposed. Second, the quality of interactions between members of a class becomes apparent. Third, baseline data or pretest information is gathered and reviewed by class members and the teacher. Finally, steps leading to the Task element are more certain because the pathway of previous learning has been illuminated. The quality of teacher facilitation can be modified to take advantage of accurate and inaccurate student knowledge, and it can be linked directly to student interest. For example, students can be grouped by interest and yet still be expected to learn about the same topic. This puts the teacher in the role of anthropologist during the Bridge to collect data about what the students already know, how they interact, and what they need to learn.

To review, the characteristics of a Bridge element are as follows:

- A Bridge surfaces students' prior knowledge.
- A Bridge refocuses students.
- A Bridge organizes students into collaborative groups.
- A Bridge builds community among students.
- A Bridge creates a shared understanding and vocabulary.
- A Bridge gathers information about what each student knows.

Use Learning Record 3.D, Bridge Element Revision, to revise your Bridge element. Don't be concerned about doing it right; just use the questions you answered before and the summary of characteristics above to guide your writing. After you are finished, return to the Exhibit section that follows and compare your element with those examples.

Learning Record 3.D	Bridge Element Revision

Write a revision of your Bridge element draft.

Copyright © 2006 by Corwin Press. All rights reserved. Reprinted from *Constructivist Learning Design: Key Questions for Teaching to Standards*, by George W. Gagnon and Michelle Collay. Thousand Oaks, CA: Corwin Press, www.corwinpress .com. Reproduction authorized only for the local school site or nonprofit organization that has purchased this book.

Now, look at some example Bridge elements from colleagues' work.

EXHIBIT SECTION: EXAMPLE BRIDGE ELEMENTS

This section includes 12 Bridge elements from the complete CLDs provided in the Resources. These designs address four different levels of students. The primary (K–3) CLDs are from Reading/Retelling the Story, Fine Arts/Drawing Animals, and Physical Education/Imitating Animals (Examples P-1, P-2, P-3). The intermediate (3–6) examples are from Science/Moon View, Media Technology/Logo, and Special Education/ Vending Machines (Examples I-1, I-2, I-3). The middle school (6–9) samples are from Language Arts/Fairy Tales, Math/Base Blocks, and Industrial Technology/Scooter Motor (Examples M-1, M-2, M-3). The high school (9–12) illustrations are from Social Studies/Trading Partners, Foreign Language/Spanish Songs, and Business Education/Creating Spreadsheets (Examples H-1, H-2, H-3). Refer to the 12 examples on the following pages.

Review these 12 Bridge elements and note that each involves the students in activities to find out what they already know about the topic of the learning episode. Then consider how each example aligns with these characteristics. Do these Bridge activities surface students' prior knowledge, focus students on the topic, organize students into collaborative working groups, build community among students, create a shared concept base and vocabulary among students, and gather information about what each student knows? Analyze which of these characteristics are included in the following examples to decide whether each Bridge satisfies the criteria.

Study these 12 Bridge element examples and compare them to your Bridge element revision. Then use Learning Record 3.E, Bridge Element Final, on page 103, to write the final version of your Bridge element based on what you noticed as you compared your writing with the examples.

After writing a revision element, review some precedents that informed the Bridge.

REFLECTION SECTION: PRECEDENTS
FOR A BRIDGE ELEMENT

Finding out what students already know about a concept, process, or attitude that you want them to learn is a basic principle of constructivist teaching and learning. Whenever learners encounter something new, they make sense of it by connecting it with something they already know.

	Bridge Element Examples
Bridge *5 minutes* P-1	The teacher reads *Brown Bear, Brown Bear, What Do You See?* to the children. Some teachers might create a simple melody and sing the story. The teacher asks the children to listen for the various types and colors of animals "looking at me."
Bridge *4 minutes* P-2	The teacher and students read the new version of *Brown Bear* using the new animals and colors on the pages of the new book that they created together.
Bridge *12 minutes* P-3	The teacher shows the pages of the new book. Children try to remember where their animal went and what it ate after seeing another animal. Teacher and children brainstorm and chart words that tell how each animal moved, where it went, and what it ate.
Bridge *15 minutes* I-1	Students are asked to explain why we have seasons. This is based on a similar question posed to students and faculty at a Harvard graduation ceremony in a film called *A Private Universe*, in which 1 out of 20 people gave a correct account while others had misconceptions. After students present their explanations, they watch *A Private Universe*.
Bridge *20 minutes* I-2	Students make a list of computer languages that they might know or have heard about. Students are given a list of Logo primitives, shown how to enter them into the program, and asked to explore what each of these functions does to the cursor: FD #, BK #, RT #, LT #, PU, PD, PE, HT, ST, CS, HOME, and CLEAN. The teacher leads a brief review of each command and what students thought it meant.
Bridge *30 minutes* I-3	The first part of this Bridge focuses on breaking down a $5 bill into smaller denominations and counting the money. The second part of the Bridge includes a whole-class visit to a vending machine area so that each child or young person can put coins or paper into a machine, get at least one product out of the machine, and retrieve any change.
Bridge *10 minutes* M-1	The teacher describes personal experiences with fairy tales and asks students to read what they wrote the previous day about their personal memories of fairy tales.
Bridge *First day* M-2	Students are each given a sheet with numbers from 0 to 100 on it and asked to work in remainder groups to write each of these numbers in the assigned base. After each group completes the count sheets, they gather all of the pieces that model places in their base from a large pile of base blocks. Students model some of the numbers under 100, and then the teacher reviews the places and exponents for different bases.

(Continued)

(Continued)

	Bridge Element Examples
Bridge *First week* M-3	Each team of two to three students is given a part of a small engine. Looking at a schematic, they must identify the part, describe its function, and tell which other parts it interacts with. They also might explain the part to see whether it is in good condition or worn and in need of replacement.
Bridge *One week* H-1	Groups conduct a preliminary study of current trading activities within their continent. For instance, the South America group might choose citrus if the curriculum includes the role of trade agreements and foreign subsidies among different nations. Citrus is also a good choice for Florida or California students.
Bridge *First day* H-2	Invite students to talk about what they know about tejano music or Selena. Watch the film *Selena* if they are not familiar with Mexican American tejano music. Students should discuss Selena's experience as a Mexican American who learned Spanish as a second language and debate whether she would have been successful singing only Spanish lyrics or only English lyrics.
Bridge *First day* H-3	The teacher hands out index cards and asks students to write down anonymously the amount of money they spend each week. Then the teacher tallies these results with the class and discusses what categories might be used to present this information. For instance, under $20, $20 to $40, $40 to $60, $60 to $80, $80 to $100, and over $100. The teacher creates a spreadsheet with the tallied information and draws a chart showing the distribution. Teacher and students will brainstorm the possible categories of income and spending: food, clothing, entertainment, transportation, games, computers, books, and sports.

A young child talks about building cranes or backhoes "resting" or "sleeping" when they are not working. He or she also recognizes that a movie or television show is over when the credits roll. When commercials for discount CDs of popular hits of the past decades come on and scroll song titles on the television, the child is convinced that a show is ending and turns it off! Adults do the same thing in their own learning when they build on what is already known to make sense of new experiences.

As teachers begin a constructivist learning episode, their first step is to find out what their students already know or think they know about

Learning Record 3.E   Bridge Element Final

Write the final version of your Bridge element.

Copyright © 2006 by Corwin Press. All rights reserved. Reprinted from *Constructivist Learning Design: Key Questions for Teaching to Standards,* by George W. Gagnon and Michelle Collay. Thousand Oaks, CA: Corwin Press, www.corwinpress .com. Reproduction authorized only for the local school site or nonprofit organization that has purchased this book.

what they are going to learn. Sometimes they know much more than we expect, and other times they have a great deal of misinformation. Either way, we are better prepared to support learners if we understand what students already know or think about a concept, process, or attitude. For example, we taught a learning episode on fractions many times to prospective teachers in elementary math methods. The Bridge question addresses what the top number and the bottom number are called and what each means. Usually the words "numerator" and "denominator" surface quickly. When questioned about why those terms are used, students speculate freely about numerating and denominating. Few students have ever described the bottom number as denominating the total number of parts in the whole and the top number as numerating the number of parts designated by that fraction. The balance of the learning episode is spent investigating wholes and parts, with the purpose of clarifying this relationship.

Piaget's notion of "disequilibrium" between existing schema and current experience and Vygotsky's idea of scaffolding to support students who are building new learning on old knowledge are based on the constructivist theory that prior knowledge has a profound influence on new learning. Individuals experience the world based on what they already know and believe. New experiences are perceived through the lens of old knowledge, so that individuals make different meanings from the same event based on their prior knowledge. Constructivist Learning Design positions the Bridge as an important initial assessment for the teacher. Teachers can take a quick inventory of what students already know to decide how the learning episode should proceed. They get a sense of what knowledge most individuals bring with them and what the class in general understands. This assessment can be helpful in deciding which group of students to spend more time with or how to modify a task for each different group. Sometimes you have to change your whole approach—for example, during a circumference lesson, it became clear that students did not understand what pi was or how it was derived. Understanding how to derive pi became the topic of the next lesson. You need to test the water temperature before jumping in. Don't assume that you know what students know at the beginning of a learning episode.

All lesson-planning schemas attend to beginnings and endings, and generally represent two camps—external and internal control over learning. An example of the external way of thinking about learning is evident in the work of Dwight Allen (1969), who introduced the concept of "microteaching" in the 1960s. His teaching represented a "systems" approach to teacher education that trained teachers to display certain behaviors that research had linked to student learning. It called for videotaping lessons, which were then analyzed for the presence of eight presentation behaviors. The student teacher would "reteach" the lesson based on feedback from this analysis. The first of the eight steps was called a "Set" and required the teacher to set up the new lesson, sometimes by asking the students what they remembered from a previous lesson and sometimes by stating facts or giving information. Although that strategy was an improvement over "Open your books to page 47," it provided the teacher with little useful information about student thinking.

Madeline Hunter's *Mastery Teaching* (1982) was a guide for teachers to improve their lesson planning. Although teacher preparation and inservice were shaped by her work for over a decade, teachers have often spoken critically about being "Hunterized" by their districts. Her efforts to systematize lesson planning and observation were heroic, if behaviorist. Her methods to enhance full-group instruction, however, did contribute to improving teacher practice. For example, she offered teachers strategies for assessing the individual attainment of concepts. This improved on the inadequate full-group "dipstick method," which depended on the choral response to questions such as "Does everyone understand?" or "Who can tell me about . . .?" Although this method got at some student knowledge, it was often limited to surface knowledge that could be reported quickly.

Both of these approaches are reflected the work of Robert Gagné (1985) and David Ausubel (1968). Gagné suggested a system of nine instructional events that began with Event 1, "gaining attention"; Event 2, "informing learners of the objective"; and Event 3, "stimulating recall of prior learning." The third event was focused on asking students to recall any relevant prior knowledge. Ausubel suggested the use of an "advanced organizer" that he described as a verbal or graphic overview that abstractly relates new concepts to previous learning. Related strategies include graphic organizers, structured overviews, pretests, timelines, directed reading lessons, and directed viewing lessons. All of these methods assume external control over learning as teachers try to force a fit between new content and what their students should already know. This assumption also deprives students of their internal control over learning, their responsibility for learning, and the individualized work of connecting new learning with prior knowledge.

Internal control over learning is a better fit with CLD. We assume that students not only have prior knowledge about a concept, process, or attitude, but also that students differ in how they make meaning and construct new knowledge. Your initial assessment during a Bridge should elicit individual student knowledge, assumptions, values, beliefs, and motivations to learn more about a topic. Your Bridge should also indicate how and when to move into the Task that students will accomplish during the learning episode.

You should have a sense of the theory and precedents that are the foundation for this Bridge element. Use Learning Record 3.F, Bridge Element Reflection, on the next page, to reflect on what you have thought and learned in drafting, revising, and finalizing the Bridge element you have built to surface the prior knowledge that students bring with them and connect it with current learning.

Now that you've designed a Bridge, check in with your partner or Learning Circle for some feedback before drafting the last three elements. Read the concluding remarks and take a break from the CLD.

Learning Record 3.F   Bridge Element Reflection

As you were thinking and writing about your Bridge element,

What feelings were in your spirit?

What images were in your imagination?

What languages were in your internal dialogue?

Copyright © 2006 by Corwin Press. All rights reserved. Reprinted from *Constructivist Learning Design: Key Questions for Teaching to Standards*, by George W. Gagnon and Michelle Collay. Thousand Oaks, CA: Corwin Press, www.corwinpress .com. Reproduction authorized only for the local school site or nonprofit organization that has purchased this book.

CONCLUDING REMARKS: THOUGHTS ON BUILDING BRIDGES

After you teach a constructivist learning episode, you may have an opportunity to talk with colleagues about their teaching, and you can compare notes on the ways they surface prior knowledge and assess existing understandings of their students. You can talk with others in your department or grade level about ways they find out what students already know or think about a concept, process, or attitude as they begin a learning episode. Others teaching the same topic may use different language to talk about ways to engage students. Some may describe an advanced organizer, some an anticipatory set, and others may refer to a motivator. You can open their "bag of tricks" and revisit those activities to look for ways to use them in keeping with the characteristics described previously. For example, one of your colleagues may use the movie *Dead Poets Society* as a motivator for a unit on poetry or teenage tendencies toward self-destruction. You might consider modifying this activity by showing a clip of students tearing pages out of their textbooks and using it as a springboard to a discussion about whether poetry needs passion or prescription to capture readers' attention.

Another reflective conversation to have with your colleagues is to brainstorm what they know about poetry and how they learned it as preparation for a similar discussion with students. We are frequently surprised by the variety of things that teachers surface in this kind of brainstorming. Students know about poetry from high school or college courses, from movie or television programs, from reading poetry by friends or partners, from going to poetry readings or slams, from attending fringe festivals or listening to public radio, and from trying to write and read their own poetry. These experiences offer you a Bridge to find out what and how your secondary students know about poetry.

Another good focus question for a discussion with your colleagues is to identify ways that your Situation purpose or learning goal helps your students meet state or national standards. This conversation might give you information about what your students really study before they are in your class and what they are expected to know for subsequent classes. The more you understand about what your students already know or will need to know, the better you can design your learning episodes to take advantage of the expectations your education colleagues have at the federal, state, or local level. If you can give your colleagues feedback about what students really understand when you involve them in learning, then you are in a better position to influence the quality and the content of their learning.

The pressures of schooling limit the time that teachers can devote to organizing for learning. Schedule bells, unrelated content, textbook length, disciplinary programs, and other external factors deplete the time required for a careful set up of each learning episode. A Bridge is an investment in student engagement that pays handsome dividends in student learning time. Time invested up front in the manner described will reduce time lost to disruption, low motivation, and discipline problems.

You now have answered three key questions about designing a Bridge element:

1. Audience: Who are your students?

2. Preconceptions: How will you surface students' prior knowledge?

3. Connections: How will you connect the topic to students' lives?

Your answers may be apparent in the element you wrote and will guide you as your students move through the Task that you will frame for them.

Constructivist Learning Design uses the notion of building a Bridge between prior knowledge and new learning as an active construction metaphor for this element of learning design. You can provide the body of learning to cross and the points to anchor a span, but individual students must construct their own Bridge between prior knowledge and new learning. These vary in time and space for each individual. We urge you to draw on opening or introductory activities that have been successful for you in the past and to modify them as necessary to accommodate our characteristics. Let your students create their own Bridge between prior knowledge and new learning.

4 Crafting Tasks

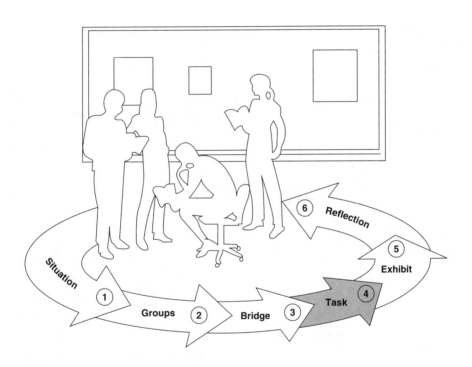

A learning task is an open question put to learners who have all the resources they need to respond. The open question in the learning task is the heart of the matter, inviting critical thinking, demanding reflection, stimulating creativity.

—Jane Vella, "Taking Learning to Task" (2001)

This chapter describes the fourth element of our Constructivist Learning Design (CLD), Task. The Task supports the examination

Figure 4.1 CLD Schematic

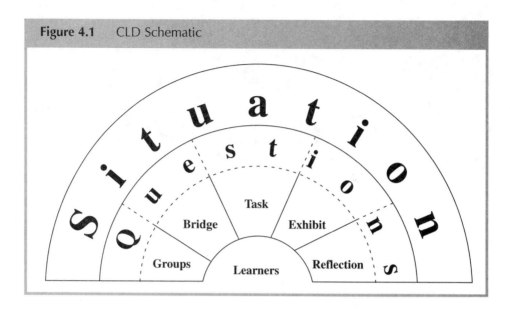

of an open question, as Vella describes, or "the heart of the matter." When writing a CLD, the Task focuses your purpose, topic, and assessment in the Situation overview. Students actually do the Task after the Groups and Bridge elements and before the Exhibit or Reflection elements. The Task is the centerpiece or keystone of the arch shown in Figure 4.1, CLD Schematic.

The Task is similar to an activity or exercise for students to do that often begins the thinking about a design for learning. However, a CLD Task emphasizes questions that you anticipate from students during the learning episode. The point is what students learn from doing the Task, not just from its completion. Think through your responses to the questions that you expect students to ask so that you can respond to them in ways that promote further thinking rather than give a definitive answer. Previous versions of the CLD template focused more on the questions dimension of a Task, so the title of this element represents a modification of CLD. Questions are still the heart of doing the Task when teachers move among Groups of students to monitor and support their learning. Much of the constructivist teacher's work is creating learning situations and then asking and responding to questions to support student thinking. In the Task element in particular, teacher questions play a critical role in shaping the learning episode for students. The kinds of questions that artful teachers use to guide student learning are described later in this chapter as well as in Chapter 7, "Teaching a Design." The Task is the fourth element in CLD to emphasize the importance of painting the big picture in the Situation, the Groups, and the Bridge elements before arriving at the Task itself.

The three key questions in crafting a Task element are designed so that you can imagine how your Task will play out with your students. Questions focus on how to engage them in making meaning, how to anticipate their questions, how to project answers that will surface their thinking, and to how record their learning.

1. Engaging: How will students engage in making meaning?

2. Learning: What kind of record will document student learning?

3. Thinking: What questions will students ask and how will you reply?

SITUATION SECTION: CRAFTING A TASK

The most powerful CLD has extensive preparation. Michelle, for example, recalls her father teaching her to paint a room. He was meticulous in preparing equipment, laying out tools, and rounding up brushes, rags, drop cloths, and the like. The room itself would be secured, floor and furniture covered, and tape applied to protect surfaces next to the area to be painted. Window and door hardware, tacks, and other unwanted protrusions were removed and carefully stored. Then the sandpaper and mud or spackle would come out. Every surface destined for new paint would be repaired, filled, and sanded. The day would pass and the can of paint hadn't even been opened! However, as she learned the hard way, the quality of the finished product was only as lovely as the quality of the preparation. Skipping any part of the preparation resulted in a lousy paint job.

The same quality of preparation is necessary in crafting a Task. For students to succeed, they must have all the resources they need to respond. The primary preparation is assessing the nature and quality of the Task for students to complete. The suggested sequence of preparation is as follows:

1. Review the purpose and topic that you framed in the Situation element and then craft a Task to engage students in learning that topic (concept, process, or attitude) to accomplish your purpose;

2. Anticipate questions from students as they are thinking about making meaning and then project how you might respond so that they can describe their current understanding; and

3. Develop a record that students will use during this Task to document their learning for the assessment you selected.

Purpose of a Task element

Why are you crafting this Task element? How can students engage in learning the concept, process, or attitude that you determined was your topic in the Situation? You must know how individual students think and the values of the larger society to which they will connect. You need to organize for both individual and collective learning, anticipating the personal meaning each student might make and the collective considerations likely necessary for your class.

Will students find the Task interesting? The Task should attract their attention and keep them focused. A delicate balance between challenge and frustration must be considered as you design the Task. The thinking required to accomplish the Task may not be easy but should be developmentally appropriate for your students. You can anticipate that some students in the class will find the Task more challenging than others.

How long will it take students to do the Task? Estimating this can be tricky. Sometimes we drastically underestimate the difficulty involved, and other times we see small groups move to completion without in-depth thinking. Have you done the learning Task before with another class or gone through a similar experience yourself? Some of students' favorite learning episodes were adapted from conference presentations for adults or classroom observations. There is value in rehearsing a Task and looking for the pitfalls and promises. Sometimes teachers don't have the time or resources to do a dry run, yet even rehearsing the Task in your imagination can highlight some obvious complications that preplanning can reduce or eliminate. Whenever possible, plan the same CLD with a colleague and his or her students so that you can compare notes and learn from each others' experiences.

Topic for a Task element

The topic for a Task element is to clarify the nature of the students' thinking as they make meaning and accomplish your purpose. What will students do that engages them in making meaning about the topic individually and collectively? As students go about accomplishing a Task, the role of the teacher in monitoring group thinking and guiding class learning is to ask questions that surface students' understanding. Teachers should ask questions not only to gauge students' learning but also to guide, clarify, and integrate their thinking. The purpose of such questions is to discern student thinking and to determine the quality of learning within the Task. Instead of focusing on speed or accuracy in student responses, these questions determine the nature and quality of thinking that students do as they engage in learning a concept, process, or attitude. *Guiding questions* shape the quality of the Situation, Groups, and Bridge and set up how students will engage with the Task. *Clarifying questions* with the power to frame conceptual learning must be designed carefully if student learning goals are to be achieved. This tension or balancing act reflects the challenge teachers face as they structure student learning with a specific purpose while still supporting students as they each make meaning in their own way and from their own experience.

For example, we sometimes use a clear plastic container of tennis balls to demonstrate a constructivist learning episode for teachers. The purpose of our Situation is to provide a concrete demonstration of the difference between perceptual impressions and conceptual thinking. The topic of our Situation is for the teachers to make meaning based on a physical comparison of perceptions and conceptions. The assessment of our Situation is how we monitor the teachers' thinking based on our questions and their explanations. We have teachers form groups and ask them to decide if the can is taller, farther around, or the same. They study the container without touching it and usually notice the slight indentation on the bottom, the slight space on the top, and the slight space between the tennis balls and the side of the container. The teachers usually agree that the container appears to be taller than it is farther around. As we ask them to explain their thinking, they usually begin to talk about the difference between the distance of three tennis balls stacked up and the distance across one tennis ball. As we ask them about the relationship between the distance across one tennis ball and the distance around it, they begin to move toward a more conceptual approach to answering the question. They think about the relationship between pi and the diameter and circumference of a circle. Then they factor in the slight distances between the balls and the container. Often, their conclusion is that the height of the container and the distance around it is nearly the same. When we finally demonstrate with a piece of paper how the circumference exceeds the height, most are convinced but still surprised that their conceptual thinking was more reliable than their perceptual impressions.

Assessment in a Task element

How will you assess the learning that students are doing by accomplishing your Task? As you plan a Task for students to accomplish, assessment of that accomplishment should result in a record that students produce. Students can present this record to the class as evidence of learning accompanied by explanations of their thinking. We often design Learning Records to let us review the learning accomplished by individual students. These Learning Records may be different from the artifact produced by a group of students to Exhibit their thinking. In the tennis ball learning episode, we ask each group of students to present a diagram of their thinking. The Learning Record is an index card that captures individual reflections about students' thinking as they compare their perceptual impressions to their conceptual thinking. However, much of the assessment during a Task is based on teacher observations and questions.

When teachers ask *clarifying questions* to discern and understand student thinking, there are several different kinds of assessment taking place. Teachers try to get inside the heads of students and assess how students are making meaning and what understandings they are developing. This involves discerning what prior knowledge students bring with them, what new learning is taking place, and how they are reconstructing knowledge. Teachers also assess what students are thinking, why they are thinking that way, and how they are responding to their own thinking. Teachers sort out the concepts, processes, and attitudes embedded in the knowledge that students construct. They further assess how students relate to others, communicate with others, and motivate themselves. Much of the assessment takes place informally as teachers observe the dynamics of small groups, decide when to participate or intervene in the group interaction, and ask questions to clarify group thinking.

When teachers ask *integrating questions*, a different kind of assessment occurs. These questions are more focused on synthesizing students' collaborative thinking into a shared meaning among those in each group. Integrating questions prepare small groups to present their thinking during the Exhibit. Teachers determine whether most of the students in a group understand the shared meaning by asking individuals to analyze, synthesize, and evaluate that group's thinking. Students who are most reluctant to participate may be the least able to articulate the group's thinking and shared meaning. Teachers also assess the accomplishment of a Task and decide when to move forward to an Exhibit of student artifacts and explanations. By imagining *anticipated questions* from students, clarifying questions and integrating questions emerge more easily than if they were forced.

Choosing and refining a quality learning Task is at the heart of developing an effective learning episode and a challenge to any constructivist learning designer. Crafting an engaging Task gets easier with experience, but it is never simple. Write a rough draft of a Task element for your CLD in Learning Record 4.A, Task Element Draft, on the next page.

Learning Record 4.A	Task Element Draft

Write a rough draft of a Task element.

Copyright © 2006 by Corwin Press. All rights reserved. Reprinted from *Constructivist Learning Design: Key Questions for Teaching to Standards*, by George W. Gagnon and Michelle Collay. Thousand Oaks, CA: Corwin Press, www.corwinpress .com. Reproduction authorized only for the local school site or nonprofit organization that has purchased this book.

In the next section, think with at least one other colleague before you revise the Task element of your CLD.

GROUPS SECTION: THINKING TOGETHER TO MAKE MEANING

The key consideration in crafting a Task element is deciding how students will think together to make shared meaning. A Learning Circle of your colleagues is in the best position to think about this challenge with you. A Task is not just information to memorize, skills to perform, or dispositions to adopt. A good Task is open ended and encourages students to think together as they construct their own shared meaning about a topic.

For example, teachers could ask primary-level students how many combinations of two numbers that total 13 they can list. This question has many answers that offer a variety of different ways to approach the topic. These range from simple ways such as $8 + 5 = 13$ to more complex ways such as $136 - 123 = 13$. These combinations also include $12 + 1$, $11 + 2$,

10 + 3, 9 + 4, 8 + 5, 7 + 6, 14 − 1, 15 − 2, 16 − 3, 17 − 4, and so on. Students could show these combinations with base 10 blocks, Cuisenaire rods, Unifix cubes, popsicle sticks, straws, or any other manipulative model available. This task is open-ended and more challenging for learners than memorizing any single combination, such as 8 + 5 = 13. Open-ended questions are appropriate at every level and in every discipline.

Intermediate students learning Logo programming in a computer lab could be asked to construct the largest possible equilateral triangle on their screens. Middle school music learners could be asked to develop their own clapping or drumming rhythm and annotate it so that others can reproduce it. Another middle school example is asking learners to assemble a collection of 20 heights that would produce an average height of 5 feet 4 inches rather than asking them to average 20 heights.

High school learners might be asked to identify all stakeholders in the American Revolution, including Native Americans, African Americans, and Spanish Americans, as well as the British, French, Dutch, and other Europeans, and then to speculate about the different perspectives of these stakeholders. These open-ended topics have no "right" answers. Each group of students can think about and explain its answer so that others can decide whether the answer is appropriate or accurate.

Considerations for Crafting a Task Element

Review the following considerations about writing this element and discuss them with a reflective partner or Learning Circle. A Learning Record is available at the end of this section to summarize your ideas.

Asking the right questions

Questions are the key to learning! Your questions set the tone for engaging students in a Task. These questions guide their thinking and allow adjustments as learning unfolds. As you anticipate student questions, you can respond not by giving answers, but by asking students to explain their current understanding and encouraging students to keep thinking about the Task. A colleague of ours reports that Japanese teachers have thick plan books for individual lessons they have developed in teams. Much of each book is devoted to anticipated student questions and explanations so that teachers are prepared to respond positively and to support students in thinking through their constructs.

Not giving direct answers can be difficult for teachers

Most people really enjoy the feeling of knowing something and being able to share knowledge with another person when they ask a question or seek advice. You are affirmed as a valuable person when you give an answer that satisfies another person. The principles of constructivist learning encourage teachers to take a different role. First, try to determine why students are asking that question and what they already know. Then, try to get inside the mind of the questioner and find out where they are in their thinking. Then ask the *next* question rather than answer that one. Teachers can experience feelings of confusion and frustration as they relearn or reconstruct the concept of "teacher" and replace the role of question answerer with the role of thinking questioner. Such a change is essential if teachers are to support students in constructing their own knowledge.

Sometimes a small change causes big confusion

In a math methods class with prospective teachers, we used a familiar Situation. Often we present a can of tennis balls and ask students to decide whether it is taller or farther around and then to explain their answer. One morning the tennis balls were not available, so we grabbed three oranges and asked the students to imagine a cylindrical container that would hold those oranges tightly. With one class, we used the tennis ball analogy in setting up the Situation, but in the next class we didn't. The second class took its Task as deciding whether the container for the oranges needed to have more room at the top or around the sides of the oranges to accommodate them. This led to several unpredicted questions until we figured out the source of the confusion. Substituting a new material or model can lead students away from the intended purpose. As designers, we hadn't thought through the nature of the now-modified Task. We certainly didn't think through the last-minute substitution very carefully.

Two-minute warnings

Bringing group thinking about a Task to a close can be tricky. Some students are not ready, others have to wait, and still others would benefit from some rethinking. But to have enough time for students to share their thinking, we usually "take the temperature" of the working groups by announcing a "two-minute warning" and doing a last check when most seem ready to present. Those who have finished can be encouraged to extend their thinking or refine their presentation. Those who are not ready or need rethinking can learn from the other small groups as they Exhibit their thinking. Two minutes is just about enough time to let them finish their conversations or decide what to save and what to present.

Supporting students to engage in the Task

Imagine students as rock climbers scaling a wall. At each junction or decision-making point, the climber will either place a foot in a crevice, reach for hand holds above their head, or belay another climber. The coach provides the right equipment, creates safety awareness, reviews climbing strategies, and only then encourages the climber to choose a strategy at each junction. As teachers, we sometimes believe that our function is to explain how to use the equipment, how to be safe, and how to select different strategies for climbing. We forget that most students can't make meaning and use this information to construct knowledge until they assist other climbers or climb the wall themselves. Human nature often prevents us from merely setting students to the learning Task and only then asking the right kinds of questions as they construct their own knowledge. Remind yourself that only a master climber can ask the right questions.

Now that you've read these considerations, talk with your reflective partner or Learning Circle about crafting a Task. Write your notes or ideas in Learning Record 4.B, Task Element Notes.

Learning Record 4.B	Task Element Notes

Write your notes and ideas about crafting a Task element.

Copyright © 2006 by Corwin Press. All rights reserved. Reprinted from *Constructivist Learning Design: Key Questions for Teaching to Standards*, by George W. Gagnon and Michelle Collay. Thousand Oaks, CA: Corwin Press, www.corwinpress .com. Reproduction authorized only for the local school site or nonprofit organization that has purchased this book.

The next section encourages you to start coaching climbers.

BRIDGE SECTION: QUESTIONS FOR FRAMING TASKS

The purpose of a Bridge is to connect prior knowledge with present learning. You may already have experience creating learning activities, exercises, or events for students to complete. The following questions are designed to guide your thinking about crafting a Task element for your CLD. Answer these questions in Learning Record 4.C, Task Element Questions, which follows.

Learning Record 4.C	Task Element Questions

How will the students engage in active learning?

How will you question students about what they already know?

What kind of response do you expect from students about the Task?

How will students reorganize their groupings to carry out a Task?

(Continued)

Learning Record 4.C   (Continued)

What kind of reaction do you expect from students about thinking together?

How will you interact with students as they are thinking about the Task?

What are the challenges and incentives for completing the Task?

Copyright © 2006 by Corwin Press. All rights reserved. Reprinted from *Constructivist Learning Design: Key Questions for Teaching to Standards*, by George W. Gagnon and Michelle Collay. Thousand Oaks, CA: Corwin Press, www.corwinpress .com. Reproduction authorized only for the local school site or nonprofit organization that has purchased this book.

Now continue to the next section, which describes the characteristics of a Task in preparation for writing a revision of your first draft of this element.

TASK SECTION: REVISING A TASK ELEMENT

In this section, you will review the characteristics of a Task element and then revise your rough draft. These characteristics include a description of why questions are important in teaching a Task. The power of the teacher's role as students are working on a Task is in asking clarifying and integrating questions. These questions guide student thinking about meaning making—both social meaning and personal meaning—as students think together and alone.

Characteristics of a Task element

The characteristics of a Task element are described in separate passages that follow. A summary of these characteristics is at the end of this section for your reference as you revise your draft of this element.

A Task is interesting to the students

As you design a Task, how do you expect students to feel about doing it? Teachers usually expect students to feel positive about tasks to accomplish and actually want to do it. Sometimes teachers miss the mark badly. Other times students do not want to quit. Think about tasks you have chosen that really engaged students in learning. What Task can students do that interests them in the concept, process, or attitude you selected?

A Task can be broken down into smaller parts

Often students have to engage in a sequence of separate pieces of thinking to accomplish a Task. You may have to design two or three separate parts of a Task for students to accomplish in order to make meaning effectively. The trick is to not break tasks into so many sequential parts that students lose track of the whole. The nature of successful tasks is that the students should be challenged but not frustrated in their efforts to make meaning while accomplishing a Task. Teachers can fragment a Task to such an extent that their students do not have to think. Some students benefit from that level of structure, but most need to grapple with learning about the whole. A CLD can be stretched over two or three episodes if necessary for in-depth investigation. Students must connect the smaller parts of the Task to the larger whole so that the purpose of the Situation remains clear.

A Task has an understandable outcome

Students must be able to understand the concept, process, or attitude they are learning. Although anything can be understood at some level, students should be at an appropriate developmental level to stay in the learning. At the beginning of a school year, we asked a fifth- and sixth-grade class to draw a map of the room. Some students sketched where the furniture was, others made a map of a wall, and others drew an outline of the windows and doors. We later had to ask for an "accurate map" and describe it as a "view from above." Few students were comfortable with drawing, and some did not have the cognitive development to imagine themselves with an abstract perception from above. Several students moved to the loft in the middle of the room to acquire a new perspective.

To understand the process of making a map, many students needed to make a model of the playground and then draw a map of the model.

A Task leads to learning new content

The purpose of accomplishing a Task should be to learn about a concept, process, or attitude by making personal meaning, negotiating shared meaning, and considering collective meaning. The content provokes meaning making rather than memorizing facts or figures. Students construct knowledge by thinking through content, communicating with each other to make and agree about meaning, and considering how that meaning is collectively understood in the broader society.

A Task results in a product

Designers often prepare a Learning Record for the students to complete as they accomplish the Task. In math or science lessons, the Learning Record provides a problem set for each group of students to work through at its own pace. Usually students have to think about how to build something with a math model that represents a concept. Then each student draws or sketches what the group has built with the model. Finally, each student writes a numerical record of the diagram. All students in a group should keep their own Learning Record so that they each make their meaning and are individually accountable. During the Exhibit, we may ask any student in the group to explain his or her product and then check on how well each student understood the concept based on individual Learning Records. If the product is a single project or poster, then students can spend some individual time writing a record of their learning on an index card or in a journal. We use so many index cards that students speculate we own stock in a company that manufactures different sizes and colors.

A Task provides opportunities for teacher and student questions

The role of questions in supporting students through a Task cannot be overemphasized. As students think and work, the teacher's role is not to answer questions, but to redirect students' thinking with provocative questions. Students learn when they are actively engaged in learning. Each CLD element is organized to include questions because they prompt thinking and learning. In the Task element, though, questions are more thoroughly discussed because of the different kinds of questions required to support active engagement in the Task. Students also ask different kinds of questions once they start on the tasks. For example, in the Fairy Tale CLD, Sue asked her students to recall a fairy tale from their early childhood. As the students began sharing their stories, they asked each other, "Was that story a fairy tale or just any old story?" Their peers would then apply new learning about the characteristics of a fairy tale to their peer's story to see whether it qualified.

Where do questions come from? Consider the source of questions—students, teachers, administrators, and local, state, and national constituencies—and the answers they expect. Also consider the purpose of the questions, such as guiding, clarifying, and integrating thinking. Ask questions of individuals, pairs, small groups, and the whole class. The following are some examples of different sources, purposes, and audiences for questions.

As teachers attend to local and state standards, they find themselves asking, "How will I know students have met the standard?" Standards are offered as general goals, with few mileposts or stepping stones along the way. A challenge for teachers is to break the standards into manageable parts and to craft tasks that set up ways and means for students to understand the content. For example, teachers used the Fairy Tale learning design to introduce students to one genre of fiction outlined in the seventh-grade language arts standards. One purpose of the Task was for students to derive the characteristics of the fairy tale genre.

Be prepared to use different types of questions for different reasons as you work through your CLD. What guiding questions will drive the Situation, Groups, or Bridge for students, and how will you respond to their requests for information or confirmation? What anticipated questions will you use to frame responses to questions you might expect from students so that you can encourage them to continue thinking for themselves? What clarifying questions will you use to understand student thinking, sustain active learning, and clarify students' explanations? What integrating questions will draw the Task to a close and support learners in agreeing on a shared meaning?

Constructivist Learning Design uses four unique types of questions—guiding, anticipated, clarifying, and integrating—which teachers can ask during the Task and other elements as they design for learning. Ask colleagues how they use questions. Many teachers choose one comprehensive guiding question to frame a project or a unit and then create subquestions within it. Teachers often ask "essay questions," that is, those designed to elicit student understanding about a topic, such as "Compare and contrast capitalism and communism." Teachers also ask "summary questions," that is, those designed to elicit a demonstration of content learning.

What questions will you generate for each CLD element? What guiding questions will you use to introduce the Situation, to arrange the Groups, and to set up the Bridge? What anticipated questions will you expect students to ask? What clarifying questions will you use to have students explain their thinking? What integrating questions will you use to prompt an Exhibit and then to encourage student Reflection?

Such questions were asked throughout the Fairy Tales learning episode. Rehearsing the Task of defining the genre of fairy tale, Sue began the day before with a homework assignment to ask a parent about a fairy tale the student had enjoyed as a young child that might surface their previous experience with fairy tales. Once the Task was under way, subsequent questions focused on the content of the genre: What are the characteristics and definitions of a fairy tale? Finally, the why and wherefore—the teacher's larger purpose for student learning: "There are fairy tales in every culture. How do different cultures express similar values?" Later in the term, teachers moved students into using fairy tales to make cross-cultural comparisons.

Here are the characteristics of the Task we just reviewed:

- A Task is interesting to the student.
- A Task can be broken down into smaller parts.
- A Task has an understandable outcome.
- A Task leads to learning new content.
- A Task results in a product.
- A Task provides opportunities for teacher and student questions.

Now write a revision of your draft of a Task element in Learning Record 4.D, Task Element Revision, on the next page.

Now that you've revised your draft, review the examples in the following section. Compare your revision to these examples and finalize your draft.

EXHIBIT SECTION: EXAMPLE TASK ELEMENTS

This section includes 12 Task elements from the complete CLDs provided in the Resources. These designs address four different levels of students. The primary (K–3) elements are from Reading/Retelling the Story, Fine Arts/Drawing Animals, and Physical Education/Imitating Animals (Examples P-1, P-2, P-3). The intermediate (3–6) examples are from Science/Moon View, Media Technology/Logo, and Special Education/Vending Machines (Examples I-1, I-2, I-3). The middle school (6–9)

Learning Record 4.D Task Element Revision

Write a revision of your Task element draft.

Copyright © 2006 by Corwin Press. All rights reserved. Reprinted from *Constructivist Learning Design: Key Questions for Teaching to Standards*, by George W. Gagnon and Michelle Collay. Thousand Oaks, CA: Corwin Press, www.corwinpress .com. Reproduction authorized only for the local school site or nonprofit organization that has purchased this book.

samples are from Language Arts/Fairy Tales, Math/Base Blocks, and Industrial Technology/Scooter Motor (Examples M-1, M-2, M-3). The high school (9–12) illustrations are from Social Studies/Trading Partners, Foreign Language/Spanish Songs, and Business Education/Creating Spreadsheets (Examples H-1, H-2, H-3). These examples were deliberately chosen from 12 different areas to emphasize the utility of CLD. Refer to the 12 examples on the following pages.

After considering these examples of tasks, reexamine the Task element you wrote and revised. Compare the types of questions used to frame the Task elements in the examples with your written Task. Is the Task clear? Will the questions support, extend, or synthesize students' understanding of the Task? Which questions appear most likely to frame deeper and more useful learning for students? When you have finished your comparison, complete a final version of your Task element in Learning Record 4.E, Task Element Final, on page 129.

	Task Element Examples
Task *20 minutes* P-1	The teacher reads Brown Bear, Brown Bear, What Do You See? again. This time, the teacher asks, "What other animal could we put here and what color could it be?" Students are encouraged to be inventive and not to criticize "polka-dot salamanders." All the students sketch their creatures. Those who can write put their descriptions in words on their page, and others dictate their descriptions to the bookmaker. Anticipated student questions: Should I make my parrot green like the picture book or a new color? Teacher questions: Is your animal real or imagined? What sounds does your animal make? Where might your animal live?
Task *10 minutes* P-2	Students think about their animal and decide where it went and what it ate. They each create movements to act out these actions. Anticipated student questions: How does my animal move around? Where would it go? What does it eat? Teacher questions: Where does your animal live? What kind of legs does it have? Where might your animal go? What do you think it eats? How many of these animals have four legs? How many of these animals live on land? How many animals were in the new book?
Task *20 minutes* P-3	Students draw a new picture showing where their animal went and what it ate after seeing another animal "looking at me." The writers in each group write the descriptions on the new pictures. Anticipated student questions: How can I write down the words to tell how my animal moved, were it went, or what it ate? Teacher questions: What words describe how your animal moved, where it went, and what it ate? Can you try to write them on a piece of scrap paper?
Task *30 minutes* I-1	Groups are asked to draw a diagram of the relationship between the sun, earth, and phases of the moon. Anticipated student questions: What are the phases of the moon? Isn't the curve on the moon just the result of the shadow of the earth? Why do we see the moon during the day? Do people on the other side of the earth see the moon in the same phase as we do? Why isn't the moon always in eclipse when the earth is between the moon and the sun? What is an eclipse of the sun? Where is the moon in the sky? How big is the moon compared to the earth? How far is the moon from the earth?
Task *30 minutes* I-2	The teacher asks students to accomplish the tasks, including measuring the display screen vertically, horizontally, and diagonally. Then they review the repeat command and try to write a program for the largest equilateral triangle they can make on the display screen. Next, they review a recursive command and write one for the largest circle they can make on the display screen.

(Continued)

(Continued)

	Task Element Examples
	Anticipated student questions: What does equilateral mean? How many degrees are in a triangle? Why did my triangle look weird? Teacher questions: What two root words are in the word "equilateral," and what might they mean? If you took a triangle at one corner and unfolded it flat, what would you have? If you were trying to walk in a triangle, how would you turn corners? Writing the same thing over and over can be tedious, so how might you repeat a routine?
Task *30 minutes* I-3	Teachers take students to a vending machine area, give them a $5 bill, and expect them to work in pairs, make change, and purchase from three different vending machines a sandwich, drink, and dessert or chips. Teacher questions: What do you already know about using a vending machine? Where is information about the product and the cost? What are clues to use if you can't read? What do you do if the machine doesn't take the kind of money you have? What will you do if the machine eats your money but doesn't give you anything?
Task *15 minutes* M-1	Students organize into groups and get paper, markers, and tape. They develop their definition of fairy tales and list common characteristics. Teacher questions: What were your previous experiences with fairy tales? How would you define a fairy tale? What are common characteristics in fairy tales? How do your definitions compare to those of experts? After seeing and reading others what would you add to your own definition or list? Which definition was more meaningful to you and would be more helpful in writing your own fairy tale? Why are we studying fairy tales? Where did fairy tales come from? What are fairy tales from other cultures?
Task *3 days* M-2	The teacher reviews the places and exponents for different bases and students model problems in addition, subtraction, multiplication, and division. Each group is asked to model the problem, its solution, and the relationship between the two. Anticipated student questions: How do we count in our base? Teacher questions: What do we do when we fill up the first place in base 10? What digits do we use in base 10? What digits can you use in your base? Guiding questions: Students are given the following four problems to solve by modeling the problem, solution, and relationship between the two. Rosalie goes to the store and buys a can of pop for 43 cents and a candy bar for 34 cents. How much does she spend? Rosalie gives the clerk a dollar bill for her purchase. How much change does she receive? Rosalie goes outside and her brother Jamie asks whether he can have her can when she is done.

(Continued)

(Continued)

	Task Element Examples
	He puts it with 11 other cans and will get 7 cents per can from the recycler. How much money will he receive? Jamie has to split this money equally with his three friends who helped him collect the cans. How much money will each get from the recycling?
Task 4–5 weeks M-3	Teams are given a motor to disassemble, reassemble, bench test, mount, and field test by themselves. How does a small gas engine work? Where does the fuel go? What does the spark plug do? What is exhaust composed of? Why does modifying the spark plug or the fuel blend affect performance? What would happen if a motor were larger or smaller? What else could you do with the motor?
Task 2 weeks H-1	Students select an occupation and evaluate its relationship to international trade. What are the roles and responsibilities of your occupation? What goods or services does your company produce or offer, and how are they used in the local region? Nationally? Internationally? Is there a link between what you do and the products of any of the six continents we talked about? How will your occupation be affected by changes in international trade?
Task 5–6 days H-2	Students transcribe the song "La Carcacha" from Spanish into English and then conduct research on the Internet to consider how Hispanic culture has influenced mainstream American music. Anticipated student questions: How would we translate this verse? Teacher questions: Can you make your translation fit the melody and rhythm? How has Hispanic culture influenced mainstream American music? Is there such a thing as mainstream American music when many styles, such as jazz, reggae, or R&B, are rooted in other cultures? Would the music be as interesting and successful if the lyrics were always in English?
Task 3 days H-3	Students create and update their spreadsheets with a week of income and expenses. Anticipated student questions: If I don't have a job, what should I do? Teacher questions: Do you have an allowance, or do you get money from your parents for lunch or the bus? What categories will you develop to describe your spending?

Now is the time to present your work so far to your reflective partner or Learning Circle. Recall the description of crafting tasks as preparing a room for painting at the beginning of the chapter. What was the purpose of your Task? Will you show your colleagues the newly painted room or a series of photos of various stages of the job? Do you want to portray your

Learning Record 4.E	Task Element Final

Write a final version of your Task element.

Copyright © 2006 by Corwin Press. All rights reserved. Reprinted from *Constructivist Learning Design: Key Questions for Teaching to Standards*, by George W. Gagnon and Michelle Collay. Thousand Oaks, CA: Corwin Press, www.corwinpress .com. Reproduction authorized only for the local school site or nonprofit organization that has purchased this book.

improved technique in painting window trim with a working demonstration or by showing the cleanliness of your brushes and rollers after use? If the purpose of the Situation were to "get the room covered with new paint any way you can," then documentation about accomplishing the Task can begin and end with a visit to the room. If the purpose of the Situation is to learn and demonstrate quality of craftsmanship, then a quite different Exhibit may be required. Both process and product tell the story.

As you prepare to show your Task documentation to colleagues, think about the nature of the Exhibit. Are you sharing all the notes you took and reflections you made throughout the chapter? Do you consider a description of the Task itself to be the only Exhibit? This is a preview of the decision making required to imagine how your students will Exhibit documentation or evidence that they accomplished a Task.

REFLECTION SECTION: PRECEDENTS FOR A TASK ELEMENT

Thinkers about learning tasks come from all walks of education, including adult education, math, science, and the fine arts. Now that you've crafted your own learning Task, take time to read about the work of others who have thought deeply about the role of tasks in learning.

Jane Vella's work was introduced at the beginning of this chapter. An educator of children and adults for many decades, Vella described her movement from "writing teaching tasks in my lesson plans to designing learning tasks" (2001, p. xiii). She examined her assumptions about students and changed her stance to reflect the following beliefs:

- Students have the capacity to learn
- Students learn when they are actively engaged
- New content can be learned through learning tasks
- Learning tasks promote accountability

These beliefs are simple yet powerful. Teachers who care deeply about learning are more comfortable advocating the first two stances than the latter two. Teachers must believe students can learn if they come to work every day. Observation of the "buzz" of real learning demonstrates engagement in tasks to even the most didactic teacher. Teachers begin to doubt the third assumption. Colleagues ask, "Don't we have to explain to students what the new content is before they can use it?"

Teachers' images of what their teachers did are more about talking and telling than about student learning. Novice and experienced teachers alike respond to the CLD by saying, "But what does the teacher do?" after they've engaged in designing learning for students. Yet when teachers recall their most vivid learning experiences, they are always doing things such as building something, performing in the choir, or editing the school paper. There was plenty of new content, but it was not dished out in full helpings. Rather, teachers recall picking up small servings of new information along their journey through school. They may or may not recall the powerful coaching that supported their ability to do something new because learning happened as they did the tasks. The smart facilitation required to support that applied student work was often subtle and intended to empower the doer, not to showcase the teacher.

Vella's fourth assumption about accountability may challenge many teachers. Teachers are held accountable for enrolling students, making sure they come to class and follow directions, and conferring a grade. They have been less accountable for real learning that can be linked to their facilitation. Teachers also have been less accountable for imparting the skills that will ensure continued learning by students. Admittedly, learning is a complex thing, and no one teacher can claim responsibility for every student's learning. However, Vella commits herself to designing learning tasks that ensure learning, transfer, and impact. Those outcomes demand a different kind of teacher accountability.

In addition to Vella's work, note the centrality of the "task" in the thinking of John M. Dearn (1996), a member of the faculty of applied science at the University of Canberra. The first two of his "several statements about learning" pinpoint the importance of tasks and especially the use of questions within the tasks. In his first statement—Students learn when they are motivated to ask questions that they perceive of as valuable and relevant to their goal—Dearn begins with questions students ask. This is a powerful statement about the nature of learning and learners. Students' "need to know" is often overlooked in the rush to impart knowledge that can be measured through standardized assessment.

Dearn's second statement focuses on the task itself: Students construct knowledge while they are engaged in authentic tasks. Dearn explains, "In order to learn students need to apply their knowledge and gain confidence in using it. Knowledge that is not put to use will not be learnt and students need to be engaged with practicing rather than studying, which is usually equated with memorizing." Dearn's attention to confidence is revealing. Building confidence with new knowledge comes from rehearsal and practice doing it, not hearing about it. Adult learners know that unless they use new knowledge on a regular basis, they will not retain it.

Gary Flewelling, a faculty member at Brock University in Ontario, has written extensively about mathematics learning. In a piece based on his and coauthor William Higginson's *Handbook on Rich Learning Tasks*, he describes the importance of teachers providing "rich learning tasks" in the context of school. He says,

I define any learning task as "rich" if it gives students the opportunity to:

- use (and learn to use) their knowledge in an integrated, creative, and purposeful fashion to conduct inquiries, investigations, and experiments and to solve problems and in so doing

- acquire knowledge with understanding, and in the process
- develop the attitudes and habits of a life-long sense maker (p. 130)

Flewelling's work aligns directly with CLD thinking about how students construct meaning or make sense. He leads students through the "sense making game," a Situation created for students to use "knowledge and experience in integrated, creative, authentic, and purposeful ways to solve problems, conduct inquiries, carry out investigations, and perform experiments" (p. 130). As in the earlier examples, the student is "producer, not consumer." Students who do real work move from thinking about it to doing it, from studying to enacting. Michelle, for example, recalls saying in front of her bassoon teacher, "I'm learning to play the bassoon." He replied, "No, you're playing the bassoon. Someday you'll play it better!"

Reviewing these precedents will help you think more deeply about the quality of your Task element and offer you more information for evaluating your effort.

Reflect on writing your Task element and imagine teaching it. As we noted earlier, many teachers start to plan for instruction with a Task as the centerpiece. Choosing the right Task for each topic is a challenge that can be addressed through a deliberate process described in CLD. In Learning Record 4.F, Task Element Reflection, on the next page, write feelings you had, images you conjured, and languages you used as you answered the three key questions for this element about engaging, thinking, and learning.

Now, read the concluding remarks and reflect on your learning.

CONCLUDING REMARKS THOUGHTS ON CRAFTING TASKS

Research on teaching suggests that teachers ask between 300 and 400 questions daily (Levin & Long, 1981). Most of these questions encourage recall of facts or information previously given by the teacher or ingested by the students. Think carefully about the questions you ask students. As you move through a learning episode, the nature of questions changes from guiding student thinking to clarifying their thinking to integrating their thinking. These kinds of questions are not focused on answers, but on making the process of student thinking more visible for

Learning Record 4.F Task Element Reflection

As you were thinking and writing about a Task element,

Describe the feelings in your spirit:

Describe the images in your imagination:

Describe the languages in your internal dialogue:

Copyright © 2006 by Corwin Press. All rights reserved. Reprinted from *Constructivist Learning Design: Key Questions for Teaching to Standards*, by George W. Gagnon and Michelle Collay. Thousand Oaks, CA: Corwin Press, www.corwinpress .com. Reproduction authorized only for the local school site or nonprofit organization that has purchased this book.

individuals, smalls groups, the whole class, and the larger community. This approach is intended to support student learners by clarifying their thinking as they make their own meaning and construct knowledge together.

You have answered and reflected on three key questions about crafting a Task element:

1. Engaging: How will students engage in making meaning?

2. Learning: What kind of record will document student learning?

3. Thinking: What questions will students ask and how will you reply?

Your answers may be apparent in the element you wrote and will guide you as students proceed to an Exhibit of their thinking and learning.

5 Arranging Exhibits

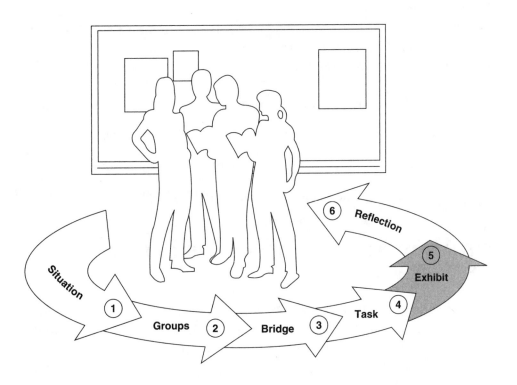

Finally, human beings are by nature social, interactive learners. We observe how others do it and see if it works for us. We learn to drive and cook this way. And how to handle ideas. We check out our ideas, argue with authors, bounce issues back and forth, ask friends to read our early drafts, talk together after we've seen a movie, pass on books we've loved, attend meetings, and argue things out, share stories and gossip that extend our understanding of ourselves and others.

—Deborah Meier, *The Power of Their Ideas* (1995)

This chapter describes the fifth element of Constructivist Learning Design (CLD), the Exhibit. The term "Exhibit" may conjure up a gallery, museum, artist's portfolio, architect's studio, or any collection of artifacts on display. The notion of the Exhibit describes student presentations of meaning they made to accomplish the Task framed by a Situation. As Meier suggests, the social construction of knowledge requires showing others what you know and sharing what you are thinking. Without this opportunity to temper thinking in the fires of consideration by others, the strength of new learning is limited. Only through a public vetting of work do students connect individual and small-group learning to greater community- or culturewide understandings or common meanings.

The three key questions to answer in arranging an Exhibit element ask you to imagine how your students will carry out an Exhibit as they produce an artifact, present it to others, and explain their collaborative thinking about meaning making:

1. Artifacts: What will students produce as a result of their learning?

2. Presentations: How will students present their artifacts?

3. Explanations: How will students explain their thinking?

Answering these questions is the focus of this chapter.

SITUATION SECTION: DEFINING THE NATURE OF AN EXHIBIT

Requiring students to show results is common in education. It is usually done at the conclusion of an assignment, unit, or term when students turn in homework, papers, or tests to the teacher for grading or scoring. An Exhibit in CLD requires students to share their work with others besides a teacher. Students also must include materials or a presentation that portrays their process of thinking, how they made meaning and how they now understand the material. Integrating evidence of student thinking within the Exhibit demonstrates how the purpose of the Situation has been met. Each facet of an Exhibit moves student work from a collection of material to a more comprehensive portrayal of thinking and learning. Teacher and students are accountable to each other, and a larger audience emerges for the product and the thinking process that led to it.

Purpose of an Exhibit element

The primary purpose of an Exhibit element is for students to make their thinking visible. Then the teacher can assess how they learned and what they now know. This is different from asking for the correct response or proper explanation. The more we value speed and accuracy in memorizing facts about any subject, the less we communicate to students that their thinking is important. The Exhibit is different from traditional assessment in two ways. First, exhibits occur in cycles and represent the completion of one in a series of tasks. Engagement with students as they create an Exhibit of their thinking will inform how you design subsequent learning. Second, the collaboration required to construct a more open and public Exhibit shapes learning in profoundly different ways from individual, private work. Students who engage with the ideas, questions, and observations of others emerge with a deeper understanding of their work. They learn the skills of critical thinking, communicating, and relating required for an effective portrayal of understanding. When the results of a learning process are private and hidden, students and teachers can't engage in and learn from this fundamental social process of framing and explaining.

Topic for an Exhibit element

The topic of this Exhibit is the artifact students will produce and how they will present it to other students. The ways that teachers ask students to Exhibit their thinking is a crucial piece of CLD. What can students create that will show you and others how they learned and what they now know? For example, you may want them to draw a diagram to solve a math or physics problem. In other cases, you may ask them to write a paragraph or essay describing an era in social studies or a character in language arts. Maybe you want them to brainstorm a list or develop criteria for identifying types of species in science or parts of speech in language arts. One unusual artifact is to portray the structure of an organization by using tinker toys, building blocks, or poster paper and markers. Sometimes students write ideas on sticky notes and put them on poster paper to create categories. In math, we ask students to represent the problem, solution, and relationship between them by constructing models. Sometimes we ask students to write or draw their information on an overhead transparency or on a white board. Other times, students display their computer work for the class.

When students provide a record of their thinking, they and their teacher have access to and accountability for learning. We often use physical models, visual representations, index cards, sticky notes, poster paper, overhead transparencies, and different colored markers so that each group can have a simple way to record and display their ideas. The materials students use to document their accomplishment of the Task must be readily accessible in the classroom. We encourage you to prepare materials for this Exhibit as students work on the Task. We find that students learn more if they have to determine the structure and format for their presentation. Think divergently about the many kinds of exhibits students may use first. Constructivist teaching and learning must be planned so that you don't limit students to a narrow conception of the Exhibit. Some groups will conceive of the Task in very different ways than you imagined, and the more brainstorming you and colleagues do ahead of time, the more possibilities you create for students' learning.

Assessment in an Exhibit element

Appropriate assessment is necessary to document student learning in relation to a benchmark or standard. It's not enough to complain that standardized tests don't tell the whole story—they never have. Teachers are responsible for structuring authentic methods of assessment that portray students' learning of required material. The product that students create to show their thinking to others is an artifact. This artifact should record or document students' thinking about a Task that they are to accomplish. The students present their artifacts, and the teacher and class examine them to determine what and how students are thinking about the topic. What do students know about the concept, skill, or attitude that completing the Task demonstrates? These two processes are at the heart of assessment in an Exhibit. Teachers and other students examine artifacts to assess presentations and explanations. Collectively, they determine what students understand in relation to the standards and decide what is necessary to support next steps in learning.

The construction of these artifacts offers the teacher a window into students' thinking about the Situation. The presentation of artifacts is not always what the teacher expects, and that is also instructive. Teachers watch students work on a Situation and see how they are thinking throughout the process. When working with prospective teachers and giving them an assignment to work individually or in groups, teachers circulate around the classroom to see what they are producing or listen in to their conversations as they discuss the Situation or explain their thinking to each other. When students of teaching use CLD to plan, you can readily observe those who are comfortable specifying a purpose, identifying a topic, and arranging an assessment of student learning. Others have panic attacks, offer vague notions, or select an activity without specifying the purpose. Immediate and informal assessment in that moment guides questioning and timing to move students toward a Situation that meets a standard.

The key to any Exhibit is that students produce an artifact in class so that you can examine their thinking as it unfolds. This requirement harks back to the old math teacher adage, "show your work." Teachers don't ask for just a final product, but for a display of understanding to use in assessment and to design subsequent learning episodes. For example, to determine what students of teaching know about rational numbers, give them a problem and then ask them to solve it by drawing diagrams rather than by using numbers or algebra. One problem used the example of Planet Xiar, where two thirds of the men were married and one half of the women were married. All marriages were between men and women. Students determined what fraction of the whole population was unmarried men. As some students presented the diagrams they created to solve this problem, a common assumption emerged. They decided that one half and two thirds of the same whole left one sixth of the population as unmarried men. They clearly were taking different parts of the same whole without considering that the men and women represented different wholes. Students who had thought about the problem in a different way introduced other solutions and led others to reconsider their thinking.

Peer review is a powerful part of assessment. Students present their own thinking during the Exhibit and then listen to other students explain their thinking about the same Task. The Exhibit element creates an opportunity for feedback so that students can learn more sophisticated ways to assess their thinking. Students listen differently to each other and may respond to suggestions from peers more openly than when teachers say the same things. Hearing a series of presentations also broadens students' understanding of especially complex ideas—often there is more than one way to resolve an issue, interpret a poem, or solve a problem. As a succession of artifacts is presented, that lesson is retaught and relearned in depth.

Assessing when to draw a Task to a close and move into an Exhibit can be a real challenge. Student groups may complete tasks at different times, and some may never be ready to present their work. Because of questions from other students, these presentations may take longer than planned. Teachers must decide when to proceed to an Exhibit, allowing enough time for Reflection afterward. New teachers often rush through a learning episode to include everything rather than simply postpone the Exhibit and Reflection until the next class session. They risk never including these elements because of pressure to move on and "cover" the next section. One way to consolidate activities is to choose a shorter Task or a series of tasks that are linked to a single Bridge, Exhibit, and Reflection. Learning episodes lasting a week or more could have a "Friday reflection" as long as there are times for presenting and reflecting on daily accomplishments.

Choosing an artifact for students to present their learning and explain their thinking is key to an effective Exhibit and shows how the Task leads to new learning. Write a rough draft of an Exhibit element for your CLD in Learning Record 5.A, Exhibit Element Draft.

Learning Record 5.A	Exhibit Element Draft

Write a rough draft of an Exhibit element.

Copyright © 2006 by Corwin Press. All rights reserved. Reprinted from *Constructivist Learning Design: Key Questions for Teaching to Standards*, by George W. Gagnon and Michelle Collay. Thousand Oaks, CA: Corwin Press, www.corwinpress .com. Reproduction authorized only for the local school site or nonprofit organization that has purchased this book.

In the next section, we ask you to share your thinking with at least one other colleague before you revise this Exhibit for your CLD.

GROUPS SECTION: THE POWER OF STUDENTS PRESENTING THEIR THINKING

This section describes ways for students to Exhibit an artifact of their learning or a product of their thinking about the topic framed in a Situation. At the end of this section, there are questions for you and your reflective partner or Learning Circle to address in thinking about revising your Exhibit element. They can support you in arranging more creative types of artifacts, especially if you represent different disciplines.

In real-world learning, exhibits are formal, finished products. In the world of work, exhibits demonstrate many things. A product crafted by a tradesperson displays his or her quality, utility, and art. For a business owner, the monthly income and expense sheet is a clear record of "success," or at least viability. For a salesperson, the number of units sold is usually displayed on a chart. For an administrative assistant, phone logs and e-mail messages record his or her work. Doctors and nurses rely on patient charts and written or dictated notes as a record of patient visits.

Considerations for arranging an Exhibit element

Several observations are described for you to consider in arranging an Exhibit element. Use the following ideas to think more expansively about how students can display their learning.

Recording and reporting thinking

During their thinking about an explanation in a group, students should keep individual records of their work to Exhibit. Good note taking or recording takes discipline and is a process that can be learned. Teachers and students can model different ways to keep notes, and teachers should monitor every student to ensure that all are meeting a minimum standard of documentation. The information being recorded must have some intrinsic value, or the process will be reduced to a required exercise. All students make a record of their thinking, not just one designated recorder. When students display their thinking during an Exhibit, teachers ask each group to report randomly by choosing the oldest, youngest, or closest birthday to today; the tallest, shortest, or "middlest;" the person who lives closest, farthest, or in between; or some other criterion that is likely to produce a random reporter. Sometimes teachers ask specific individuals to report because of the unique or complex character of thinking they observed in a group. This approach is "individual recording and selective reporting." The teacher's role is to ensure that different voices and cultural perspectives are heard in the report, not just the usual school-smart students.

Using the record of thinking

Students should be encouraged to learn and use basic note taking processes, termed "record keeping." For this process to be compelling, everyone must make use of the notes. For example, if the group recorder writes down a list of ideas from a brainstorming session, these can be transcribed and made public for the rest of the group. The items on the list should be used in subsequent thinking. In a recent class, students generated characteristics of a good collaborator. Each student wrote five, and each group recorded 10 and then placed its list on the classroom whiteboard. These characteristics were discussed and typed into a long list, then sent by e-mail to the entire class. Students made use of the collaborative list to select and prioritize a handful of characteristics that they would practice in a more focused way. These characteristics appear in the textbook, but the level of ownership is greater with this strategy. Artifacts in this example include individual note cards or notebook entries, recorded notes, full group whiteboard and e-mail messages, and individual learning plans. Finally, a study group of students could be formed around each common characteristic, a useful strategy for differentiating learning.

Teaching to learn

Moving from personal note taking or record keeping to a public display of learning is a critical step in constructivist learning and teaching. Although the need to hold individual students accountable might be the most important reason, there are others. "To teach is to learn twice over" is the main reason. Jotting down a few notes does not require the same depth of understanding that one needs to explain a concept to others. When students present publicly, they prepare more carefully, anticipate some debate, and learn quickly that everyone doesn't make the same meaning they did. Therefore, students must be prepared to explain and defend their thinking. English-Language Learners need as many opportunities as possible to use English to express their thinking and to be heard by peers and teachers.

Keeping a positive tone

Positive group interactions that build strong learning communities depend on the exchange of valuable information. Students must be recognized and rewarded for sharing their best learning, not encouraged to hoard the "right answers" in an atmosphere of competitive bell curves, where speed counts and only a single representation of learning is valued. The variety of presentations in an Exhibit respects divergent thinking styles and honors different points of view. Brainstorming and shared thinking require trust and respect for one another, so this classroom culture must be fostered and nurtured by the teacher. Students will become accustomed to this value system, and they will share responsibility for sustaining their learning community. Be prepared for resistance. Students who are most successful at playing the "school game" often are the most resistant to collaborative work.

Valuing and encouraging divergent thinking

School can be a place where imitation is a religion and divergence is discouraged. Teachers and other adult role models must encourage and reward individuality rather than fall into the trap that similarity means rigor. Similar exhibits might lull teachers and students into thinking they are meeting a standard. Creative or different students must be recognized as legitimate and other students reminded of the benefits of divergent thinking. One way to document diverse contributions is to have students create individual records of their own thinking and a collective record of the group's meaning making. One student or several can report their explanations to others, or several students can present their group artifact to the class. Teachers can introduce students to different ways of producing artifacts that document learning, then invite students to offer their own ideas. Several different ways of explaining the same thinking may emerge from one class as each group finds its own approach. One artifact may require each group to create a pie chart for ease of comparison, while another artifact may expect them to design their own chart as part of interpreting data.

Identifying exhibits in the real world

Young people are the ultimate consumers of everything from media to fast food. Although many teachers don't appreciate such consumerism, they can still look to well-funded commercial exhibits and borrow ideas from Madison Avenue. Students can report on images from MTV, advertising campaigns, magazine ads, or Web site captions, then describe their effectiveness in delivering a message. They can borrow methods that best represent their work.

Now talk with your reflective partner or Learning Circle about arranging an Exhibit. Write your notes or ideas in Learning Record 5.B, Exhibit Element Notes, on the next page.

Learning Record 5.B	Exhibit Element Notes

Write your notes and ideas about designing an element.

Copyright © 2006 by Corwin Press. All rights reserved. Reprinted from *Constructivist Learning Design: Key Questions for Teaching to Standards*, by George W. Gagnon and Michelle Collay. Thousand Oaks, CA: Corwin Press, www.corwinpress .com. Reproduction authorized only for the local school site or nonprofit organization that has purchased this book.

This reflective dialogue should support you in revising your Exhibit element.

BRIDGE SECTION: QUESTIONS FOR ENCOURAGING EXHIBITS

To assist you in thinking about an Exhibit, answer the questions in Learning Record 5.C, Exhibit Element Questions, on the next page. The prompts are more explicit to support you in thinking divergently about the kinds of exhibits students can use. Initially, students are dependent on the materials you have available to construct their exhibits, so a certain amount of legwork is required.

Learning Record 5.C	Exhibit Element Questions

How will students record and exhibit the artifact they created to demonstrate their thinking as they accomplished the task?

What if students write a description on index cards or on poster paper and give a verbal presentation?

What if students make a graph, chart, or other visual representation to present?

What if students act out or role play their impressions?

What if students construct a physical representation with models to show their thinking?

What if students make a videotape, audiotape, photographs, or website to display their thinking?

Copyright © 2006 by Corwin Press. All rights reserved. Reprinted from *Constructivist Learning Design: Key Questions for Teaching to Standards*, by George W. Gagnon and Michelle Collay. Thousand Oaks, CA: Corwin Press, www.corwinpress .com. Reproduction authorized only for the local school site or nonprofit organization that has purchased this book.

Now proceed to the following section, which describes the characteristics of an Exhibit element, and use them to refine your thinking.

TASK SECTION: REVISING AN EXHIBIT ELEMENT

The Exhibit element focuses on each group of students making a public presentation of the artifacts they have generated to document their accomplishment of a Task during a learning episode. When students have an opportunity to "show what they know" to others, they take their accomplishment of tasks and documentation of learning more seriously. The product of their own thinking becomes a basis for their presentations and provides an opportunity for others to review their work. Students listen more attentively to each other and support one another in explaining their thinking when they present their work to peers. They also engage in more authentic work when they are preparing an explanation of their thinking for one another. This public presentation provides a time and place for students to respond to questions from the teacher or their peers about their artifacts or thinking. The teacher can use student presentations of artifacts to decide what has been learned, to design future learning episodes, and to guide whole-class and individual student consideration of the learning episode. Teachers also can ask students to make explanations of their thinking that respond to state or national standards.

Characteristics of an Exhibit element

You have considered different ways to have students display what they have learned and explain how they have made meaning. Review the characteristics that follow to assess your thinking. Below is a description of each characteristic with a summary at the end for revising your draft.

Students generate artifacts to document accomplishing of a tasks

Artifacts are as varied as the thought terrain traveled during the learning episode. Some examples include the following:

- Writing a description on cards and giving a verbal presentation
- Making a graph, chart, or other visual representation
- Acting out or role playing their impressions
- Constructing a physical representation with models
- Making a videotape, photographs, or audiotapes to display thinking and meaning making
- Crafting an electronic portfolio

Artifacts must reflect the Task and address the goals of the students and teacher. One way to display understanding of a concept is through a visual metaphor. For example, juniors and seniors in a high school career course might draw a picture of the tools they will use in certain professions. Some might sketch a toolbox and talk about carpentry tools, some might draw a computer keyboard or monitor as they think about technical careers, still others might sketch a stethoscope and talk about their hope to work in health professions.

If the Task to be accomplished is a step-by-step process and requires analysis or problem solving, a Venn diagram might be a useful artifact for students and teacher. Two middle school science teachers asked students to sort a list of animals by type: pets, domesticated, and wild. They found a pig in all three categories. Upon reviewing their diagram for the class, students had to explain why some animals fit only one category, while others appear in the intersection of one or more circles.

An artifact can capture understanding about a concept or idea from the early stages of thinking to a very complex analysis. For example, high school social studies teachers might ask each student to write a sentence or paragraph about the colonizing of North America. Such an open-ended question will generate a tremendous amount of feedback. Teachers can assess the content that each student carried from previous study and identify the source of information such as a textbook, miniseries, or visit to living history exhibits. Teachers can judge the sophistication of knowledge and gauge the student's expository writing ability. Teachers also can ask students where they got their ideas before they write or discern that information on gathering responses.

Students present artifacts publicly and explain their thinking

After most of the class has accomplished the Task framed in the CLD, students present the artifacts they generated and explain their thinking. This public explanation of their thinking is the key to our construct of the Exhibit. Students realize they are expected to think, produce artifacts that document their accomplishment of tasks, present these artifacts publicly, and explain their thinking. Learning takes on an immediate urgency, social character, and personal relevance that often is not anticipated or appreciated by students who are not engaged in learning or invested in making meaning when they just sit and listen to a teacher.

Students respond to questions from their teacher or peers

As each question is asked, the exhibitor is challenged to retell the story of accomplishing the Task, articulate the reasons certain things were done, and look for ways to help the questioner make sense of the Exhibit. This responsibility moves the student quickly into the role of active presenter rather than passive listener. Teachers have the opportunity to ask clarifying questions or modify integrating questions that reflect the sophistication of the learning and individualize the framework of inquiry.

Teachers determine learning based on presentations of artifacts

The evaluation of learning is much more straightforward when multiple measures are available. Skillful teachers assess student learning informally, intuitively, and sometimes without the benefit of documentation. Teachers use subtle assessments to make myriad decisions—when or whether one student or many students have mastered a concept, process, or attitude; which parts of a complex curriculum might be focused on or abandoned; and what kinds of tasks have been most effective in supporting new learning. Teachers can make their judgment visible to students by showing how student artifacts and presentations of thinking influence subsequent learning episodes.

Students need to develop skills of self-evaluation. Because little time is available to unpack or reflect on teacher or student observations, students may not be aware of the evaluation that has occurred and don't gain capacity in self-assessment or peer assessment. When students present their documentation of learning when accomplishing tasks, they move into the realm of analysis and interpretation.

Teachers act as anthropologists, keeping both anecdotal and statistical records of student work. If teachers and students don't have a paper or electronic trail to show gradual or rapid growth in student learning, then students, parents, and teachers are at the mercy of a single measurement, such as a one-time standardized exam that shows what they *don't* know. Parents, some of the most important stakeholders in student assessment, can become powerful advocates for appropriate assessment if they are introduced to quality documentation of their child's learning. For all of these reasons, teachers and students continuously offer evidence of current and new learning.

Teachers guide reflective considerations based on student explanations

In almost every learning episode, students can make a record of both their previous and new understanding. These artifacts are made by individuals demonstrating existing knowledge about a concept ("know, want to know, learned"), by Learning Circles working cooperatively to complete tasks, or by a larger group or class. An Exhibit can be structured to provide teachers and other students with both individual and group assessments. For example, in our Spanish Songs CLD, each student translates the same song but is encouraged to think independently about their interpretation of the lyrics. Teachers and students are reassured that each is doing a common exercise of translation and an individual exercise of interpretation.

In another example, students study the civil rights movement. As a Bridge, students jot down their key understandings and sources of information about the civil rights movement. The teacher can then group them by interest in a topic, by source of information, or randomly so they can compare responses and generate artifacts that show their combined understanding of the topic at hand. Each group could brainstorm key activists in the civil rights movement and present their list to the class. A new group can be formed to study each activist. As part of their documentation, each study group might make a placard that each activist would have carried. This Exhibit is specific to the teacher's purpose—that students understand the importance of individuals in this particular movement. The teacher can set about revisiting the social, historical, and economic context with students and add new information, ideas, and images along the way.

Teachers align explanations and presentations with standards

Teachers are often ambivalent as they seek to broaden their classroom assessment practices in an educational system that is increasingly pressured by external standardized testing. As you interact with the formal assessment frameworks in your district, you can incorporate realistic examples into classroom assessment practices. Some states have good, comprehensive problem-solving assessments for middle school math. These assessments are appropriate and useful in daily math teaching and align with standardized test questions.

Efforts to improve technological literacy can be combined with a social studies curriculum. Unlike mathematics, there are few standardized curricula or assessments for technology teaching and learning. A group or individuals can create a Web site or a multimedia presentation about Native Americans, key stakeholders in American history who are often overlooked. Students conduct research to learn about the contemporary treaty rights of tribes in their region. Then they document how their communities are affected by treaty rights, such as fishing policies in Washington and Minnesota or casino policies in California and North

Dakota. Students can create a public relations Web site to educate members of the community and work with the teacher to decide how the Web site will be evaluated and what standards of quality each project must meet for both social studies and technology. When students are invited to assist teachers in constructing the evaluation framework, teachers and students refine the assignment and expand their vision of learning from completing a high school assignment to learning something that will be useful for a lifetime.

In all three of the cases just described, regional or national standards can be used to frame the choice of content and the type of evaluation methods used. Teachers can encourage students to design the Exhibit itself, not just follow a recipe to complete one. Assessment of student learning in relation to standards can be done with teacher-generated rubrics or, more effectively, with a rubric designed by students and teachers together. The work of Ted Sizer (1992) offers standards-based Exhibitions that are linked directly to external standards. Deborah Meier (1995) suggested that standards emerge from collaborative decision making by students, teachers, parents, and community members about what kinds of displays best demonstrate student learning.

Multilevel accountability policies are driving educators, parents, and other consumers of the products of schooling to set minimal standards for recent graduates. Using standardized test scores and more qualitative portfolios, college admissions committees and employers want to know what young adults can do. Amid the frenzy of high-stakes testing, candidates for college or work are still required to bring different skills to the table. Students can carry these exhibits in many forms as they move into future roles and responsibilities. Professionals making admissions and hiring decisions get not only a clear view of what students know but also a glimpse of how they make sense about what they have learned.

To summarize, the characteristics of an Exhibit are the following:

- Students generate artifacts to document accomplishing tasks.
- Students presents artifacts publicly and explain their thinking.
- Students respond to questions from their teachers or peers.
- Teachers determine learning based on presentations of artifacts.
- Teachers guide reflective considerations based on student explanations.
- Teachers align explanations and presentations with standards.

Now that you've reviewed these characteristics, use Learning Record 5.D, Exhibit Element Revision, on the next page, to rewrite your first draft of an Exhibit element. Use the questions you answered before and the summary of characteristics described above to guide your writing.

Learning Record 5.D | Exhibit Element Revision

Write a revision of your Exhibit element draft.

Copyright © 2006 by Corwin Press. All rights reserved. Reprinted from *Constructivist Learning Design: Key Questions for Teaching to Standards*, by George W. Gagnon and Michelle Collay. Thousand Oaks, CA: Corwin Press, www.corwinpress .com. Reproduction authorized only for the local school site or nonprofit organization that has purchased this book.

Now, take a look at some of the examples of Exhibit elements we've drawn from colleagues' work.

EXHIBIT SECTION: EXAMPLE EXHIBIT ELEMENTS

This section includes 12 Exhibit elements from the complete CLDs provided in the Resources. These designs address four different levels of students. The primary (K–3) elements are from Reading/Retelling the Story, Fine Arts/Drawing Animals, and Physical Education/Imitating Animals (Examples P-1, P-2, P-3). The intermediate (3–6) examples are from Science/Moon View, Media Technology/Logo, and Special Education/ Vending Machines (Examples I-1, I-2, I-3). The middle school (6–9) samples are from Language Arts/Fairy Tales, Math/Base Blocks, and Industrial Technology/Scooter Motor (Examples M-1, M-2, M-3). The high school (9–12) illustrations are from Social Studies/Trading Partners, Foreign Language/Spanish Songs, and Business Education/Creating Spreadsheets (Examples H-1, H-2, H-3). Examples from 12 different teaching areas were deliberately used in the Exhibit Element Examples on the next page.

	Exhibit Element Examples
Exhibit *12 minutes* P-1	All the students sketch their creatures and describe the color and name. Those who can put descriptions on their page, and others dictate their descriptions to the bookmaker. They all describe their animal orally when presenting the final version to the bookmaker. Read the new version of *Brown Bear, Brown Bear, What Do You See?* with new animals and colors. For each "What do you see?" the children show their drawing of the creature "looking at me."
Exhibit *25 minutes* P-2	In the order of the new book, first the individuals and then the whole class acts out the movements of each animal after it sees another animal looking at it.
Exhibit *10 minutes* P-3	In the order of the new book, students bring up their new drawings and read their new page to the class. The teacher puts each new page into the book so it follows the student's first drawing of a new animal.
Exhibit *25 minutes* I-1	After each group has had an opportunity to work out how to represent the relationship between the sun, the earth, and the moon, the person in each group whose birthday is closest to the day of the learning episode presents the explanation to the class.
Exhibit *20 minutes* I-2	When most are done trying to make the largest equilateral triangle, they show the triangle they made and the program used to draw it to the class. Later, students show the circle they made and the program to draw it.
Exhibit *10 minutes* I-3	If the teams return to the teacher with any or all of the three parts of the meal, they have a literal exhibit and can describe their experience in words, written or oral. If they don't have the items, they can tell what happened.
Exhibit *10 minutes* M-1	Student groups tape the chart papers with their definitions and lists of common elements on the white board and present their thinking to the rest of the class.
Exhibit *Last day* M-2	After each group has had an opportunity to work out how to represent the problem, a solution, and the relationship between the two, the groups have a "see what we made parade" so that each group can explain its thinking.
Exhibit *1–2 weeks* M-3	The teams can exhibit individual parts of the engine, descriptions of their analysis, and repairs throughout the term. The final exhibit, of course, is the fully functioning scooter. They should prepare a presentation and demonstration for the whole school.
Exhibit *2 weeks* H-1	Each continent group prepares a multimedia presentation about the influence that international trading activities will have on their occupations. The class develops a rubric to assess each presentation.

(Continued)

(Continued)

	Exhibit Element Examples
Exhibit *2 days* H-2	Groups sing their transcribed song in English. In Spanish, they present their findings about how Hispanic musical styles have influenced mainstream American music.
Exhibit *Last day* H-3	On Friday, students create and print a graph of their spreadsheet and print six copies for classmates. They work in teams of four to consolidate the separate spreadsheets into a common class spreadsheet and present their results to the class.

Review these examples of an Exhibit and note that each includes the presentation of an artifact and some explanation of thinking. Then consider how each example aligns with our characteristics. Do students create an artifact and present it to explain their thinking? Do students respond to questions from peers and teachers? Are teachers able to use these presentations to determine learning, lead considerations of learning, and align learning with standards? Compare the following examples to these characteristics and judge whether each Exhibit satisfies our criteria.

Study these examples to inform your own work and extend your thinking by comparing them to your draft of the Exhibit element. Then use Learning Record 5.E, Exhibit Element Final, on the next page, to revise your draft based on what you noticed as compared with your writing.

REFLECTION SECTION: PRECEDENTS FOR AN EXHIBIT ELEMENT

Throughout this chapter, an Exhibit of learning has been described as prominent in real life and in many parts of the elective curriculum. In workplace settings, employees at all levels must demonstrate their ability to do their job–whether that is punching picture buttons on the cash register at McDonald's or carrying a portfolio of graphic art to a potential employer on Madison Avenue. In fine arts, industrial arts, personal finance, journalism, athletics, or home economics, the proof is in the pudding. Are the dancers' steps synchronized? Can the mechanic fix the small engine, can the business student balance a spreadsheet, can the philosophy student write a coherent argument, and can the athlete win a competition? These exhibits are already evident in applied courses in the comprehensive high school curriculum. An Exhibit that captures a greater breadth of learning can strengthen assessment in disciplines that often depend on print-only approaches such as science, math, social studies, and language arts or English.

Learning Record 5.E	Exhibit Element Final

Write a final version of your Exhibit element.

Copyright © 2006 by Corwin Press. All rights reserved. Reprinted from *Constructivist Learning Design: Key Questions for Teaching to Standards,* by George W. Gagnon and Michelle Collay. Thousand Oaks, CA: Corwin Press, www.corwinpress .com. Reproduction authorized only for the local school site or nonprofit organization that has purchased this book.

Now that you've had a chance to try your hand at designing an Exhibit element, check in with your reflection partner or Learning Circle for some feedback before reflecting on your thinking and learning.

Judging an Exhibit requires courage. Many teachers fall back on grading schemes based on less significant factors such as attendance, homework completion, and quizzes because they are more quantifiable or objective and because authentic assessment is harder and more subjective. To work primarily with a student's real product requires two things: the product and the knowledge to judge it against a standard. English teachers are notorious for marking grammatical errors and split infinitives—but do they acknowledge the young writer who can tell a compelling story? Can they engage with students who share frightening personal information?

Do they trust their own intuition about the potential of a young person to make a contribution to the literary world through prose or to the technological world by writing useful manuals? This step requires the courage of one's convictions in a system that rewards easy-to-measure success and adherence to easily scored tests.

Parents and other teachers put pressure on classroom teachers to measure details and to avoid the challenge of creating and judging fully developed products. However, the quality of thinking presented at science fairs, debate meets, or journalism competitions makes a strong case for students displaying their own work for others to examine against a professional standard. Authentic productions are more parallel to the real world or community life. Parents and other constituents appreciate such displays of real learning—they must support their legitimacy as academic evaluation.

Ted Sizer (1992) and other leaders in the Coalition of Essential Schools emphasize Exhibitions as part of the learning process. "This Exhibition allows a student to demonstrate not only qualities of mind but also of persistence, habits of organization, and the ability to apply 'classroom knowledge' well beyond the confines of the school" (p. 80). Sizer's approach gained national prominence because of the work of essential schools, as well as the work of others such as Deborah Meier at Central Park East School. The completion of "passages" in the Jefferson County Open School in Colorado and "validations" in St. Paul Open School in Minnesota has been required of graduates for 35 years. These forms of authentic assessment are advocated by a variety of sources, including Grant Wiggins (1998). Documentation from Brenda Engel (1994), portfolios from Patricia Carini (1986), and alternative assessments from the North Dakota Study Group on Evaluation convened by Vito Perrone (1991b) offer models that teachers can use to structure an exhibit of student learning.

In the last decade, portfolios have been the focus of "authentic assessment" and what we refer to as "appropriate assessment," particularly for teacher educators. But all portfolios are not alike. Mary Dietz (1995) describes several kinds of portfolios for different uses, including the presentation portfolio (résumé or album), the working portfolio (evidence that fulfills prescribed competencies, standards, or outcomes) and the learner portfolio (an envelope of the mind). These three different purposes allow students and teachers different ways to capture and portray new learning. The presentation portfolio is the one most people think of as they imagine a photographer carrying his or her best offerings to a magazine editor, or a third grader proudly showing a well-edited essay. The working portfolio is an Exhibit in the tradition of Exhibitions for the Coalition of Essential Schools, those designed to show that students have met a standard of achievement. Finally, the learner portfolio captures formative assessment by student and teacher, demonstrating the learner's knowledge of a topic.

Another example of an Exhibit emerged from Project 2061, a collaboration of the American Association for the Advancement of Science (AAAS), the National Research Council, and the National Council of Teachers of Mathematics that synthesizes what students should know and be able to do in science and mathematics. In her review of the role of assessment within the project, Natalie Nielsen (2000) stated, "Nearly everyone recognizes that to effect meaningful improvement in science and mathematics education, curriculum and assessment have to be aligned with specific goals for specific learning." In addition to this alignment, *Blueprints for Reform: Science, Mathematics, and Technology Education* (AAAS, 1998) recommends that assessments should include a variety of techniques, encourage students to go beyond simple recall of data or facts, close the gap between the classroom and the real world, and include opportunities for students to perform tasks and solve problems.

Another group of educators designed a curriculum approach requiring exhibitions in action, Expeditionary Learning Outward Bound. This model is used by many urban schools seeking to improve the quality of student learning and supports the accomplishment of tasks and documentation of learning. Expeditionary Learning Outward Bound is another powerful example of a constructivist learning process designed to unfold within a standards-based curriculum. Its examples of multiple assessments include ongoing assessment using probing questions; focus on thinking, not just on answers; analysis of student work to assess understanding and to evaluate and refocus instruction; employment of performance assessments; matching purpose and function of assessments to learning targets; and documentation of student progress (www.elob.org). Assessment practices in Expeditionary Learning Outward Bound are based on a comprehensive framework that includes multiple assessments, reflection and critique, portfolios, and preparation for high-stakes tests.

One learning episode can use the portfolio for different kinds of assessment. In the Fairy Tales example, a portfolio could contain the final student-authored fairy tale, versions of the same story from its inception through refined completion, and student reflections about the evolving work. Convincing students to keep drafts for public review is not easy—the first time we asked adult students to include their "sloppy copy" of an essay, the class exploded. Many individuals were uncomfortable allowing the gaze of another to fall on their most intimate struggles as writers. Young authors feel the same way. Teachers need to create a culture that supports the exposure of early efforts, making clear that early efforts are valued.

There is no limit to the ways teachers can ask students to Exhibit their thinking. The challenge comes in choosing an appropriate assessment that aligns with your purpose and topic from the Situation. The purpose is based on specific content outlined by professional organizations and reiterated in state standards and district outcomes. In addition to students, other teachers are a vital source of novel learning displays. Often, they are teaching within the same curricular framework that you are. They have access to the same materials and budgets and are working within the same assessment frameworks, such as portfolios or standardized tests. Teachers can stretch their notions of ways to demonstrate knowledge by looking outside our schools and districts to observe the documentation strategies used by others. In addition to the formal materials seen in museum displays, children's learning settings, or libraries, the educational design projects listed previously all offer ways to Exhibit thinking and learning.

Teachers can work with central office personnel and regional support providers to embed district evaluation efforts within CLD. In light of the tremendous emphasis on test scores, teachers are challenged to maintain a practice of intermediate assessments or "dipstick" efforts that capture student learning throughout the unit or the year. A proactive rather than reactive response to external evaluation structures allows teachers to blend useful, strategic methods to assure themselves of what and how students are learning. A substantive, continuous cycle of formative assessment will give students and teachers more confidence as they approach summative assessments.

A final reminder is to bring the community into the students' work. A tenet of authentic assessment is that the judges come from beyond the school's walls. A middle school art teacher had her students set up an art show and act as critics for their own and others' work. Using the "discipline-based art education" framework, students learned about the elements of artistic works, created their own drawings, paintings, and sculptures, and then examined each other's work through that lens. At the end of the unit, parents and community members were invited to an Exhibit of the children's work. Students' grades were linked directly to their role as critics as well as producers of art.

In Learning Record 5.F, Exhibit Element Reflections, on the next page, reflect on what you thought and learned by writing, revising, and finalizing an Exhibit element. Write about feelings, images, and languages in your thoughts when you were answering the three key questions as you arranged an artifact of student learning, a presentation of their learning, and an explanation of their thinking during the Exhibit for others to consider.

Learning Record 5.F Exhibit Element Reflection

As you were thinking and writing about an Exhibit element,

Describe the feelings in your spirit:

Describe the images in your imagination:

Describe the languages in your internal dialogue:

Copyright © 2006 by Corwin Press. All rights reserved. Reprinted from *Constructivist Learning Design: Key Questions for Teaching to Standards*, by George W. Gagnon and Michelle Collay. Thousand Oaks, CA: Corwin Press, www.corwinpress .com. Reproduction authorized only for the local school site or nonprofit organization that has purchased this book.

Now read the concluding remarks and take a break from the CLD.

CONCLUDING REMARKS THOUGHTS ON ARRANGING EXHIBITS

For too long, a quality Exhibit has remained the province of the fine arts, industrial technology, and now computer-based coursework, while teachers in the required courses have clung tenaciously to research papers and multiple choice tests. Although there are places in comprehensive assessment frameworks for the latter approaches, they must take their place alongside the many other assessment procedures available to teachers. As teachers imagine students taking their knowledge as writers, historians, and scientists into the real world, they know from their own experiences and from what the greater community tells them that they will be required to show what they know. Teachers are doing students and themselves a big favor if they enter into the spirit of showing what students know in their daily, weekly, monthly, and end-of-term practice of evaluation and assessments. This kind of performance assessment linked to explanations of student thinking is even becoming evident in state tests to determine whether graduation benchmarks or grade-level learning requirements are being met.

You have answered and reflected on three key questions about arranging an Exhibit element:

1. Artifacts: What will students produce as a result of their learning?

2. Presentations: How will students present their artifacts?

3. Explanations: How will students explain their thinking?

Your answers may be apparent in the element you wrote and will guide you as students advance to Reflection on their thinking and learning.

6 Leading Reflections

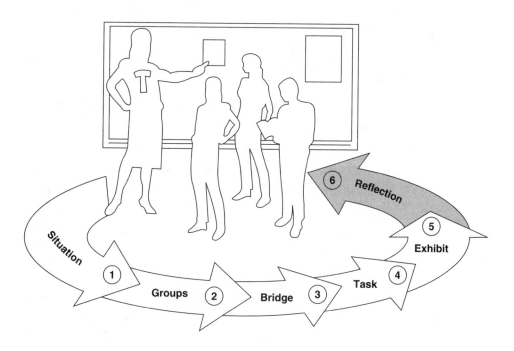

In a good process of design, the conversation with the situation is reflective. In answer to the situation's back-talk, the designer reflects-in-action on the construction of the problem, the strategies of action, or the model of the phenomena, which have been implicit in his [or her] moves.

—Donald Schön, *The Reflective Practitioner* (1983)

This chapter describes the sixth and last element of Constructivist Learning Design (CLD), Reflection. This final, critical element offers both students and teachers the opportunity to think again about their individual and collective learning, to begin the integration of new learning with existing knowledge, to plan for the application of new knowledge, and, in many cases, to design strategies for the next learning episode. As Schön suggests, through Reflection, the designer or creator converses with the Situation. When students are active designers of their own learning, their knowledge is fluid, flowing backward and forward in time. This knowledge must be situated in a continuum of learning episodes. Reflection is a process of integrating new knowledge.

The three key questions to answer in writing a Reflection element are intended to ask you to project how your students will reflect on their thinking through feelings in their spirit, images in their imagination, and languages in their internal dialogue as they consider their making meaning during a learning episode.

1. Feelings: How will students reflect on their emotional/physical experiences?

2. Images: How will students reflect on their sensory experiences?

3. Languages: How will students reflect on their communication experiences?

Answering these questions is the intent of this chapter.

SITUATION SECTION: LEADING REFLECTION ON THINKING

There are many tangible ways to guide, prompt, enhance, and document Reflection. However, taking time to reflect, reconsider, and create links between learning episodes is often overlooked or given short shrift in the workaday hustle and bustle of a classroom. This section attempts to make explicit the importance of this element in the learning and teaching process and to offer many ways to structure Reflection. Moreover, Reflection plays a specific role in your assessment of student learning and in students' assessment of their own and others' learning. Constructivist Learning Design puts particular emphasis on thinking and the metacognitive engagement involved in reviewing and analyzing students' thought processes during meaning making.

Purpose of a Reflection element

The purpose of a Reflection element is to invite students to reflect on their thinking and learning as they made personal, shared, and collective meaning during the learning episode. As you think about the kinds of Reflection that will be most useful and productive, look back at the Situation you initially designed. Student Reflection is a critical dimension of assessment, especially of your teaching. Telling yourself or your students "I covered that" when you or they can't produce evidence of their new learning may not be very useful. As with questions during other elements, Reflection is another opportunity for you to find out directly from students and for students to find out from each other what they learned. What students actually learn is presented as individual understandings that emerge within the co-construction of new knowledge.

Topic for a Reflection element

The topic for a Reflection element is to determine how you will lead students in reflecting on their thinking and learning. We usually begin by having a conversation with students to compare the similarities and differences in their presentations and explanations during the Exhibit element and to consider their thinking as they moved from personal meaning to shared meaning in their Groups. Sometimes, students are able to make collective meaning as a class and may be ready to consider standard meaning that is common in their culture. Other times, students may not agree and need the teacher to lead a consideration of their shared meanings to see whether they can find common ground in collective meaning. This aspect of a Reflection element is often put aside as teachers hurry to close out a class. One of the essential ingredients in a learning design is to compare students' collective meaning to the standard meaning in their culture. Students may not agree, but they should be aware of the "conventional wisdom." However, teachers must realize that some of the most important scientific and artistic revolutions occur when someone questions the current paradigm. As researchers were designing a pre-engineering curriculum for middle school students around a "design, build, test" format, the engineers encouraged them to add "analyze" to that list. The notion that you have to review and reflect on the results of your research was critical to improving the design in engineering. The same is true in education. Analyzing what students were thinking and learning during a learning episode leads to a better understanding of learning, teaching, and the learning-design process.

Assessment in a Reflection element

Reflection really involves two different kinds of assessment. The first kind is a public or group Reflection to consider the explanations of thinking made during the Exhibit. The teacher may draw the learning episode to a close and bring learners to a collective understanding of the concept, process, or attitude addressed in the Situation. As learners raise questions or objections, teachers assess their understanding again and support them in struggling to construct collective knowledge after they have made personal and shared meaning.

The second kind of Reflection is an analysis of personal thinking, which is usually solicited in writing as a capstone to a learning episode. This Reflection is a private process compared to the public consideration of individual or collaborative thinking presented during an Exhibit. Teachers are able to assess how individual learners were thinking as they worked to accomplish the Situation and Exhibit. This appropriate assessment of personal thinking also demands a great deal of honesty and trust from the students, respect and empathy for the students from the teacher, and integrity from both the teacher and student. When we ask students to think about the feelings, images, and languages they experienced in their thinking, we are moving the relationship between teacher and student to a different level. Only by opening our thinking to others can we clearly examine our strengths and weaknesses. As teachers "get into the heads" of students, they assume an awesome responsibility to be careful, patient, and supportive of learners. As students reveal their thinking, teachers must assess both thinking and potential misunderstandings to clarify and guide new thinking in a productive and positive way. How students think, make meaning for themselves, and construct knowledge with others all must be assessed, accepted, and applied to support their learning. Public and private Reflection offers yet another opportunity for teachers to assess the thinking and learning of their students.

Collecting individual reflections is a critical piece of the assessment puzzle. The comments we often collect on index cards at the end of a learning episode give us a quick glance at what students took away or what still confuses them. Many times, we have notes from students indicating they are still struggling with the concept, process, or attitude addressed by the Situation, or they comment on the difficult time they had revisiting a previous assumption to consider a new understanding or way of thinking. Students may experience being shut down or marginalized because of their race, gender, class, or other perceived difference. Because students are often reticent to display these concerns or any lack of content understanding, individual, private data collection is essential.

Now, turn your attention to reflections on meaning making. Write a rough draft of a Reflection element for your CLD in Learning Record 6.A, Reflection Element Draft.

Learning Record 6.A	Reflection Element Draft

Write a rough draft of a Reflection element.

Copyright © 2006 by Corwin Press. All rights reserved. Reprinted from *Constructivist Learning Design: Key Questions for Teaching to Standards*, by George W. Gagnon and Michelle Collay. Thousand Oaks, CA: Corwin Press, www.corwinpress .com. Reproduction authorized only for the local school site or nonprofit organization that has purchased this book.

GROUPS SECTION: REFLECTING ON MAKING MEANING

This section describes ways that a teacher can lead student Reflection on thinking and learning as they made meaning to accomplish tasks arranged by the teacher. At the end of this section is a Learning Record for readers to record their notes or ideas about leading reflective analyses as they are thinking about writing a Reflection element. Talk with your reflective partner or Learning Circle about your experiences leading Reflection.

Considerations for Leading a Reflection Element

Many teachers have asked, "What did you learn?" and heard back, "Nothing," or something else that is noncommittal. The other common response offered by well-behaved students is, "Here are the three things you told us to learn. Now can we go to recess?" These responses are not satisfying, nor are they reliable indications of what really went on in that student's mind and heart during the learning episode. Inviting Reflection is an art and a craft, requiring careful structures that enable multiple points of response. Inviting Reflection also requires the teacher to put his or her ego and trust on the line—if you ask students honestly about what they learned, you must be prepared to listen to their answers. Teachers need strength to accept learners' "truth"—that, in fact, they may not have learned what you had expected or understood information or ideas in the way you had intended. When you and your students develop a mutual understanding that both parties are responsible for the construction of knowledge, honest Reflection becomes a joy.

Time and space for reflecting

Individual and collective Reflection is a very important part of the learning episode. Often, students spend so much time on their explanations and presentations that there is little time left for reflections. If you can, leave at least five minutes for personal Reflection and schedule at least five minutes of class consideration time on days when learning designs are ending. Students' metacognitive activity should focus on what they were thinking as they were explaining the Situation. Constructivist Learning Design considers thoughts to be the feelings, images, and languages that learners experienced while they were making meaning with their small groups. These reflective activities must be carefully structured so that each learner is held accountable and individual learning is documented.

Closing circles

This closing activity is a quick and useful way to circle around a classroom so that each student says one thing he or she now knows about the topic or intends to do to apply it. Sometimes called a "Whip or Wave," the prompt should ask students to say something they learned, something they still have a question about, or something they will do differently as a result of the lesson. Some teachers model a short, focused response or use a timer so that each person has equal time and the class isn't held beyond the agreed-upon concluding time.

Index cards

Students may respond to a prompt on an index card and turn it in, or they can tell another class member next steps toward completing their thinking. Index cards or Reflection records can be used for one response or used over time to collect initial plans, new information, and final thoughts about a project. For example, a class may observe its group process for three meetings. On a 5×8 card, students first write the group name, their role in the group, the names of members, and the configuration of furniture. They will add new pieces of information and analyze changes as the group develops. They also will use that card to write up their final report. You can easily vary the length of Reflection by your choice of prompts and by selecting index cards of different sizes—3×5, 4×6, or 5×8—depending on the time available.

Journal entries

Other examples of Reflection include asking students to make a single entry in their journal. For example, language arts students could write about something they now know about the main character in a story or a question they have for the author of a book. Special education students could note what kind of currency they will need to buy lunch from vending machines or who they would like to pair with for the trial run. Fine arts students could describe a possible subject for a sketch or what color they would choose if they could only use one. Depending on the developmental level of the students, they can write or tell a teacher or another student what they think and why.

Write a letter to myself or to the subject of study

After-class activities give students more opportunities to think about the topic, and a letter is a personal and metacognitive activity for students to complete. When students read a class play, they can choose one of the minor characters and write a letter from themselves. They also could become that character and write a letter to the main character of the play. Depending on the teacher's purpose, the letter can be structured to include content aligned with local or national standards.

Now that you've read our considerations, talk with your reflective partner or Learning Circle about inviting Reflection. Write your notes or ideas in Learning Record 6.B, Reflection Element Notes, on the next page.

Learning Record 6.B	Reflection Element Notes

Write your notes and ideas about leading a Reflection element.

Copyright © 2006 by Corwin Press. All rights reserved. Reprinted from *Constructivist Learning Design: Key Questions for Teaching to Standards*, by George W. Gagnon and Michelle Collay. Thousand Oaks, CA: Corwin Press, www.corwinpress .com. Reproduction authorized only for the local school site or nonprofit organization that has purchased this book.

The next section encourages you to answer questions based on your anticipation of writing a Reflection element.

BRIDGE SECTION: QUESTIONS FOR INVITING REFLECTION'S

To assist you in thinking about leading a Reflection, please answer the questions in Learning Record 6.C, Reflection Element Questions, on the next page.

Learning Record 6.C	Reflection Element Questions

What kinds of questions can you ask yourself to invite Reflection?

How will students reflect on what they thought about while they accomplished the Task and after seeing others present artifacts of their thinking?

How can you lead students in considering their collaborative thinking and reflecting on their collective learning?

What did individual learners remember about the *feelings, images,* and *languages* of their thoughts as they were making meaning?

What concepts, processes, and attitudes will students take out the door?

What did students learn today that they won't forget tomorrow?

What did students know before, what did they want to know, and what did they learn today?

Copyright © 2006 by Corwin Press. All rights reserved. Reprinted from *Constructivist Learning Design: Key Questions for Teaching to Standards,* by George W. Gagnon and Michelle Collay. Thousand Oaks, CA: Corwin Press, www.corwinpress .com. Reproduction authorized only for the local school site or nonprofit organization that has purchased this book.

After answering these questions to your satisfaction, proceed to the following section, which describes the characteristics of a Reflection element.

TASK SECTION: REVISING A REFLECTION ELEMENT

Reflection is the last element in CLD, although it happens throughout the entire learning episode. Reflection captures what students were actually thinking and learning, not what material was presented or "covered." Reflection has two parts. In the first part, the teacher engages the full class in interpreting and making sense of what has happened. Teachers review the learning episode with students to determine what concepts, processes, and attitudes students will take with them. The primary reason for this review is for teachers to construct their own knowledge of student understandings that emerged during the learning episode. This process will assist teachers in evaluating the purpose, flow, and effectiveness of their learning design. Another reason for teacher-led Reflection is so teachers can revisit or restate some ideas or understandings that were presented in limited or inappropriate ways by the teacher or by student exhibits. For example, a group of students may inadvertently give factual misinformation or perpetuate racial or gender stereotypes. Teachers have the challenge and the responsibility to reframe the new information in a way that saves face for the presenters yet leads the students along a path that is deliberately chosen. A final reason is for teachers to link student learning with big ideas or educational standards.

Teacher-led Reflection can occur in a variety of ways, including class conversations, collective processing, group dialogues, or individual writing that is then shared publicly. Teachers need to be strategic and equitable about gathering student feedback during the full-class activity. In this first part of reflection, teachers and students consider what has gone on in the Exhibit element of CLD. For students, these considerations offer a supportive framework to think together and to make collective meaning of the learning episode that has just taken place. This is especially important for students whose ideas are less popular. The teacher must show respect for these ideas so that other students listen to them.

In the second part, students reflect on what they thought about while accomplishing a Task and seeing an Exhibit of presentations and explanations. Most teachers say they value teaching their students the process of "learning how to learn." Such deliberate Reflection must be practiced to become a habit of mind. Reflection includes what students remember from their thoughts about feelings in their spirit, images in their imagination, and languages in their internal dialogue. Students also might reflect on what they learned today that they won't forget tomorrow or what they knew before, what they wanted to know, and what they actually learned.

Characteristics of a Reflection element

What will students do with their newfound knowledge? In Schön's words, the students have a conversation with the Situation. These conversations are captured in print so that students have a record of their learning and can self-assess. Learning Records can be used to compare students' knowledge before and after the learning episode. They create a sense of accountability for both students and teacher. When students take time to document their Reflection in a systematic way, accountability and assessment are built into the episode and the unit.

This most critical aspect of learning is often missed because of the nature of classroom teaching. As mentioned earlier, most classroom teachers don't feel they can afford time to "just reflect" and teach to the bell. This behavior is also driven by classroom-management traditions that encourage teachers to keep learners busy right until the end of class so they don't become unruly. This habit must be changed for reflective activities to take place on a regular basis. Be assured that a well-designed Reflection is compelling and will keep learners' attention well focused. Conducted thoughtfully, reflections are a productive way to manage classroom time and keep learners engaged at the end of a class session.

The six characteristics of a Reflection element are offered in separate passages below to check your thinking. Each characteristic is described in detail, with a summary at the end to use in revising your draft.

Teachers lead a collective consideration of learning

In the first part of this element, teachers use the information about student learning that they gleaned from the Exhibit to lead a class conversation about the learning episode. This might play out as a class discussion of the different artifacts and explanations of thinking presented by students, as a debriefing in which each group compares its work with others, or as a question that asks each group to decide about holding or abandoning their perspective. There are many different ways to consider a learning episode with a class, including discussing what students learned, asking them how they might approach a similar task, asking several students to explain their current thinking, or surveying each group to see whether their thinking changed after the Exhibit. The key to this reflective process is checking the understandings that students gleaned from the learning episode and determining what knowledge they have constructed about the concept, process, or attitude being considered.

Recently, we were consulting in a seventh-grade math class when the teacher was giving a lesson on circumference. The teacher reviewed two formulas for circumference, $c = \pi d$ and $c = 2\pi r$. Students were to use these formulas when the diameter or the radius was given. Then two values for pi were provided, either 3.14 or 22/7, depending on whether the measurement was given in decimals or fractions. After surveying a majority of students as they worked the practice problems, most of them had some understanding of calculating the answer but very little understanding of pi, what it was, and how it was derived. This information surfaced from informal interactions rather than a formal Reflection, but their lack of understanding about the concept of pi was clear. We talked with the teacher about a follow-up lesson in which students could investigate the relationship between diameter and circumference for a variety of circles. The reflective activity of analyzing student understanding based on considering the learning episode with your class may be the most critical process in CLD.

Teachers gather data about individual student understanding

Individual Reflection offers teachers a look at student learning and data to document that learning. For example, teachers often assume they've covered certain material and that most of the students will take similar knowledge of that material away from the classroom. This is seldom borne out when individual assessments are conducted. Teachers can quickly see and hear the similarities and differences in the meaning students have made of specific learning episodes or of entire units. These differences are not always misunderstandings and generally reflect what students already knew about a topic or their personal beliefs.

One example of gathering data during Reflection is making a schematic that captures student knowledge about the content in a curriculum unit. The schematic or web provides places for key topics, related topics, topic flow, and key questions. As students complete this schematic, each graphically organizes course information in ways that make sense. Teachers can then collect and review the schematic data to assess the continuum of student understanding about the unit. The point is not for all the students to do it the same way! This is not an exercise such as diagramming sentences but an engaging activity that invites students to show connections and links to prior knowledge. Teachers experience success when students start individually, compare with a neighbor, and then present to the class as pairs. This is also an assessment activity to do at the beginning and end of a learning episode.

An Exhibit can demonstrate to teachers that the benchmarks they've set or designed have been met and that students are reaching school and district learning goals and regional, state, and national standards. Reflective activities can be aligned with these goals and standards, offering appropriate data not only for teachers but also for students and other stakeholders. With the steady movement toward standardized testing, teacher-designed assessment is even more essential. Comprehensive evaluation can include different types of assessment for student learning within a well-thought-out CLD, including tasks that prepare students for standardized testing.

Teachers address big ideas and common misconceptions

Reflection offers the teacher a road map for next steps. Evidence may reassure the teacher that most students already have a clear understanding of a topic he or she had intended to pursue further. Likewise, a concept, process, or attitude the teacher thought was well understood might be unclear, misunderstood, or partially understood. A subsequent learning design can be shaped more effectively to give students another opportunity to revisit that topic. This is a critical moment for teachers to differentiate teaching, that is, design multiple approaches for students who have greater or lesser understanding of a concept. One size does not fit all, and CLD offers a framework with flexibility for such modifications.

The schematic just described can include a "big idea" space for students to write about the main idea of a unit or a "future learning" space for specific topics they would like to learn more about. The future learning corner, like the prompt "A question you still have," gives the teacher good information about ways to proceed, and students feel valued when teachers use their suggestions.

Students individually consider their thinking

Individual Reflection captures feelings, images, and languages from student thinking about making meaning during the learning episode. Each student makes different meaning and understanding of any learning event, and teachers can offer students some systematic ways to capture those differences. Students can reflect aloud as they speak with a peer, their study group, or the full class. Students can reflect by writing on an index card, by responding to guiding prompts on a single sheet, or by jotting one thought on a sheet of butcher paper or an overhead transparency for the class to review. Students also can reflect privately in a journal and see patterns emerge over time.

Choosing the prompt is itself a reflective activity. Students can respond to a teacher's or another student's prompt or initiate the Reflection themselves. There are often ideas in texts or other curriculum materials that can frame useful reflective activities. Reflection on learning can be as creative as any individual can make it. For example, elementary students can reflect on a story just read by writing a different ending to the story and telling why they chose that ending. As in any thoughtful teaching, shape and structure should improve students' chances to succeed rather than limit opportunities. Reflective activities come alive by building on the teacher's strengths and values. Questions from the back of the chapter, deadly boring when presented as homework, can be reconfigured into opening gambits. Instead of "Name the six continents that have trading partners," the prompt could be "Look at a globe and figure out which continent is least likely to have trading partners, then draw a picture of someone who lives there and show it to the class." You might get a penguin phoning in for pizza or a scientist living in a research station studying snow. You will certainly get more students engaged in learning, and there is a greater chance that every student will remember images of the continent Antarctica.

Records of student thinking can document learning

Reflection can be used to document student learning over time. Although the Exhibit generally focuses on learning within a specific episode, systematic documentation of Reflection can show change over time. Reflective "metacognition," or making meaning of learning by thinking about thinking, can be done only as a systematic process with sustained effort. Engaging students in a regular analysis of their own thinking is integral to "learning to be a learner," a value many teachers purport is the purpose of education.

Reflection can be completely private, partially shared, or publicly shared with the entire class. Obviously, there is not enough time to ask every student to speak in front of the whole group after every learning episode. Teachers must choose the level of public and individual Reflection based on the quality of the learning episode, the need for individual accountability, the nature of a public sharing to inspire or teach others, and the use of data that will emerge from the sharing. Teachers must be sensitive to the level of trust among students and whether patterns of public sharing reflect race, gender, or language bias. Any teacher who strives to document what students learn on a regular basis knows the challenge of doing so during a busy day. Teachers must be selective to make the most of their own energy and the data they gather. Treating student data as an assessment of learning for both students and teachers and as an evaluation of learning for a broader audience of parents and the school community can encourage documentation.

Students revisit their thinking after a learning episode

After teaching and reflecting on this last (but not least) element of CLD, we recognize that students do not quit thinking when they walk out the door of the classroom. We sometimes assign reflective papers after class to encourage student thinking over time. Reading their papers privately, we may learn that many students took pains to judge their thinking during the learning episode. They chose to affirm the inertia of their idea, to adopt new ideas presented by others, or to remain ambivalent or uncommitted to any idea. They might be "persisters, persuaders, or prevaricators," but invariably, they continued to review the learning episode and revisit their thinking about the topic considered long after the class was over. People do this after most real-life learning experiences. For example, you may try to make sense out of winds, waves, and tides when sailing on the San Francisco Bay, but you often learn what you did right or wrong when you revisit the experience in your imagination and reflect on theory you were trying to apply.

Careful reconsideration must be acknowledged and used in subsequent learning episodes. When the next class convenes or the sailboat is put back in the water, the press of the new agenda or changed weather must not be allowed to push aside previous learning. These experiences confirm CLD's commitment to Reflection by both the class and individuals during a learning episode to capture the benefits of previous considerations and to maintain structures for ongoing analysis of their thinking and learning.

The summary of characteristics for a Reflection element follows:

- Teachers lead a collective consideration of learning episode.
- Teachers gather data about individual student understanding.
- Teachers address big ideas and common misconceptions.
- Students individually consider their thinking.
- Records of student thinking can document learning.
- Students revisit their thinking after a learning episode.

Now that you've reviewed these characteristics, review the first draft you made about leading a Reflection. Does it have these characteristics? Use Learning Record 6.D, Reflection Element Revision, on the next page, to revise your Reflection element draft. Don't be concerned about doing it

Learning Record 6.D	Reflection Element Revision

Write a revision of your Reflection element draft.

Copyright © 2006 by Corwin Press. All rights reserved. Reprinted from *Constructivist Learning Design: Key Questions for Teaching to Standards,* by George W. Gagnon and Michelle Collay. Thousand Oaks, CA: Corwin Press, www.corwinpress .com. Reproduction authorized only for the local school site or nonprofit organization that has purchased this book.

right, just use the questions you answered before and our summary of characteristics in this section to guide your writing.

After you are finished rewriting, please return to the next section and compare your element to some of the examples of Reflection elements we've drawn from colleagues' work.

EXHIBIT SECTION: EXAMPLE REFLECTION ELEMENTS

This section includes 12 Reflection elements from the complete CLDs in the Resources. These designs address four different levels of students. The primary (K–3) CLDs are from Reading/Retelling the Story, Fine Arts/Drawing Animals, and Physical Education/Imitating Animals (Examples P-1, P-2, P-3). The intermediate (3–6) examples are from

Science/Moon View, Media Technology/Logo, and Special Education/ Vending Machines (Examples I-1, I-2, I-3). The middle school (6–9) samples are from Language Arts/Fairy Tales, Math/Base Blocks, and Industrial Technology/Scooter Motor (Examples M-1, M-2, M-3). The high school (9–12) illustrations are from Social Studies/Trading Partners, oreign Language/ Spanish Songs, and Business Education/Creating Spreadsheets (Examples H-1, H-2, H-3). Examples from 12 different teaching areas were selected to emphasize the utility of the CLD in the Reflection Element Examples that follow. You should choose at least one CLD to follow each element and watch as it unfolds. Compare the following examples to your revised element and consider whether they satisfy CLD characteristics.

	Reflection Element Examples
Reflection *10 minutes* P-1	How did you decide which animal to draw and what color it should be? Think about extending your creature's behavior in various ways. For instance, after seeing an "aqua elephant looking at me," grey goose might waddle off to a pond or follow other geese down to a garden.
Reflection *10 minutes* P-2	Do the actions you created for your animal fit with their habitat? For example, would an orange cow fly or a silver turtle run? Why do you think so? How did you feel imitating your animal?
Reflection *5 minutes* P-3	How does it feel to write a new book together? How did you choose the words to tell about your animal? How would you change the color or movement of your animal if we did this again?
Reflection *10 minutes* I-1	The teacher leads a debriefing of the phases and positions of the moon related to the earth and sun. Students write individually on index cards about why people have misconceptions about the phases of the moon.
Reflection *10 minutes* I-2	The teacher asks students to compare different programs that draw the same figure. How did it feel when you were in control of what happened on the computer? What image did you have in your mind of the way the cursor was moving based on your commands? Why is Logo called a "computer language"?
Reflection *10 minutes* I-3	The teacher invites students to discuss their experiences. Why were you or why weren't you successful? What would help you to be successful next time? What are some characteristics of vending machines? What are some strategies that will help you use vending machines in future?

(Continued)

(Continued)

	Reflection Element Examples
Reflection *10 minutes M-1*	Students read the articles and compare and contrast with their own definitions and lists. Then they write about what they would add to their definitions or lists from other groups or from the article. Students describe why their own definition or an expert's definition was more meaningful to them as they think about writing their own fairy tale.
Reflection *15 minutes M-2*	The teacher discusses the concept of counting in bases with the whole class. Then students write individually on index cards about what they learned and what they were thinking during their work together.
Reflection *1 week to write,* *edit, and post* *on a Web page.* *M-3*	The teacher leads an ongoing analysis of gas engine repair based on problems that students encounter. What did you know about small gas engines at the beginning of the term? What was the most difficult concept to understand? How did you make sense of that concept, teach it to others on your team, or demonstrate that you understood it? If you were to teach a class about small gas engines, how would you proceed? Given the movement away from use of small engines toward electric, is small gas engine repair an important skill?
Reflection *1 week H-1*	Reflect on your continent, country, and region in relation to the original question. Given what we have learned about trade between your region and the world, what are the implications for your chosen occupation? Document your reflections as a list of implications, recommendations for job preparation, or plans for a job search. Complete a form including name, date of birth, chosen occupation, international trading factors influencing that occupation, and your personal goals for training for that occupation.
Reflection *1 day H-2*	The teacher leads a discussion on the challenges of transcribing lyrics into English. Students write journal entries to answer these questions. Why did Selena's music "cross over" into the mainstream music scene in the United States? How has your music listening influenced your knowledge of subcultures in the United States? What is the place of music in cross-cultural understanding?
Reflection *Last day H-3*	The teacher leads the class in considering the similarities and differences in group spreadsheets. In what categories did you expect to find the most income or spending? What surprised you most about the class's expenses or income? How would you use a spreadsheet to balance a checkbook?

After exploring these 12 Reflection elements, revisit the complete designs to see how they bring closure to each CLD. Study these 12 Reflection examples and compare them to your draft of a Reflection element. Does each element include teachers arranging collective and individual considerations of learner thinking during the learning episode? Then consider how each example aligns with our characteristics. Do teachers gather data about individual student understanding, connect to big ideas, and address common misconceptions? Do students record their Reflection and revisit their thinking? Then use Learning Record 6.E, Reflection Element Final, to prepare a final version of your element based on what you noticed as you compared your writing with these examples.

Learning Record 6.E	Reflection Element Final

Write a final version of your Reflection element.

Copyright © 2006 by Corwin Press. All rights reserved. Reprinted from *Constructivist Learning Design: Key Questions for Teaching to Standards*, by George W. Gagnon and Michelle Collay. Thousand Oaks, CA: Corwin Press, www.corwinpress .com. Reproduction authorized only for the local school site or nonprofit organization that has purchased this book.

Now that you've had a chance to try your hand at designing a Reflection element, check in with your reflective partner or Learning Circle for some feedback before reflecting on your own thinking and learning. Review the characteristics and see whether your Reflection element meets some or all of those criteria.

REFLECTION SECTION: PRECEDENTS FOR A REFLECTION ELEMENT

Reflection is the act of describing the following:

- What you have already felt, seen, or talked to yourself about?
- How you are making new meaning, changing your current understanding, or adding to current knowledge within a learning episode?
- What you will do or think more about because of a learning episode?

One powerful example of reflective activity that is evident in constructivist teaching is the thinking you do about the learning and teaching process before a learning episode begins. As you shape or design a learning episode, you talk to yourself or others about what you hope to accomplish. You consider your own knowledge, the content you are addressing, and the students you are teaching. You draw on past experience with your own strengths as a teacher, how the content can be made accessible to students, and the class history with the same or related content. Based on your repertoire in each area, you use your judgment to frame the next learning episode.

Throughout a learning episode, you constantly measure, assess, and take stock of how the students are interacting with the material. Tiny, incremental decisions are made within a web of newly emerging information and assumptions you already hold about the content and the students. Each learning episode provokes different responses to the students as you seek the most productive way to move students to the next level or layer of understanding.

At the end of each episode, you ask students to reflect on their own thinking as they moved through the learning process. As they reflect and write about their thinking, they produce documentation of their learning. Often, students tell you they were not clear on the concept, process, or attitude until the class considered it together. Without the benefit of class consideration and personal Reflection, that realization might be discarded or ignored.

Finally, after the learning episode is completed, you relive the episode by revisiting the feelings, reviewing the images, and rehearing the languages of self-talk about your understanding of what went on. Teacher and students strengthen their confidence in this knowledge and construct greater understanding of the complex processes used to gather it as both proceed to the next learning episode.

In his essay "Why Reflective Thinking Must be an Educational Aim," John Dewey (1933) outlines three purposes of Reflection. Reflection makes possible (1) action with a conscious aim, (2) systematic preparations and inventions, and (3) enrichment of things with meanings. Maxine Greene (1995) has interpreted and presented the work of John Dewey in many of her articles. "Learning, after all, is a reflected-on process that moves on into conscious praxis in an unpredictable world" (p. 68). Both Dewey and Greene focus on the pathway of knowledge, from a lived experience, through Reflection on it, toward plans for the future. Many perspectives on the relationship of thinking to language are illuminating. Alex Kozulin's 1986 translation of Vygotsky's *Thought and Language* (1934) allowed Western readers insight into Vygotsky's powerful thinking about the psychology of language. Vygotsky's description of "inner thought" suggests that cognition or knowing is a complex process that begins with an inner dialogue with one's self. Those supporting students must understand this often-invisible form of Reflection. Hans Furth (1966) reminded us that deaf learners reflect on "thinking without language."

Schön's work on "reflection-in-action" (1983) begins this chapter. Schön studied the thinking of professionals including architects, psychotherapists, and engineers, and investigated how people in the professions articulate knowledge that has remained invisible or tacit. Richard Schmuck, in *Practical Action Research for Change* (1997) talked about the need for educators to move in a cycle from reflections to inquiry to improvement. He believed that mature teachers focus on effective practice and seek strategies to improve student learning and evaluate their success. Professionals act, reflect on those actions, and then plan new actions. Without the systematic Reflection suggested by both Schön and Schmuck, improvement in practice remains elusive.

Narrative has become more widely understood and used in our field during the past two decades. Carol Witherell and Nel Noddings (1991) edited *Stories Lives Tell: Narrative and Dialogue in Education*. This volume offers students of education a rich collection about the usefulness of narrative. Whether through autobiographical reflections or through the stories of others, teachers can use deeply individual, personal Reflection as a medium to connect students and teacher or students with ideas. Jean Clandinin and Michael Connelly (1994) legitimized individual Reflection as "personal experience methods" in the *Handbook of Qualitative Research*. They described the "inquiry into narrative" required for us to become students of our lives. In "Recherche: Teaching Our Life Histories" (1998), Michelle Collay explained how her research activities became a systematic method of engaging new teachers in Reflection throughout their first year. As teacher-educators have observed over many years, you teach who you are. Teachers must stop and reflect on the "who" they are teaching to their students.

Jerome Bruner (1996) also took up the theme of narrative as Reflection in *The Culture of Education*. He revisited his three modes of mental representation: *Enactive* is the representation of physical action; *iconic* is the representation of visual imagery; and *symbolic* is the representation of language. These three modes of representation echo our three symbolic systems of feelings, images, and languages. We agree that these three internal systems serve as the processes of thought. We argue that feelings and images are also symbolic systems, not just modes of representation. Feelings are symbolized by facial expressions or body language, and icons without words are symbols that communicate across cultures. When students reflect on their own thinking and learning, we ask them to talk or write about their awareness of feelings, images, and languages that are the symbolic systems we construct to represent external experience as internal thoughts.

Critical Reflection also focuses on systematizing reflective practice and using the information or ideas that are revealed to improve practice or make decisions. Steven Brookfield's *Becoming a Critically Reflective Teacher* (1995) emphasizes this strategy. He describes the importance of confronting our own assumptions or taken-for-granted beliefs, lest we enact our praxis thoughtlessly. As George Gagnon's colleague at the University of St. Thomas in St. Paul, Minnesota, Steven was in a group of faculty who met weekly for lunch to reflect on their practice. Mezirow and associates (1990) published a series of articles about Reflection and adult learning. Their book, *Fostering Critical Reflection in Adulthood*, contains many useful ideas and shows Reflection in many different contexts of personal and professional learning.

After getting a sense of the theory and precedents that are the foundation for the Reflection element, please use this background to reflect on your thinking and learning.

Metacognition is often described colloquially as "thinking about thinking." *Meta* is the Greek word for "beyond" or "after," and *cognition* comes from the Latin word for "knowledge" and refers to the process of knowing in the broadest sense, including perception, memory, and judgment. The whole process of Reflection must support analyzing, synthesizing, and evaluating our thinking. These higher-order thoughts focus on the process of thinking itself, not the recollection, comprehension, or application of information. Both collective and individual Reflection is part of CLD because of the important role that metacognition plays in understanding and using what you experience and learn.

In Learning Record 6.F, Reflection Element Reflection, reflect on what you have learned by writing and revising a Reflection element. Write about the feelings, images, and language in your thoughts about leading students in collective and individual reflective consideration of their thinking and learning.

Learning Record 6.F	Reflection Element Reflection

As you were thinking and writing about a Reflection element,

Describe the feelings in your spirit:

Describe the images in your imagination:

Describe the languages in your internal dialogue:

Copyright © 2006 by Corwin Press. All rights reserved. Reprinted from *Constructivist Learning Design: Key Questions for Teaching to Standards*, by George W. Gagnon and Michelle Collay. Thousand Oaks, CA: Corwin Press, www.corwinpress .com. Reproduction authorized only for the local school site or nonprofit organization that has purchased this book.

Now read the concluding remarks and take a break from the CLD.

CONCLUDING REMARKS THOUGHTS ON LADING REFLECTIONS

Teachers often think of Reflection as the "so what?" of the lesson, unit, or course. Least understood and most often overlooked, this final element is the reason you work so hard at all the other elements of CLD. Students need a chance to say what they learned—if they can't, then the learning is incomplete. You need a framework so that you can listen to what students say. Such a framework allows students to express what worked and what they need more of. You may seldom ask your students what they've learned because you are afraid of what they might say. Use careful language in this stage of your development so that you don't open yourself to negativity or thoughtless criticism. For example, if you ask students to write down something they now know about a topic, then they're likely to give a proactive response. If you ask students, "Did you learn anything?" then they might not be so forthcoming.

Experience has shown that expectations breed success. When you perceive students as knowledgeable and able contributors, they contribute. When you document those contributions and talk about their goodness, students are more likely to feel successful as learners. Feelings of success are simple yet elusive. Students learn something from every exchange, and they will tell you about their learning if you ask them. Together, teacher and students can structure learning experiences that result in fluent and diverse Reflection on new knowledge.

You have answered and reflected on three key questions about leading a Reflection element:

1. Feelings: How will students reflect on their emotional/physical experiences?

2. Images: How will students reflect on their sensory experiences?

3. Languages: How will students reflect on their communication experiences?

Your answers will be apparent in the element you wrote and will guide you in thinking about using all of the CLD elements together in a learning episode.

7 Teaching Designs

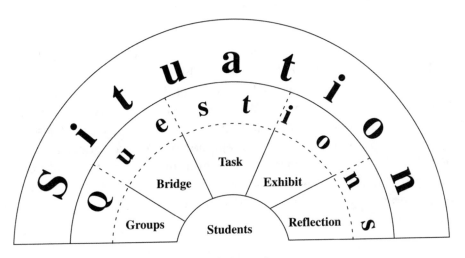

CLD Schematic

It is one of the great truths that what it is impossible to teach the child through words will be learned easily through the language of movement.

—Isadora Duncan, *The Art of the Dance* (1926)

Constructivist learning episodes actively engage students in a purposeful *Situation* that involves collaboratively formulating questions, explaining phenomena, addressing complex issues, or resolving problems. Organizing *Groups* of students with materials and furniture is a prelude to building a *Bridge* between what they already know and what you want them to learn. Students make their own meaning of a well crafted *Task* and actively construct knowledge together as the teacher asks guiding, clarifying, and integrating questions. Then teachers arrange an *Exhibit* of student learning and explanations of their thinking. Finally, the teacher leads class and individual *Reflection* about students' thinking as they made personal meaning, shared meaning, and collective meaning during the learning episode.

This final chapter first describes how a Constructivist Learning Design (CLD) unfolds chronologically or is taught during a learning episode. Then it revisits the Fairy Tales CLD presented in the Introduction to give details about how one design unfolded in different ways. The chapter concludes with personal reflections on learning about CLD. These descriptions are presented using the metaphor of a dance rehearsal or production. Comparing the image of choreographing and performing a dance to designing and teaching a learning episode is a powerful metaphor for understanding the complex and artful design process of organizing for constructivist learning.

DANCING A DESIGN

Teaching a learning design is like rehearsing a dance production. The teacher is both choreographer and leading dancer as he or she plans the sequence of elements in a CLD. A choreographer has danced in many recitals, studied with great dancers and choreographers, listened to thousands of pieces of music, and directed many productions. Choreographers, like teachers, know their own likes and dislikes. They choose from available musical scores or commission a new score, select a venue for performance, decide how best to use the space, time, and materials available to the company, and only then begin rehearsing the troupe. Choreographers have their own image about how the dance will take form, yet only when they see dancers in action do they know just how the dance will flow. The dancers become leaders in the production, not puppets responding to simple commands. At the end of the performance, the dancers are the stars and get most of the credit for the quality of the dance.

Choreographers and teachers have much in common. Each has choices to make and limitations to overcome. Both work to their own strengths and with the abilities of the troupe or students. They choose music or curricular approaches best suited to their group and expect a certain level of skill and performance from each member. Some individuals are stars, and others are part of the chorus line. Both dancers and students know the repertoire of basic steps, but they need modeling and coaching to move to the next level of performance.

PACING, RHYTHM, AND FOOTWORK

The performance art involved in leading a dance troupe or teaching a learning design depends on pacing, rhythm, and footwork. A dance production succeeds or fails if these pieces are not precisely interconnected. The same techniques are just as important in teaching a successful learning episode. Both choreography and teaching require careful development of a thoughtful design, and each requires quick judgments and decisions as the dance performance or learning episode unfolds. Pacing is highly variable and reflects the rhythm of each successive element in your design. When you begin the dance of a learning episode, your description of the purpose, topic, and assessment of the Situation depends on many variables. The students' presence, mood, and attention are all factors in the decision. Sometimes a burning social issue needs to be addressed, and other times housekeeping chores need to be done.

When you form Groups and where you position them in the room are also considerations. A good production needs props and costumes. A good choreographer knows how to inspire dancers by having them feel the rhythm as they rehearse. How you arrange materials beforehand, have students collect materials for their group, or distribute materials to each group are all matters of pacing. Any rehearsal or practice has its own tempo so that performers use their energy well and have something left at the end. When you begin the warm-up or Bridge and how long you continue it is another variable. When you draw the Task to a close and decide that most students are ready to Exhibit their work is a question of pacing. At the end of each rehearsal, performers meet in the greenroom and take notes from the rehearsal leader, director, or choreographer. For a teacher, the focus of these notes or Reflection varies depending on how much time is left to complete the learning episode. All of these decisions require watching the clock and managing increments of time, minute to minute or hour to hour.

Footwork is the artistic part of teaching a learning design, the improvised dance between students and teacher. This modern dance—a learning episode choreographed by a teacher—is more fluid than a ballet because students dance to the same music in different ways from one day to the next. The dynamic interplay between dancers and choreographer keeps you on your toes, responding to the unique rhythms of learning performers. Students are not spectators but participants in the performance art of co-creating a dance that you have choreographed. They are guided by your design and encouraged to interpret and improvise. How you question students, when you decide to engage with a group, whom you choose to question, how you set up exhibits, whom you invite to reflect, and how you respond to students' questions are all footwork in the performance design. As in dance production, the order in which members or small groups present can have a profound effect on the quality of the presentations. For example, if the teacher starts individual presentations by calling on a low-talking student who has a unique perspective on the solution to a problem, subsequent students may be more inclined to risk sharing creative answers. If you ask each person to present, all opinions are equal, not just those of high talkers with hands raised, so the majority or more privileged are recognized. A creative choreographer will shape the performance so that all dancers present themselves at their best.

Many teachers practice the performance art of teaching using deep, tacit professional knowledge acquired through lengthy experience. Words on a page cannot express the dynamic interchange that evolves in seconds and minutes in each classroom. A dance score recorded on paper does not suggest the personal dynamics between dancers during a performance. Similarly, no written learning design can possibly capture or predict the nuances of personal and emotional reactions that take place during a learning episode among students or between students and teacher. The nature of being a professional is that you make these decisions quickly, without time to reflect on each choice yet with confidence in your judgment.

CHOOSING MUSIC FOR THE DANCE

Constructivist Learning Design can be applied to any subject and to classes or units of any length. CLD is a process of teacher inquiry about actively engaging students to accomplish learning tasks.

- *Writing* teachers might ask students to construct the simplest sentences and compare their structure.
- *Literature* teachers might ask students to explain the motives of a character.
- *Social studies* teachers might ask students to assume the roles of two adversaries in a meeting.
- *Science* teachers might demonstrate a phenomenon and ask students to explain what was observed.
- *Math* teachers might ask students to find examples of sloping lines in the world around them and then introduce grids to determine equations.
- *Foreign language* teachers might engage students in conversational immersion without resorting to English translations.
- *Art* teachers might ask students to transform clay with their hands without looking at it.
- *Music* teachers might ask students to notate rhythms in a piece of music using their own symbols.

The constructivist approach can be adapted to any subject area or curriculum by engaging students as active participants in making meaning and constructing knowledge. Successful students are never passive recipients of information given to them by the teacher but engage ideas individually and make meanings different from other students.

Constructivist Learning Design can be incorporated into 45- or 50-minute class periods, 100-minute block schedules, and half- or whole-day sessions to teach a particular concept, process, or attitude. A single Bridge or assigned Groups of students may apply to a unit that lasts two days or three weeks. Other learning episodes may present each element on a daily basis and link together into a CLD to teach topics in a chapter or piece of literature. Organizers of professional development often structure three-hour morning or afternoon sessions with a single design and include more than one Task to accomplish so that teachers move through a sequence of related tasks that increase in complexity. Sometimes they develop designs for a weekend retreat or a weeklong institute with several different teachers.

REHEARSING THE DANCE

This section is designed to walk you through a process of teaching a CLD from the notes you have written as you imagined moving through a learning episode with students. Think of teaching a design as more of a dance rehearsal than a performance. You and your students should feel relaxed and comfortable as you practice your moves together. The six elements of CLD unfold consecutively as you rehearse the dance during a learning episode and occur in the order you will practice each one. You may decide to change the sequence as you engage with students and materials so that the CLD sequence becomes more logical than magical.

1. This element emerges at the beginning of the rehearsal as you announce the purpose, topic, and assessment that you framed for your students in the *Situation*. These are the *big ideas* that guide your rehearsal. This can be the most difficult element of CLD for new teachers. Clarifying the purpose, determining a worthwhile topic, and engaging students in some kind of active inquiry around these big ideas is not an easy process. As with most things, experience is the greatest teacher, and the more you rehearse, the greater your proficiency.

2. The next element to unfold in rehearsing a learning episode is *Groups*. Your design described how students might think collaboratively and what materials or furniture might support their thinking. Arranging Groups of students, materials, and furniture takes careful planning, too. "Put the kids in groups!" is advice given to a teacher who is unprepared and needs a quick plan. However, creating productive Groups requires a different kind of preparation and sophisticated teaching. Think about students, materials, and furniture in advance so you don't spend valuable time during the learning episode deciding how to organize students, scrambling for materials, or rearranging furniture. Students may grumble but will get their gear, move around to find their places, and settle into a new group. If the classroom contains flexible tables and chairs rather than individual desks, then forming and getting into Groups is easier. Teachers form productive small groups with tables and chairs, with moveable chair desks, in large open rooms with chairs or no furniture at all, and in lecture halls with stadium chairs and arm desks. Don't let the classroom configuration and furniture become a barrier to working in small groups.

3. Building a *Bridge* to make connections between old and new learning is the next element in rehearsing a learning episode. A hallmark of constructivist teaching and learning is creating a thoughtful stage to surface prior knowledge. Students can express what they already know about a topic individually or collectively. Small-group conversations can offer a safe way for students to express their ideas and to test their thinking with others, especially if community-building activities have constructed a strong foundation of trust. Direct prompts generate real documentation, offer a more thorough introduction and review of the Situation, engage

more students, and don't take longer than a whole-group discussion. Specific directions and required documentation reduce the time students spend chatting about unrelated topics. The Bridge can take a few minutes if the CLD is one class period, a day if the CLD takes a week, or a few days if the CLD lasts a term. How you build a Bridge with your students is not as important as doing it early in the rehearsal so that students can connect prior knowledge to new learning.

4. The *Task* element unfolds next in rehearsing a learning episode. Articulate the Task as clearly as possible, knowing that different students will make different meanings of your language and examples. Good questions lie at the heart of CLD and let you envision what students might think and do as they accomplish a Task. By anticipating student questions, you are ready to ask guiding questions, respond with clarifying questions, and pose integrating questions to wrap up work on tasks. As with any dance, the more time spent in design, the better the rehearsal will play out. The key is to expect the unexpected and to cherish divergent thinking that emerges from students. You need to be flexible and embrace decisions that redirect the course of a learning episode. As in a dance rehearsal, some movements might not convey your feelings, yet several other movements may. Some groups take a long time, while other groups finish quickly and may need additional tasks to engage or focus, so you might have some content-related sponge activities at the ready. You may move the learning episode toward closure before some students are ready because they will benefit from listening to what other groups have thought and done. Demonstrate through your actions that the Task is productive because of the quality of each student's thinking, not because it is completed quickly. Some classroom-management concerns may still arise and need to be resolved. If students are more engaged in thinking together, fewer management issues tend to emerge.

5. The next element that unfolds in rehearsing a learning episode is the *Exhibit*. This opportunity for students to show their work provides a record of their thinking, gives a sense of completion, and reassures stakeholders about what and how students are learning. Practice taking a bow. Constructivist teachers often use physical models, visual representations, index cards, sticky notes, poster paper, overhead transparencies, and different colored markers so that each group can have a simple way to record and display their work. Some forms or copies may need to be run off ahead of time, but students tend to learn more if they have to decide for themselves on the structure and format for their presentation. Small groups will accomplish a Task in very different ways from those you imagine, but students benefit from divergent thinking. Timing the Exhibit can

UNIVERSITY OF WINCHESTER
LIBRARY

be a challenge. You must decide when to proceed to an Exhibit and allow enough time for Reflection afterward. New teachers may rush through a learning episode, just to include everything rather than simply postponing the Exhibit and Reflection. They risk not teaching these elements at all because of pressure to move on and cover the next section. Learning episodes lasting a week could have a longer Reflection session on Friday, but make sure students reflect on thinking every day so that they connect new learning with prior knowledge.

6. The final element in rehearsing a learning episode is *Reflection*. This is truly a case of last but not least! Performers call this "notes" when they meet to debrief that night's performance and make corrections or changes. Students need time to critically reflect on their thinking throughout the learning episode in order to complete the cycle of constructing knowledge. As students move from making personal meaning to shared meaning to collective meaning, Reflection on their thinking is necessary for them to complete the social construction of knowledge. This Reflection has two major parts. First, teachers lead a large-group consideration of how the learning episode unfolded. They revisit the big ideas, link this episode with previous ones, make connections and applications, challenge misconceptions that became evident during the Exhibit, and commend minority opinions so that those students know they have been heard and feel legitimized. Second, individual students make sense of their personal understanding. Ask students to write about, draw, or represent in some other way their individual thinking during the learning episode. This personal documentation creates time and space for each student to communicate the feelings they had, images they sensed, and languages they used as they thought during the learning episode. Individual students are held accountable. This final phase of the learning episode is a capstone experience that should bring together the elements of a CLD into a coherent whole. Making time and space for whole-class and personal Reflection on thinking is essential.

This general description of rehearsing a learning design from start to finish is illustrated by a specific example in the next section.

A TALE OF THREE DANCERS

The same choreography or learning design can be danced or taught in many ways depending on interpretation. The Introduction presented a Fairy Tales CLD designed by three teachers and told the composite story of teaching this learning design. Now, we revisit the story with more detail about how each teacher taught her own version of this CLD. The *Situation* element of their CLD focused on engaging students with the genre of fairy tales. They explained to students that the purpose was to understand core elements and common themes that define this area of literature. Their ongoing purposes of strengthening writing, improving reading ability, and teaching study skills were evident throughout the CLD. The topic was analyzing fairy tales for common elements. The assessment was comparing their analysis with that of experts.

In the Fairy Tales CLD, each teacher took a different approach to *Groups*. Ellen grouped the students randomly by handing out slips of paper with characters from several well-known fairy tales and asked the students to find others whose characters were from the same story. This activity was fun for the students and tested their knowledge of the general literature. Gail grouped students by location in the room. She was confident her class would be productive in almost any configuration. Sue had her students meet in writing workshop Learning Circles she had set up earlier in the term.

Ellen, Gail, and Sue required students to complete the same prewriting activity. In the Fairy Tales CLD, students first wrote about a fairy tale from their own experience. This *Bridge* activity allowed students to share thinking already begun rather than considering a question for the first time. Ellen had her students complete the prewriting activity the previous Friday because she had a substitute that day. Gail and Sue had their students write at home the night before.

Bridge activities can take several forms, and some teachers use more than one in a learning episode. First, all of these teachers asked their students to write a reflective piece about their memories of hearing a fairy tale. This essay served as a Bridge for individual students to connect their prior learning to the Task of identifying characteristics of fairy tales. Then, all three teachers used a second, different Bridge. During the class period, Ellen told about her grandfather's stories as a Bridge to that day's activities, while Gail called on some of her students to share what they had written. In a third classroom, Sue put her students in their regular writer's workshop Learning Circles immediately and asked them to talk about their essays in those groups. She used familiar writer's workshop strategies, and they critiqued each other's opening paragraphs and offered suggestions.

During the *Task* the small groups within the three classrooms behaved quite differently from one another and from those in the other two classrooms. Ellen's newly formed random groups bantered in a friendly competition to see which group could list the most characteristics commonly found in fairy tales. She stopped them after about 10 minutes and asked the students to debate the question of quality versus quantity that was evident on the chart paper. Some of Gail's groups worked quickly on the list of characteristics with little discussion, while other groups took more time debating various characteristics. She asked the most efficient groups to apply their characteristics to *Snow White and the Seven Dwarfs* because it had just been rereleased and most of them had seen the movie. Sue's groups spent most of their time editing each other's opening paragraphs and only a few minutes on the Task of generating characteristics. Questions in each of the three classrooms ranged from "What is a characteristic?" to "Does this group's very long list contain more useful information than another list where group members spent more time debating the entries?" All three teachers asked individual students whom they knew to be "low talkers" to name a fairy tale and describe one characteristic.

Ellen and Gail got to the *Exhibit* during the same day, while Sue put that element off until the next day. Her writer's workshop Learning Circles needed time to generate more characteristics. Ellen's classroom is small, and the chart paper sheets were easily visible from every seat. The group recorder talked about the list and how it was generated. In Gail's classroom, the wall with room for chart paper is not easily seen from the desks, so small groups toured the room and examined each list. Gail asked each group to note characteristics that were consistent across all or most sheets. In all three rooms, some of the characteristics listed on the groups' chart papers were not valid. For example, in Ellen's classroom, the students themselves questioned other groups about whether "death of the lead character" was really a characteristic of all fairy tales. Gail revisited that debate after all groups had presented their Exhibit and asked her students to place sticky dots next to the characteristics that appeared on each sheet. Sue talked about the writing process and students shared how they had used their writer's group to clarify their thinking.

In teaching the Fairy Tales CLD, each teacher added something to the *Reflection* they had designed together. All three had their students read articles about fairy tales and compare the definitions and characteristics that the class had developed with those listed by the experts. In addition to writing about two definitions for the next day, Ellen had students link back to the characters in their prewriting activity. She asked students to analyze their group's fairy tale using three characteristics from their new lists. Gail had students write down something that they would make sure to include when writing their original fairy tale. Sue had students draft the next section of their writing assignment, a sketch of the plot of their original fairy tale. They each described how the teacher trio had designed the CLD, what they anticipated in the learning episode, and their interpretation of how it had come out. Each teacher told her class that the teachers would meet afterward, review the videotapes, and compare notes.

DANCING TOGETHER

One of the great joys we have in sharing a career is teaching together. By creating and coteaching a CLD, we can witness and discuss how the learning episode we had imagined together then unfolded in real life. Every learning episode we design and rehearse is a new dance. As in most creative endeavors, sometimes it succeeds beyond our expectations, and sometimes it flops. Most of the time, we see things that worked well and things we would change if we did it again. The process of creating a CLD with a colleague can be a wonderful experience, especially because most of us work alone. Because teaching is usually a solo performance, teachers also tend to plan for teaching as a solitary act. But designing for learning with another teacher can be like dancing with a partner.

Often, planning is done in the shower, while driving to work, or when reading student papers after your children are in bed. The opportunity to think together about teaching is seldom part of teacher culture. Teachers spend preparation time planning lessons, organizing materials, or squeezing out a few minutes to manage their personal lives. Meeting times are spent on school business, district procedures, or general professional development. Few graduate degree programs focus specifically on the process of teaching and learning.

Find a teacher colleague to create one CLD with you. Invite a member of your department or grade-level team to think about how you might teach a learning episode. The language of CLD might not be familiar to your colleagues. You can talk with them about how they would find out what students already know or how students would present their work during a lesson rather than using the terms Bridge or Exhibit or learning episode. Constructivist Learning Design uses different language because we are reframing familiar procedures of planning for teaching into a process of designing for learning. New language may become a barrier for some teachers, and during daily conversations, language isn't as consistent as it can be when we are writing. Many colleagues refer to "constructivist *lesson* design" or "lesson plans" and make other connections with previous planning formats they have used effectively. We see them making their own meaning and never insist on uniformity as they engage in the nuances of new language.

To get started, select a concept, process, or attitude you intend to teach in about a month and share your understanding of how to create a CLD with your colleague. Think through the CLD elements in sequence and then imagine how your choices will play out. Imagine a few Situation, Groups, or Bridge elements and anticipate the effects of each one. How can you get the results you want? Do you foresee any problems with particular students or learning? After you agree on a CLD, try it out in your classes. Observe each other teaching if possible, and then revise the design based on your observations and student feedback. The exchanges you have while creating and improving a CLD with a colleague is professional collaboration at its best.

We found a similar focus on colleagueship in *The Teaching Gap* by James Stigler and James Hiebert (1999). These educational researchers analyzed videotapes from math classrooms in the United States, Germany, and Japan that were recorded as part of the Third International Mathematics and Science Study (TIMSS). They learned that "teaching is not a simple skill but rather a complex cultural activity that is highly determined by beliefs and habits that work partly outside the realm of consciousness" (p. 103). They contend that teaching is so constant in our culture that teachers can't imagine or believe it should be changed and that educational reform efforts fail because most reforms have little, if any, effect on actual classroom teaching. These researchers advocate a process of "lesson study" they adapted from the Japanese *jugyou kenkyuu*. Teams of teachers work on developing, piloting, observing, and revising a single "research lesson" for several months until they feel it improves student learning. The suggestions in this section echo their focus on collegial lesson study to improve the quality of teaching and learning in schools.

Several teachers are now beginning to embrace lesson study as part of their professional development. At the University of California, Berkeley, academic staff initiated weekly sessions with math teachers at one middle school. These teachers talked with their colleagues and soon were joined by math teachers from other middle schools. Several interested faculty and staff joined the discussions. They spent six months designing and refining their first research lesson for everyone to observe. The format they decided to use was very similar to CLD. Some teachers found the process so valuable that they formalized lesson study as their professional development model during the following school year.

After designing a CLD with colleagues, look for opportunities to actually teach a learning episode together. If you can teach a CLD that you have developed together, it may be less intimidating to have your collaborator watch you teach. Usually, teachers take responsibility for different elements of the learning episode, so one is teaching while the other is observing the group process and student reaction. When you teach that CLD to another class, you might switch roles and teach the elements you watched before. You tend to get a better feel for the flow of CLD as it unfolds during a learning episode when you are on the inside looking out rather than on the outside looking in.

INVITING ADMINISTRATORS TO THE DANCE

Principals may need to be educated about the process of CLD and what they should expect to see when they observe the flow of a learning episode. Most principals are working from an older model of instruction and supervision. They may not know constructivist learning theory or understand how its principles can be applied to engage students in learning. Thinking in groups, surfacing prior knowledge, accomplishing tasks without specific instruction, displaying learning, and reflecting on thinking may all be new constructs for building administrators to consider in evaluating teachers. These issues need to be addressed in the preconference and reviewed in the postconference so that your principal is clear about your teaching methodology and learning expectations. Your classroom and teaching style may look much different from what the principal anticipates without this preparation and debriefing.

INVITING OTHERS TO THE DANCE

We hope you enjoyed using our book and will appropriate some of these ideas for your teaching. We thought and learned more about the process of Constructivist Learning Design than we had ever expected. We clarified our understanding of different elements and the social construction of knowledge. The power of reflecting and writing together as a vehicle for our own collaborative thinking and learning was reaffirmed for us, giving new meaning to *collaboration* or *laboring together.*

This enterprise represents our own meaning making about engaging readers to reflect on how they learn. We offer one structure for collective design work and encourage you to continue to build your knowledge of design. Through self-exploration you looked inward, through collaboration you looked outward. Regulating the "inside-out" and "outside-in" of the learning cycle will allow you to bring these elements together in artful and productive ways. We are better learners and teachers when we know ourselves and engage fully in community with others. Resource 13 on page 212 is a summary of the CLD Key Questions and three key questions for each element that provide the framework for our Constructivist Learning Design. Please refer to this summary to guide you in preparing other CLD's.

Thank you for being a part of the "class" for our Exhibit of thinking. We invite your Reflection as a reader with us, offers of your own CLDs for other teachers to consider, or analysis of one of your learning episodes. Please visit our Web site at www.prainbow.com/cld to post your reflection, design, or analysis. We wish you and your students the joy and fulfillment that arises from your personal experience and mutual exploration of constructivist teaching and learning!

Resources

RESOURCE MATRIX

CLD Matrix for Examples of Elements (Chapters)			
Level	*Situation (1) &* *Task (4)*	*Groups (2) &* *Exhibit (5)*	*Bridge (3) &* *Reflection (6)*
Primary Grades *Resources* *1, 2, 3*	Fine Arts *Drawing* *Animals*	Physical Education *Imitating* *Animals*	Reading *Retelling* *the Story*
Intermediate Grades *Resources* *4, 5, 6*	Science *Moon View*	Media Technology *Logo*	Special Education *Vending* *Machines*
Middle School *Resources* *7, 8, 9*	Language Arts *Fairy Tales*	Mathematics *Base Blocks*	Industrial Technology *Scooter* *Motor*
High School *Resources* *10, 11, 12*	Social Studies *Trading* *Partners*	Foreign Language *Spanish* *Songs*	Business Education *Creating* *Spreadsheets*

RESOURCE 1

Level: Primary Grades
Subject: Fine Arts
Title: Drawing Animals

Situation *50 minutes*	The purpose of this sequence of three Situations is for young students to make further meaning of the rhythmic, patterned story *Brown Bear, Brown Bear, What Do You See?* "Brown bear, brown bear, what do you see? I see a yellow duck looking at me." They engage in rich literature activities by listening to the story or song, drawing new animals, writing a parallel phrase, acting out new behaviors, describing these new behaviors in words, and retelling the story through new pictures and words. The topic is for students to choose a new animal and a color for that animal and then create a page for a book about new animals. In the assessment, the teacher or assistant collects the sheets into a book and students write on their page or dictate a story pattern for their new animal and color.
Groups *3 minutes*	To create work groups, students pull from a basket an index card naming one of nine animals in the original story. Materials such as markers, crayons, construction paper, drawing paper, and glue are available for the groups to use to create a depiction of their invented animals. Students can create one picture per child or one per group. Students can sit in groups of four or fewer per table.
Bridge *5 minutes*	The teacher reads *Brown Bear, Brown Bear, What Do You See?* to the children. Some teachers might create a simple melody and sing the story. The teacher asks the children to listen for the various types and colors of animals "looking at me."
Task *20 minutes*	The teacher reads *Brown Bear, Brown Bear, What Do You See?* again. This time, the teacher asks, "What other animal could we put here and what color could it be?" Students are encouraged to be inventive and not to criticize "polka-dot salamanders." All the students sketch their creatures. Those who can write put their descriptions in words on their page, and others dictate their descriptions to the bookmaker.
	Anticipated student questions: Should I make my parrot green like the picture book or a new color?
	Teacher questions: Is your animal real or imagined? What sounds does your animal make? Where might your animal live?
Exhibit *12 minutes*	All the students sketch their creatures and describe the color and name. Those who can put descriptions on their page, and others dictate their descriptions to the bookmaker. They all describe their animal orally when presenting the final version to the bookmaker. Read the new version of *Brown Bear, Brown Bear, What Do You See?* with new animals and colors. For each "What do you see?" the children show their drawing of the creature "looking at me."
Reflection *10 minutes*	How did you decide which animal to draw and what color it should be? Think about extending your creature's behavior in various ways. For instance, after seeing an "aqua elephant looking at me," grey goose might waddle off to a pond or follow other geese down to a garden.

RESOURCE 2

Level: Primary Grades
Subject: Physical Education
Title: Imitating Animals

Situation *50 minutes*	The purpose of this sequence of Situations is for young students to make further meaning of the rhythmic, patterned story *Brown Bear, Brown Bear, What Do You See?* "Brown bear, brown bear, what do you see? I see a yellow duck looking at me." They engage in rich literature activities by listening to the story or song, drawing new animals, writing a parallel phrase, acting out new behaviors, describing these new behaviors in words, and retelling the story through new pictures and words. After drawing new animals in the previous learning episode, the topic is for students to think about how their animal moved, where it went, and what it ate after it saw the next animal. For example, the red goat might bounce to the garden and eat flowers after seeing "a pink salmon looking at me," and the grey goose might waddle off to a pond and eat slugs after seeing "an aqua elephant looking at me." In the assessment, individuals act out what their animal did after it saw another animal looking at it, and then the whole class imitates each action in the order of the new book.
Groups *1 minute*	Students work in the same small groups as the Drawing Animals learning design to create actions for their new animals. Materials needed are space and clothes for free movement.
Bridge *4 minutes*	The teacher and students read the new version of *Brown Bear* using the new animals and colors on the pages of the new book that they created together.
Task *10 minutes*	Students think about their animal and decide where it went and what it ate. They each create movements to act out these actions. Anticipated student questions: How does my animal move around? Where would it go? What does it eat? Teacher questions: Where does your animal live? What kind of legs does it have? Where might your animal go? What do you think it eats? How may of these animals have four legs? How many of these animals live on land? How many animals were in the new book?
Exhibit *25 minutes*	In the order of the new book, first the individuals and then the whole class acts out the movements of each animal after it sees another animal looking at it.
Reflection *10 minutes*	Do the actions you created for your animal fit with their habitat? For example, would an orange cow fly or a silver turtle run? Why do you think so? How did you feel imitating your animal?

RESOURCE 3

Level: Primary Grades
Subject: Reading
Title: Retelling the Story

Situation *50 minutes*	The purpose of this sequence of three Situations is for young students to make further meaning of the rhythmic, patterned story *Brown Bear, Brown Bear, What Do You See?* "Brown bear, brown bear, what do you see? I see a yellow duck looking at me." They engage in rich literature activities by listening to the story or song, drawing new animals, writing a parallel phrase, acting out new behaviors, describing these new behaviors in words, and retelling the story through new pictures and words. The topic is for students to use a new sheet of paper to draw a picture of their new animal and then to write down how their animal moved, where it went, and what it ate after seeing another animal. The words should describe the story they made up when imitating their animal's actions in the previous learning episode.
Groups *3 minutes*	Students work in small groups of two or three formed by the teacher so there is one writer in each group. Materials include pencils, markers, crayons, pieces of paper to fit in the book, glue, and scissors. Small groups can meet at tables.
Bridge *12 minutes*	The teacher shows the pages of the new book. Children try to remember where their animal went and what it ate after seeing another animal. Teacher and children brainstorm and chart words that tell how each animal moved, where it went, and what it ate.
Task *20 minutes*	Students draw a new picture showing where there animal went and what it ate after seeing another animal "looking at me." The writers in each group write the descriptions on the new pictures. Anticipated student questions: How can I write down the words to tell how my animal moved, were it went, or what it ate? Teacher questions: What words describe how your animal moved, where it went, and what it ate? Can you try to write them on a piece of scrap paper?
Exhibit *10 minutes*	In the order of the new book, students bring up their new drawings and read their new page to the class. The teacher puts each new page into the book so it follows the student's first drawing of a new animal.
Reflection *5 minutes*	How does it feel to write a new book together? How did you choose the words to tell about your animal? How would you change the color or movement of your animal if we did this again?

RESOURCE 4

Level: Intermediate Grades
Subject: Science
Title: Moon View

Situation *90 minutes*	The purpose of this Situation is to provide investigation of a basic science concept rarely understood by adults and often explained with misconceptions relating to shadows of the earth on the moon. The topic is for students to work in groups to determine the relationship between the sun, the earth, and the phases of the moon. In the assessment, groups are asked to explain their thinking through a diagram.
Groups *10 minutes*	Students are put into groups of four based on their zodiac signs. Groups work with drawings, pictures, or any objects they spontaneously use to construct models of the relationship. Small groups can push desks together.
Bridge *15 minutes*	Students are asked to explain why we have seasons. This is based on a similar question posed to students and faculty at a Harvard graduation ceremony in a film called *A Private Universe*, in which 1 out of 20 people gave a correct account while others had misconceptions. After students present their explanations, they watch *A Private Universe*.
Task *30 minutes*	Groups are asked to draw a diagram of the relationship between the sun, earth, and phases of the moon. Anticipated student questions: What are the phases of the moon? Isn't the curve on the moon just the result of the shadow of the earth? Why do we see the moon during the day? Do people on the other side of the earth see the moon in the same phase as we do? Why isn't the moon always in eclipse when the earth is between the moon and the sun? What is an eclipse of the sun? Where is the moon in the sky? How big is the moon compared to the earth? How far is the moon from the earth?
Exhibit *25 minutes*	After each group has had an opportunity to work out how to represent the relationship between the sun, the earth, and the moon, the person in each group whose birthday is closest to the day of the learning episode presents the explanation to the class.
Reflection *10 minutes*	The teacher leads a debriefing of the phases and positions of the moon related to the earth and sun. Students write individually on index cards about why people have misconceptions about the phases of the moon.

RESOURCE 5

Level: Intermediate Grades
Subject: Media Technology
Title: Logo

Situation *90 minutes*	The purpose of this Situation is to let students feel competent as creators of computer programs, not just consumers of software others have made. The topic is to introduce students to programming in the Logo language and to challenge them to accomplish some basic tasks such as measuring the screen vertically, horizontally, and diagonally. Next, they preview the repeat command and try to write a program for the largest equilateral triangle that they can make on the display screen. Then they preview a recursive program and write one for the largest circle they can make on the display screen. In the assessment, students will present their programs and show the results on screen.
Groups *10 minutes*	Students work in pairs determined by self-report of advanced and basic computer skills. Students work in pairs or in small groups on the computer depending on how many are available. Students meet at the computer.
Bridge *20 minutes*	Students make a list of computer languages that they might know or have heard about. Students are given a list of Logo primitives, shown how to enter them into the program, and asked to explore what each of these functions does to the cursor: FD #, BK #, RT #, LT #, PU, PD, PE, HT, ST, CS, HOME, and CLEAN. The teacher leads a brief review of each command and what students thought it meant.
Task *30 minutes*	The teacher asks students to accomplish the tasks, including measuring the display screen vertically, horizontally, and diagonally. Then they review the repeat command and try to write a program for the largest equilateral triangle they can make on the display screen. Next, they review a recursive command and write one for the largest circle they can make on the display screen. Anticipated student questions: What does equilateral mean? How many degrees are in a triangle? Why did my triangle look weird? Teacher questions: What two root words are in the word "equilateral," and what might they mean? If you took a triangle at one corner and unfolded it flat, what would you have? If you were trying to walk in a triangle, how would you turn corners? Writing the same thing over and over can be tedious, so how might you repeat a routine?
Exhibit *20 minutes*	When most are done trying to make the largest equilateral triangle, they show the triangle they made and the program used to draw it to the class. Later, students show the circle they made and the program to draw it.
Reflection *10 minutes*	The teacher asks students to compare different programs that draw the same figure. How did it feel when you were in control of what happened on the computer? What image did you have in your mind of the way the cursor was moving based on your commands? Why is Logo called a "computer language"?

RESOURCE 6

Level: Intermediate Grades
Subject: Special Education
Title: Vending Machines

Situation *90 minutes* *(plus travel)*	The purpose of this Situation is for each student to learn independent life skills and to do some basic problem solving when confronted with a new challenge. The topic is for developmentally delayed students to choose what to eat from vending machines and then manage money to use vending machines. In the assessment, students are given a $5 bill and use three different vending machines to get a sandwich, a drink, and dessert or chips.
Groups *10 minutes*	The teacher puts students in pairs. When possible, team a more capable or street-wise student with a less able or experienced one. Each student team is also assigned a paraeducator or adult volunteer to accompany them or to shadow them so they are protected or can have assistance as needed. $5 bill or equivalent change per team is needed. Pairs can meet at tables or push desks together.
Bridge *30 minutes*	The first part of this Bridge focuses on breaking down a $5 bill into smaller denominations and counting the money. The second part of the Bridge includes a whole-class visit to a vending machine area so that each child or young person can put coins or paper into a machine, get at least one product out of the machine, and retrieve any change.
Task *30 minutes*	Teachers take students to a vending machine area, give them a $5 bill, and expect them to work in pairs, make change, and purchase from three different vending machines a sandwich, drink, and dessert or chips. Teacher questions: What do you already know about using a vending machine? Where is information about the product and the cost? What are clues to use if you can't read? What do you do if the machine doesn't take the kind of money you have? What will you do if the machine eats your money but doesn't give you anything?
Exhibit *10 minutes*	If the teams return to the teacher with any or all of the three parts of the meal, they have a literal exhibit and can describe their experience in words, written or oral. If they don't have the items, they can tell what happened.
Reflection *10 minutes*	The teacher invites students to discuss their experiences. Why were you or why weren't you successful? What would help you to be successful next time? What are some characteristics of vending machines? What are some strategies that will help you use vending machines in the future?

RESOURCE 7

Level: Middle School
Subject: Language Arts
Title: Fairy Tales

Situation *50 minutes*	The purpose of this Situation is to engage students in analyzing fairy tales so they develop an understanding of core elements and common themes that define this area of literature. The topic is for students to consider their previous experience with fairy tales, develop their definition of a fairy tale, and identify a list of common elements that are found in fairy tales. In the assessment, groups present a poster of their definition and common elements.
Groups *5 minutes*	Students put themselves into groups of three or four. The students are provided large sheets of chart paper, markers, and tape so they can write their group's definition of a fairy tale and list of common elements in fairy tales and post these for the Exhibit. Copies of articles by experts defining fairy tales and common characteristics of fairy tales are given to individual students after the Exhibit. Students can push desks together if there are no tables.
Bridge *10 minutes*	The teacher describes personal experiences with fairy tales and asks students to read what they wrote the previous day about their personal memories of fairy tales.
Task *15 minutes*	Students organize into groups and get paper, markers, and tape. They develop their definition of fairy tales and list common characteristics. Teacher questions: What were your previous experiences with fairy tales? How would you define a fairy tale? What are common characteristics in fairy tales? How do your definitions compare to those of experts? After seeing and reading others, what would you add to your own definition or list? Which definition was more meaningful to you and would be more helpful in writing your own fairy tale? Why are we studying fairy tales? Where did fairy tales come from? What are fairy tales from other cultures?
Exhibit *10 minutes*	Student groups tape the chart papers with their definitions and lists of common elements on the white board and present their thinking to the rest of the class.
Reflection *10 minutes*	Students read the articles and compare and contrast with their own definitions and lists. Then they write about what they would add to their definitions or lists from other groups or from the article. Students describe why their own definition or an expert's definition was more meaningful to them as they think about writing their own fairy tale.

RESOURCE 8

Level: Middle School
Subject: Mathematics
Title: Base Blocks

Situation *1 week*	The purpose of this Situation is to engage students in a deeper exploration of number sense and place value in a different context than base 10. The topic is that students work with models of a different number base, from base 2 to base 7 and then use these models to show how they would solve basic problems requiring addition, subtraction, multiplication, and division. Each group is asked to model the problem, a solution, and the relationship between the two and explain it to their peers.
Groups *First day*	Students get into six groups by counting off from one to how many there are in the class. Then they divide their number by six and get into groups by remainders: zero, one, two, three, four, and five. Groups work with the blocks that model a base that is two more than their remainder: remainder zero group works with base 2, remainder one with base 3, and so on. Small tables with chairs are the best arrangement for models.
Bridge *First day*	Students are each given a sheet with numbers from 0 to 100 on it and asked to work in remainder groups to write each of these numbers in the assigned base. After each group completes the count sheets, they gather all of the pieces that model places in their base from a large pile of base blocks. Students model some of the numbers under 100, and then the teacher reviews the places and exponents for different bases.
Task *3 days*	The teacher reviews the places and exponents for different bases and students model problems in addition, subtraction, multiplication, and division. Each group is asked to model the problem, its solution, and the relationship between the two. Anticipated student questions: How do we count in our base? Teacher questions: What do we do when we fill up the first place in base 10? What digits do we use in base 10? What digits can you use in your base? Guiding questions: Students are given the following four problems to solve by modeling the problem, solution, and relationship between the two. Rosalie goes to the store and buys a can of pop for 43 cents and a candy bar for 34 cents. How much does she spend? Rosalie gives the clerk a dollar bill for her purchase. How much change does she receive? Rosalie goes outside and her brother Jamie asks whether he can have her can when she is done. He puts it with 11 other cans and will get 7 cents per can from the recycler. How much money will he receive? Jamie has to split this money equally with his three friends who helped him collect the cans. How much money will each get from the recycling?
Exhibit *Last day*	After each group has had an opportunity to work out how to represent the problem, a solution, and the relationship between the two, the groups have a "see what we made parade" so that each group can explain its thinking.
Reflection *Last day*	The teacher discusses the concept of counting in bases with the whole class. Then students write individually on index cards about what they learned and what they were thinking during their work together.

RESOURCE 9

Level: Middle School
Subject: Industrial Technology
Title: Scooter Motor

Situation *1 quarter*	The purpose of this Situation is for students to understand how a small gas engine works. This Situation is structured over one quarter as the theory of small engines is reviewed and applied. The topic is for students to take apart and reassemble a small gas engine. First, teams test and replace specific parts of the engine, next bench test it, and then test it on a machine such as a scooter that they make themselves. In the assessment, teams demonstrate their engine and machine for peers and parents.
Groups *First class*	Teams of two or three students are determined by the number of students in the class, the number of engines available, and the amount of hands-on learning each student needs. For instance, one motor could be taken apart by the teacher and each team given one part. One motor could be taken apart several times, once by each team. Or four to five motors could be divided among 20 students. The groups should be small enough that each student can fully participate.
Bridge *First week*	Each team of two to three students is given a part of a small engine. Looking at a schematic, they must identify the part, describe its function, and tell which other parts it interacts with. They also might explain the part to see whether it is in good condition or worn and in need of replacement.
Task *4–5 weeks*	Teams are given a motor to disassemble, reassemble, bench test, mount, and field test by themselves. How does a small gas engine work? Where does the fuel go? What does the spark plug do? What is exhaust composed of? Why does modifying the spark plug or the fuel blend affect performance? What would happen if a motor were larger or smaller? What else could you do with the motor?
Exhibit *1–2 weeks*	The teams can exhibit individual parts of the engine, descriptions of their analysis, and repairs throughout the term. The final exhibit, of course, is the fully functioning scooter. They should prepare a presentation and demonstration for the whole school.
Reflection *1 week to write, edit, and post on a Web page.*	The teacher leads an ongoing analysis of gas engine repair based on problems that students encounter. What did you know about small gas engines at the beginning of the term? What was the most difficult concept to understand? How did you make sense of that concept, teach it to others on your team, or demonstrate that you understood it? If you were to teach a class about small gas engines, how would you proceed? Given the movement away from use of gas engines toward electric, is small gas engine repair an important skill?

RESOURCE 10

Level: High School
Subject: Social Studies
Title: Trading Partners

Situation *6 weeks*	The purpose of this Situation is to investigate how global trade will influence students' future employment. The topic is for students to explore international trade between continents and determine how it might affect their future jobs. Teachers specify regions, goods or services, and jobs. The students list jobs of family and friends, review the want ads to see the kinds of positions that employers are seeking to fill, and then choose an occupation and company for the duration of the unit. In the assessment, students list ways that their occupation and company are linked to international trade.
Groups *First day*	Maps of the six inhabited continents are cut into four to six puzzle-like pieces and distributed randomly to students. They organize into six groups by finding others with pieces of the same continent. Accompanying materials include maps, graphs, business pages, and Web site information related to international trade. Students need large library tables or floor space.
Bridge *One week*	Groups conduct a preliminary study of current trading activities within their continent. For instance, the South America group might choose citrus if the curriculum includes the role of trade agreements and foreign subsidies among different nations. Citrus is also a good choice for Florida or California students.
Task *2 weeks*	Students select an occupation and evaluate its relationship to international trade. What are the roles and responsibilities of your occupation? What goods or services does your company produce or offer, and how are they used in the local region? Nationally? Internationally? Is there a link between what you do and the products of any of the six continents we talked about? How will your occupation be affected by changes in international trade?
Exhibit *2 weeks*	Each continent group prepares a multimedia presentation about the influence that international trading activities will have on their occupations. The class develops a rubric to assess each presentation.
Reflection *1 week*	Reflect on your continent, country, and region in relation to the original question. Given what we have learned about trade between your region and the world, what are the implications for your chosen occupation? Document your reflections as a list of implications, recommendations for job preparation, or plans for a job search. Complete a form including name, date of birth, chosen occupation, international trading factors influencing that occupation, and your personal goals for training for that occupation.

RESOURCE 11

Level: High School
Subject: Foreign Language
Title: Spanish Songs

Situation *2 weeks*	The purpose of this Situation is to explore the influence of Hispanic language and culture on American music. The topic is for students to transcribe a contemporary Spanish song by Selena in the *tejano* style popular with Mexican Americans and some mainstream audiences. Students first create an English translation of the lyrics to fit the melody and rhythm of the original Spanish version. Then students conduct research on the Internet to consider how Hispanic musical styles have influenced mainstream American music. In the assessment, students video their song and research summary for presentation to peers and parents.
Groups *First day*	Students are grouped based on the number of letters in their Spanish names. No group should be larger than four. Each group needs a CD or cassette player and a computer with internet access.
Bridge *First day*	Invite students to talk about what they know about tejano music or Selena. Watch the film *Selena* if they are not familiar with Mexican American tejano music. Students should discuss Selena's experience as a Mexican American who learned Spanish as a second language and debate whether she would have been successful singing only Spanish lyrics or only English lyrics.
Task *5–6 days*	Students transcribe the song "La Carcacha" from Spanish into English and then conduct research on the Internet to consider how Hispanic culture has influenced mainstream American music. Anticipated student questions: How would we translate this verse? Teacher questions: Can you make your translation fit the melody and rhythm? How has Hispanic culture influenced mainstream American music? Is there such a thing as mainstream American music when many styles, such as jazz, reggae, or R&B, are rooted in other cultures? Would the music be as interesting and successful if the lyrics were always in English?
Exhibit *2 days*	Groups sing their transcribed song in English. In Spanish, they present their findings about how Hispanic musical styles have influenced mainstream American music.
Reflection *1 day*	The teacher leads a discussion on the challenges of transcribing lyrics into English. Students write journal entries to answer these questions. Why did Selena's music "cross over" into the mainstream music scene in the United States? How has your music listening influenced your knowledge of subcultures in the United States? What is the place of music in cross-cultural understanding?

RESOURCE 12

Level: High School
Subject: Business Education
Title: Creating Spreadsheets

Situation *1 week*	The purpose of this Situation is to familiarize students with creating spreadsheets using categories, formulas, and charts to make and account for a personal budget. The topic is for students to create a spreadsheet with categories for all their income and spending for a week. Each day they record in a notebook the money they get and spend and then transfer this information to their spreadsheet during class. In the assessment, students create a DVD for presentation to their families.
Groups *First day*	Students work in pairs on computers and with each other to develop categories, formulas, and systems to track their income and spending. Then they work in teams of four to record class information. Materials include one computer per pair, notebooks, index cards, and Monopoly money. Students need additional work space such as desk tops or tables.
Bridge *First day*	The teacher hands out index cards and asks students to write down anonymously the amount of money they spend each week. Then the teacher tallies these results with the class and discusses what categories might be used to present this information. For instance, under $20, $20 to $40, $40 to $60, $60 to $80, $80 to $100, and over $100. The teacher creates a spreadsheet with the tallied information and draws a chart showing the distribution. Teacher and students will brainstorm the possible categories of income and spending: food, clothing, entertainment, transportation, games, computers, books, and sports.
Task *3 days*	Students create and update their spreadsheets with a week of income and expenses. Anticipated student questions: If I don't have a job, what should I do? Teacher questions: Do you have an allowance, or do you get money from your parents for lunch or the bus? What categories will you develop to describe your spending?
Exhibit *Last day*	On Friday, students create and print a graph of their spreadsheet and print six copies for classmates. They work in teams of four to consolidate the separate spreadsheets into a common class spreadsheet and present their results to the class.
Reflection *Last day*	The teacher leads the class in considering the similarities and differences in group spreadsheets. In what categories did you expect to find the most income or spending? What surprised you most about the class's expenses or income? How would you use a spreadsheet to balance a checkbook?

RESOURCE 13

CLD Key Questions	1. **What are your students expected to learn?** 2. **Where are your students now in their learning?** 3. **How will students make meaning about what they are expected to learn?**

Situation **Key** **Questions**	1. Purpose: Why are you designing this learning episode? 2. Topic: What is your specific focus for student learning? 3. Assessment: How will you assess student learning?
Groups **Key** **Questions**	1. Students: How will you organize students into groups? 2. Materials: What materials will students use to make meaning? 3. Furniture: How will you arrange furniture to facilitate learning?
Bridge **Key** **Questions**	1. Audience: Who are your students? 2. Preconceptions: How will you surface students' prior knowledge? 3. Connections: How will you connect the topic to students' lives?
Task **Key** **Questions**	1. Engaging: How will students engage in making meaning? 2. Learning: What kind of record will document student learning? 3. Thinking: What questions will students ask and how will you reply?
Exhibit **Key** **Questions**	1. Artifacts: What will students produce as a result of their learning? 2. Presentations: How will students present their artifacts? 3. Explanations: How will students explain their thinking?
Reflection **Key** **Quetsions**	1. Feelings: How will students reflect on their emotional/physical experiences? 2. Images: How will students reflect on their sensory experiences? 3. Languages: How will students reflect on their communication experiences?

References

Allen, D. W. (1969). *Microteaching*. Reading, MA: Addison-Wesley.

American Association for the Advancement of Science (AAAS). (1998). *Blueprints for reform: science, mathematics, and technology education*. New York: Oxford University Press.

Aronson, E. (1978). *The jigsaw classroom*. Beverly Hills, CA: Sage.

Ausubel, D. P. (1968). *Educational psychology: A cognitive view*. New York: Holt, Rinehart & Winston.

Block, J. (1971). *Mastery learning: Theory and practice*. New York: Holt, Rinehart, & Winston.

Bloom, B., et al. (Eds.) (1956). *Taxonomy of educational objectives: The classification of educational goals, by a committee of college and university examiners*. New York: Longmans, Green.

Brody, C., & Davidson, N. (1998). *Professional development for cooperative learning: Issues and approaches*. New York: State University of New York Press.

Brookfield, S. (1995). *Becoming a critically reflective teacher*. San Francisco: Jossey-Bass.

Brooks, J. G., & Brooks, M. G. (1993). *The case for constructivist classrooms*. Alexandria, VA: Association for Supervision and Curriculum Development.

Brosterman, N. (1997). *Inventing kindergarten*. New York: Harry N. Abrams.

Bruner, J. S. (1996). *The culture of education*. Cambridge, MA: Harvard University Press.

Carini, P. F. (1986). Building from children's strengths. *Journal of Education, 168*(3), 13–24.

Case, R. (1996). Changing views of knowledge and their impact on educational research and practice. In D. R. Olson & N. Torrance (Eds.), *The handbook of education and human development* (pp. 75–99). Cambridge, MA: Blackwell.

Clandinin, D. J., & Connelly, M. (1994). Personal experience methods. In N. K. Denzin & Y. S. Lincoln (Eds.), *Handbook of qualitative research* (pp. 413–427). Thousand Oaks, CA: Sage.

Cohen, E. (1994). *Designing groupwork: Strategies for the heterogeneous classroom*. (2nd ed.). New York: Teachers College Press.

Collay, M. (1998). Recherche: Teaching our life histories. *Teacher and Teacher Education, 14*(3), 245–255.

Collay, M., Dunlap, D., Enloe, W., & Gagnon, G. (1998). *Learning circles: Creating conditions for professional development*. Thousand Oaks, CA: Corwin.

Collier, V. P. (1995). Acquiring a second language for school. *Directions in Language and Education, 1*(4), 1–10.

Cuban, L. (1984). *How teachers taught: Constancy and change in American classrooms, 1890–1980.* New York: Longman.

Dearn, J. M. (1996, July). Facilitating active learning in introductory science classes. Paper presented at the Higher Education Research and Development Society of Australasia Conference, Perth, Western Australia. Retrieved April 4, 2004, from www.herdsa.org.au/confs/1996/contents.html.

Dewey, J. (1897). My pedagogic creed. *School Journal 54*(3), 77–80.

Dewey, J. (1933). Why reflective thinking must be an educational aim. In R. D. Archambault, *John Dewey on education* (pp. 212–228). Chicago: University of Chicago Press, 1964.

Dienes, Z. P. (1967). *Building up mathematics.* London: Hutchinson Educational.

Dietz, M. (1995). Using portfolios as a framework for professional development. *Journal of Staff Development, 16*(2), 40–43.

Duckworth, E. (1987). *The having of wonderful ideas.* New York: Teachers College Press.

Duncan, I. (1926). *The art of the dance.* New York: Theatre Arts Books.

Engel, B. (1994). Portfolio assessment and the new paradigm: New instruments and new places. *Educational Forum, 59*(1), 22–27.

Flewelling, G., & Higginson, W. (2002). *A handbook on rich learning tasks.* Kingston, Ontario, Canada: Queen's University, Centre for Mathematics, Science, and Technology.

Fosnot, C. (1996). *Constructivism: Perspectives, theory, and practice.* New York: Teachers College Press.

Freire, P. (1970). *Pedagogy of the oppressed.* New York: Herder and Herder.

Furth, H. G. (1966). *Thinking without language: Psychological implications of deafness.* New York: Free Press.

Gagné, R. M. (1985). *The conditions of learning and theory of instruction* (4th ed.). New York: Holt, Rinehart & Winston.

Gagnon, G., & Collay, M. (1996). *Teachers' perspectives on Constructivist Learning Design.* Paper presented at the Second Annual Qualitative Research Conference, St. Paul, MN.

Goodlad, J. I. (1984). *A place called school: Prospects for the future.* New York: McGraw-Hill.

Goodlad, J. I. (2004). *A place called school.* (2nd ed.). New York: McGraw-Hill.

Greene, M. (1995). *Releasing the imagination: Essays on education, the arts, and social change.* San Francisco: Jossey-Bass.

Harvard-Smithsonian Center for Astrophysics, Science Education Department, Science Media Group. (1987). *A private universe.* Burlington, VT: Annenburg/CPB Math and Science Collection. Retrieved from www.learner.org/catalog/science/pup

Hirsch, E. D. (1987). *Cultural literacy: What every American needs to know.* Boston: Houghton Mifflin.

Hunter, M. (1982). *Mastery teaching.* El Segundo, CA: TIP Publications.

Johnson, D., & Johnson, R. (1998). *Learning together and alone: Cooperative, competitive, and individualistic learning.* Boston: Allyn & Bacon.

Kagan, S. (1990). *Cooperative learning: Resources for teachers.* San Juan Capistrano, CA: Resources for Teachers.

Krashen, S. (1987). *Principles and practice in second language acquisition.* New York: Prentice Hall.

Kuhn, T. (1996). *The structure of scientific revolutions* (3rd ed.). Chicago: University of Chicago Press.

Lambert, L. (1998). *Building leadership capacity in schools.* Alexandria, VA: Association for Supervision and Curriculum Development.

Lambert, L., Collay, M., Dietz, M. E., Kent, K., & Richert, A. (1997). *Who will save our schools? Teachers as constructivist learners.* Thousand Oaks, CA: Corwin.

Levin, T., & Long, R. (1981). *Effective instruction.* Alexandria, VA: Association for Supervision and Curriculum Development.

Marzano, R. (2000). *Designing a new taxonomy of educational objectives.* Thousand Oaks, CA: Corwin.

Meier, D. (1995). *The power of their ideas: Lessons for America from a small school in Harlem.* Boston: Beacon.

Mezirow, J., et al. (1990). *Fostering critical reflection in adulthood: A guide to transformative and emanicipatory learning.* San Francisco: Jossey-Bass.

Montessori, M. (1963). *Education for a new world.* Aydar, Madras, India: Kalakshetra.

Montessori, M. (1965). *Dr. Montessori's own handbook.* New York: Schocken Books.

National Center for Education Statistics (NCES). (1998). Pursuing excellence: Initial findings from the Third International Math and Science Study [CD-ROM]. Washington, DC: Government Printing Office.

Newton, A. (2005). Presentation to the University of California, Berkeley, College of Engineering, Center for Under-represented Engineering Students (CUES) Board.

Nielsen, N. (2000). Aligning assessment with learning goals. *ENC Focus, 7*(2), 47–48.

Papert, S. (1993). *The children's machine: Rethinking school in the age of the computer.* New York: BasicBooks.

Perrone, V. (1991a). *A letter to teachers: Reflections on schooling and the art of teaching.* San Francisco: Jossey-Bass.

Perrone, V. (Ed.). (1991b). *Expanding student assessment.* Alexandria, VA: Association for Supervision and Curriculum Development.

Piaget, J. (1954). *The construction of reality in the child.* New York: Ballantine.

Piaget, J. (1976). *To understand is to invent: The future of education.* (G. A. Roberts, Trans.) New York: Penguin.

Piaget, J., & Inhelder, B. (1969). *The psychology of the child.* New York: BasicBooks.

Sadker, M., & Sadker, D. (1994). *Failing at fairness: How our schools shortchange girls.* New York: Simon & Schuster.

Sapon-Shevin, M. (1999). *Because we can change the world: A practical guide to building cooperative, inclusive classroom communities.* Boston: Allyn & Bacon.

Schmuck, R. A. (1997). *Practical action research for change.* Arlington Heights, IL: Skylight.

Schmuck, R. A., & Schmuck, P. A. (1992). *Small districts, big problems: Making school everybody's house.* Thousand Oaks, CA: Corwin.

Schmuck, R. A., & Schmuck, P. A. (2001). *Group processes in the classroom* (8th ed.). Boston: McGraw-Hill.

Schön, D. A. (1983). *The reflective practitioner: How professionals think in action.* New York: BasicBooks.

Sharan, S., & Sharan, Y. (1992). *Expanding cooperative learning through group investigation.* New York: Teachers College Press.

Shulman, L. (1999). Taking learning seriously. *Change 31*(4), 11–17.

Sizer, T. (1992). *Horace's school: Redesigning the American high school.* Boston: Houghton Mifflin.

Slavin, R. E. (1995). *Cooperative learning: Theory, research and practice* (2nd ed.). Boston: Allyn & Bacon.

Steffe, L. P., & D'Ambrosio, B. S. (1995). Toward a working model of constructivist teaching: A reaction to Simon. *Journal for Research in Mathematics Education, 26*(2), 146–159.

Stigler, J. W., & Hiebert, J. (1999). *The teaching gap: Best ideas from the world's teachers for improving education in the classroom.* New York: Free Press.

Tyler, R. (1949). *Basic principles of curriculum and instruction.* Chicago: University of Chicago Press.

Vella, J. (2001). *Taking learning to task.* San Francisco: Jossey-Bass.

Vygotsky, L. S. (1934). *Thought and language.* (A. Kozulin, Ed. & Trans.). Cambridge: MIT Press, 1986.

What's so special about international business schools? (2003). *Princeton Review.* Retrieved July 6, 2005, from www.princetonreview.com/mba/research/articles/find/internationalDifferences.asp

Wiggins, G. (1998). *Educative assessment: Designing assessments to inform and improve student performance.* San Francisco: Jossey-Bass.

Wiggins, G., & McTighe, J. (2005). *Understanding by design* (Expanded 2nd ed.). Alexandria, VA: Association for Supervision and Curriculum Development.

Witherell, C., & Noddings, N. (Eds.). (1991). *Stories lives tell: Narrative and dialogue in education.* New York: Teachers College Press.

Index

**CORWIN
PRESS**

The Corwin Press logo—a raven striding across an open book—represents the union of courage and learning. Corwin Press is committed to improving education for all learners by publishing books and other professional development resources for those serving the field of PreK–12 education. By providing practical, hands-on materials, Corwin Press continues to carry out the promise of its motto: **"Helping Educators Do Their Work Better."**

UNIVERSITY OF WINCHESTER
LIBRARY